# The MCSE™ Windows® 2000 Network Cram Sheet

This Cram Sheet contains the distilled, key facts about the MCSE Implementing and Administering a Microsoft Windows 2000 Network Infrastructure exam. Review this information last thing before entering the test room, paying special attention to those areas where you feel you need the most review. You can transfer any of the facts onto a blank piece of paper before beginning the exam.

## DHCP

1. The lease process consists of four different messages:
   - IP request
   - IP offer
   - IP selection
   - IP acknowledgement

2. *Automatic Private Internet Protocol Addressing (APIPA)* is a client-side feature of Windows 98/2000 DHCP-enabled computers. The client receives an IP address from the 169.254.0.0/16 address range if a DHCP server is not reached.

3. A *DHCP scope* is a range of IP addresses allocated to DHCP-enabled clients on the network. Other components of the scope include:
   - *Scope options*—Additional IP configurations for the clients within the scope.
   - *Exclusions*—Ranges within the scope of IP addresses that are removed from the allocation to clients.
   - *Reservations*—Individual IP addresses within the scope that are reserved for a particular network card address on the network.
   - *Lease duration*—The allotted amount of time the client can use the IP address without renewing the lease.

4. BOOTP scopes and clients are supported along with BOOTP lease durations.

5. DHCP options take three different forms:
   - *Server options*—Effective for all scopes configured for the DHCP server.
   - *Scope options*—Only apply to the scope they are configured for.
   - *Reservation options*—Only applied to the specified computer.

6. All DHCP options have *class* and *vendor* options that can be configured.

7. *Superscopes* and *multicast scopes* are supported types of scopes.

8. Windows 2000 DHCP servers need to be authorized with Active Directory before they can allocate IP addresses to DHCP-enabled clients.

9. The *DHCP relay agent* is a computer that helps DHCP-enabled clients obtain an IP address from a DHCP server on another segment.

10. DHCP is integrated with DNS for dynamically updating both A and PTR records:
    - This task is always done on Windows 2000 clients.
    - This task may be configured for legacy Windows clients.

11. The **ipconfig** command is used to control the IP configuration for the client.

## REMOTE ACCESS

12. The two different types of remote access are:
    - *Dial-up access*—Uses standard telephone lines or ISDN connections.
    - *Virtual private network (VPN)*—Uses a common internetwork to link two disparate networks.

13. Remote access must either have a static pool of IP addresses or use DHCP.

14. The DHCP relay agent is a critical component of the remote access configuration. It gives the connecting client access to the DHCP server.

15. *Dial-up services* support PPP for incoming connections.

16. *VPN services* support PPTP and L2TP for connections.

17. L2TP enables the use of IPSec for securing the payload between client and server.

18. Supported PPP configurations are:
    - *Multilink*—The ability to aggregate physical connection links.

58. The *HOSTS* text file is a table that is stored on a host and used to resolve FQDNs to IP addresses.

59. *WINS proxy* is used when a client cannot register its name with a WINS server. To configure a Windows 2000 computer as a WINS proxy, you must add the **EnableProxy** value (set to 1) to the following Registry key:

```
HKEY_LOCAL_MACHINE\SYSTEM\CurrentControlSet\
    Services\NetBt\Parameters
```

60. *Manual tombstoning* prevents WINS servers from sending deleted records back to other WINS servers.

61. *WINS name registration* includes not only the name, but also the workstation service, the server service, the messenger service, the workgroup or domain that the computer pertains to, and the user who was logged on to the client when it registered its name.

62. *WINS name renewal*—When a client computer registers its name with the WINS server, the server returns a TTL value to the client.

63. *WINS name release*—Names are released when a client shuts down, when a client fails to renew its name within the TTL value, or when the WINS server marks it for extinction by giving it an extinction interval.

## DNS

64. DNS services provide name-to-TCP/IP address resolution in forward lookup zones and TCP/IP address-to-name resolution in reverse lookup zones.

65. *Standalone primary zones* write information to the DNS database. *Standalone secondary zones* receive information from the primary zone master through zone transfers.

66. *Active Directory integrated zones* are replicated to all domain controllers, which then can receive writes to their respective databases, which then replicate through the normal Active Directory replication topology.

67. To enable secure dynamic updates of the database, you must be using Active Directory integrated zones.

68. Caching-only servers do not write to their databases, nor do they replicate.

69. Additional domain name suffixes on the client allow for multiple namespace searches for similarly named hosts.

70. If additional name servers outside of the member domain need to be searched, add those entries to the root hints file, and then configure the DNS to read that file on boot rather than consult the Active Directory exclusively.

## CERTIFICATE SERVICES

71. Certificate Services must be installed for Active Directory to issue certificates for the domain.

72. If external certificate authorities (CAs) are to be used, they must be trusted by the domain in which they will be valid.

73. Enterprise certificate authorities can only issue, validate, and revoke certificates for members (objects) of that domain.

74. For external certificate issue, validation, or revocation, create a standalone certificate authority rather than an enterprise.

75. Subordinate authorities can be established for load balancing of certificate services.

76. Certificate Revocation Lists (CRLs) are used to rescind and invalidate certificates previously issued.

77. SSL is for Web and Internet services, not for domain user or machine certificates.

78. Public keys encrypt; private keys decrypt.

79. The Encrypting File System (EFS) encrypts files on a user basis, and only that user can open the file once encrypted. You can recover the file by the domain (or OU) recovery agent, but that is a separate process.

80. CA names are bound to their certificates and cannot be changed.

**CORIOLIS™**
*Certification Insider Press*

37. *TCP/IP* is a 32-bit addressing scheme represented in dotted decimal notation (W.X.Y.Z) where each letter represents an *octet*. A 32-bit number called a *subnet mask* accompanies the IP address. It masks a portion of the IP address to distinguish which part of the address is the host ID and which part is the network ID. Four classes of IP addresses are supported in Windows 2000:

- *Class A*—Contains addresses where the first octet ranges from 1 to 126.
- *Class B*—Contains addresses where the first octet ranges from 128 to 191.
- *Class C*—Contains addresses where the first octet ranges from 192 to 223.
- *Class D*—Contains addresses where the first octet ranges from 224-239.

38. *Binding order* is the order by which network protocols are used in client/server communication. The most frequently used protocols should be placed toward the top of the list.

39. You install network protocols in the Local Area Connections Properties dialog box in Network and Dial-up Connections.

40. *Packet filtering* is the ability to define what traffic is allowed into and out of each NIC based on what filters are defined.

## IPSEC

41. The purpose of IPSec, not to be confused with digital certificates, is to secure TCP/IP packet communication by:

- Protecting the integrity of the packet while en route
- Ensuring the confidentiality of the packet
- Authenticating credentials for established entities in the secured conversation
- Protecting computers against network protocol attacks

42. The ESP protocol provides data privacy by encrypting the IP packets.

43. *Cryptography-based keys* create a digital checksum for each IP packet. Any modifications to the packet data alter the checksum, which indicates to the receiving computer that the packet was modified in transit.

44. *Mutual verification* (authentication headers, or AH) is used to establish trust between the communicating systems; only trusted systems can communicate with each other. IPSec combines mutual authentication with shared, cryptography-based keys.

45. *Packet filtering* determines whether communication is allowed, secured, or blocked according to IP address ranges, protocols, or specific protocol ports.

46. *IPSec filters* control how packets are processed before the client sends them and before the server processes them.

47. *Internet Key Exchange (IKE)* is performed if matching filters exist on the client and server to force secure communication.

48. *Security associations (SA)* have control of the negotiating and processing of communications between client and server.

49. An SA negotiates in two phases. Phase I handles the initial negotiations and secure encryption of the packets:

- Policy negotiation, where encryption (such as DES) and hashing (such as MD5) of the packet occur
- DH exchange of public values
- Authentication

50. Phase II of the SA handles the next-level processing of communications between client and server:

- Policy negotiation: the IPSec protocol (AH or ESP)
- The hash algorithm for integrity and authentication (MD5 or SHA)
- The algorithm for encryption, if requested (3DES or DES)
- Session key refresh or exchange

51. Two SAs are created, one for outbound communication and one for inbound.

52. IPSec can be used either standalone or tunneled. Tunneling adds no IPSec security levels but adds outer headers to the packet for secure transmission between routers.

53. AH provides for authentication security.

54. When IPSec is tunneled, ESP should be applied first, then AH.

55. IPSec filters specify what types of packets are allowed to be processed by a receiving computer: source port, source address, or protocol used in transport.

## WINS

56. Name resolution is the process by which a host determines the IP or MAC address of another host. There are two major types of name resolution:

- *NetBIOS name resolution*—There are four nodes of NetBIOS name resolution:
  - *B-node*—Uses a local broadcast.
  - *P-node*—Uses a WINS server.
  - *M-node*—Uses a local broadcast and then a WINS server.
  - *H-node*—Uses a WINS server and then a broadcast.
- *Hostname resolution*—For clients that cannot use NBNS for name resolution. Uses DNS and HOSTS files as its primary method of resolving FQDNs (fully qualified domain names) to IP addresses.

57. The *LMHOSTS file* is a text file containing a table that is stored on a host and used to resolve NetBIOS names to IP addresses. Options for an LMHOSTS file include:

- **#PRE**
- **#DOM:<*domain_name*>**
- **#INCLUDE <*path to file*>**
- **#BEGIN_ALTERNATE**
- **#END_ALTERNATE**
- **#NOFNR**
- **#MH**

- *BAP*—Dynamically controls the multilink connection for optimized bandwidth utilization.
- *LCP*—Supports the additional features of callback and Caller ID.

19. *Remote access policies* control the communication abilities and configuration between the server and client.

20. *Conditions* are the initial portion of the remote access policy that the connecting client must meet to have the policy apply.

21. The *remote access policy profile* determines what the connecting client configuration must be for communication to be successful. Configurations include:
- Dial-in constraints
- IP settings
- Multilink settings
- Authentication settings
- Encryption settings
- Advanced settings for IAS and RADIUS configurations

22. Authentication options include:
- PAP
- SPAP
- CHAP
- MS-CHAP v1 and v2
- EAP

23. Data encryption is available via MPPE and the basic and strong encryption methods.

24. IAS uses the RADIUS protocol to centralize authorization, authentication, and accounting for the remote access servers in the enterprise.

## ROUTING

25. *Static routes* update the routing table for network communication.

26. Static routes across demand-dial interfaces support *default routes* or *auto-static routes*.

27. *Demand-dial routing* has the following characteristics and options:
- On-demand or persistent connection types
- One-way or two-way demand-dial connections
- Demand-dial filtering to allow or deny connectivity
- Dial-out hours set to control the connection and peak time bandwidth
- Support for static or dynamic routing

28. Demand-dial user account details include:
- Password expiration should be turned off.
- Change Password At Next Logon should be turned off.
- The username needs to be the same as the demand-dial interface name.

29. OSPF terminology:
- *Area*—A segment of like subnets that reduces intra-area traffic.
- *Area border router (ABR)*—An OSPF router that links an area to the backbone area.

- *Autonomous system (AS)*—A collection of networks with a common administrative authority.
- *Backbone area*—A high-bandwidth network.
- *Virtual link*—A connection to a new or changing area that is not directly connected to the backbone area. These connections should be avoided!

30. RIP has three options:
- RIP v1 is chatty and supports no peer security.
- RIP v2 supports multicast announcements, password authentication, CIDR, and VLSM.
- RIP Listener processes announcements only (Windows 2000 Professional).

31. RIP and SAP for IPX is supported.

32. ICS supports the following characteristics:
- Single IP address from an ISP
- Utilizes the 192.168.0.0/24 network on the internal interface
- Limited configuration of applications and services
- Automatically configures a static route

33. NAT supports the following characteristics:
- Built-in DHCP allocator or use of network DHCP server
- Multiple Internet IP address support
- Inbound and outbound application configuration

34. IGMP proxy and IGMP router are supported for both forwarding and multicasting

## NETWORK PROTOCOLS

35. Windows 2000 supports the following protocols:
- TCP/IP
- NWLink
- NetBEUI
- AppleTalk

36. The *OSI reference model* is divided into seven layers:
- *Application layer*—Responsible for the way network applications interact with the network.
- *Presentation layer*—Responsible for the way network information is formatted. Also responsible for compression.
- *Session layer*—Responsible for establishing and breaking network communications between hosts.
- *Transport layer*—Responsible for ensuring error-free delivery of network packets.
- *Network layer*—Responsible for addressing network packets and the route they take to their destination.
- *Data Link layer*—Responsible for taking raw data bits and packaging them into frames.
- *Physical layer*—Responsible for taking electric impulses off network media and putting raw data onto network media in the form of electric impulses.

# MCSE™
# Windows® 2000
# Network

Hank Carbeck
Derek Melber
Richard Taylor

## MCSE™ Windows® 2000 Network Exam Cram

### Limits of Liability and Disclaimer of Warranty

The author and publisher of this book have used their best efforts in preparing the book and the programs contained in it. These efforts include the development, research, and testing of the theories and programs to determine their effectiveness. The author and publisher make no warranty of any kind, expressed or implied, with regard to these programs or the documentation contained in this book.

The author and publisher shall not be liable in the event of incidental or consequential damages in connection with, or arising out of, the furnishing, performance, or use of the programs, associated instructions, and/or claims of productivity gains.

### Trademarks

Trademarked names appear throughout this book. Rather than list the names and entities that own the trademarks or insert a trademark symbol with each mention of the trademarked name, the publisher states that it is using the names for editorial purposes only and to the benefit of the trademark owner, with no intention of infringing upon that trademark.

The Coriolis Group, LLC
14455 N. Hayden Road
Suite 220
Scottsdale, Arizona 85260

(480)483-0192
FAX (480)483-0193
www.coriolis.com

Library of Congress Cataloging-in-Publication Data
Taylor, Richard, 1964–
    MCSE Windows 2000 network exam cram / by Richard Taylor, Hank Carbeck, and Derek Melber.
        p.   cm.
    Includes index.
    ISBN 1-57610-711-6
    1. Electronic data processing personnel--Certification.   2. Computer networks--Examinations--Study guides.   3. Microsoft Windows (Computer file)   I. Carbeck, Hank.   II. Melber, Derek.   III. Title.
QA76.3.T375   2000
005.7'13769--dc21                                    00-058991
                                                        CIP

**President and CEO**
Keith Weiskamp

**Publisher**
Steve Sayre

**Acquisitions Editor**
Shari Jo Hehr

**Marketing Specialist**
Brett Woolley

**Project Editor**
Toni Zuccarini Ackley

**Technical Reviewer**
Adam Burgess

**Production Coordinator**
Wendy Littley

**Cover Designer**
Jesse Dunn

**Layout Designer**
April Nielsen

Printed in the United States of America
10 9 8 7 6 5 4

The Coriolis Group, LLC • 14455 North Hayden Road, Suite 220 • Scottsdale, Arizona 85260

# *ExamCram.com* Connects You to the Ultimate Study Center!

Our goal has always been to provide you with the best study tools on the planet to help you achieve your certification in record time. Time is so valuable these days that none of us can afford to waste a second of it, especially when it comes to exam preparation.

Over the past few years, we've created an extensive line of *Exam Cram* and *Exam Prep* study guides, practice exams, and interactive training. To help you study even better, we have now created an e-learning and certification destination called **ExamCram.com**. (You can access the site at **www.examcram.com**.) Now, with every study product you purchase from us, you'll be connected to a large community of people like yourself who are actively studying for their certifications, developing their careers, seeking advice, and sharing their insights and stories.

I believe that the future is all about collaborative learning. Our **ExamCram.com** destination is our approach to creating a highly interactive, easily accessible collaborative environment, where you can take practice exams and discuss your experiences with others, sign up for features like "Questions of the Day," plan your certifications using our interactive planners, create your own personal study pages, and keep up with all of the latest study tips and techniques.

I hope that whatever study products you purchase from us—*Exam Cram* or *Exam Prep* study guides, *Personal Trainers*, *Personal Test Centers*, or one of our interactive Web courses—will make your studying fun and productive. Our commitment is to build the kind of learning tools that will allow you to study the way you want to, whenever you want to.

**Visit *ExamCram.com* now to enhance your study program.**

Help us continue to provide the very best certification study materials possible. Write us or email us at **learn@examcram.com** and let us know how our study products have helped you study. Tell us about new features that you'd like us to add. Send us a story about how we've helped you. We're listening!

Good luck with your certification exam and your career. Thank you for allowing us to help you achieve your goals.

Keith Weiskamp
President and CEO

# Look for these other products from The Coriolis Group:

**MCSE Windows 2000 Accelerated
Exam Prep**
By Lance Cockcroft, Erik Eckel,
and Ron Kauffman

**MCSE Windows 2000 Server Exam Prep**
By David Johnson and Dawn Rader

**MCSE Windows 2000 Professional
Exam Prep**
By Michael D. Stewart, James Bloomingdale,
and Neall Alcott

**MCSE Windows 2000 Network Exam Prep**
By Tammy Smith and Sandra Smeeton

**MCSE Windows 2000 Directory Services
Exam Prep**
By David V. Watts, Will Willis, and Tillman
Strahan

**MCSE Windows 2000 Security Design
Exam Prep**
By Richard Alan McMahon and Glen Bicking

**MCSE Windows 2000 Network Design
Exam Prep**
By Geoffrey Alexander, Anoop Jalan,
and Joseph Alexander

**MCSE Migrating from NT 4
to Windows 2000
Exam Prep**
By Glen Bergen, Graham Leach,
and David Baldwin

**MCSE Windows 2000
Directory Services Design
Exam Prep**
By J. Peter Bruzzese and Wayne Dipchan

**MCSE Windows 2000 Core Four
Exam Prep Pack**

**MCSE Windows 2000 Server
Exam Cram**
By Natasha Knight

**MCSE Windows 2000 Professional
Exam Cram**
By Dan Balter, Dan Holme, Todd Logan,
and Laurie Salmon

**MCSE Windows 2000 Directory Services
Exam Cram**
By Will Willis, David V. Watts,
and J. Peter Bruzzese

**MCSE Windows 2000 Security Design
Exam Cram**
By Phillip G. Schein

**MCSE Windows 2000 Network Design
Exam Cram**
By Kim Simmons, Jarret W. Buse,
and Todd B. Halpin

**MCSE Windows 2000
Directory Services Design
Exam Cram**
By Dennis Scheil and Diana Bartley

**MCSE Windows 2000 Core Four
Exam Cram Pack**

*and...*
**MCSE Windows 2000 Foundations**
By James Michael Stewart and Lee Scales

*To Michelle—making the goals is such fun with you.*
*—Hank Carbeck*

❧

*I dedicate this book to Yvette and Alexa.*
*—Derek Melber*

❧

*I dedicate this book to my Heavenly Father, my wife, and my children.*
*—Rick Taylor*

❧

# About the Authors

. . . . . . . . . . . . . . . . . . . . . . . . . . . . . . . . . . . . . . . . .

**Hank Carbeck**'s debut to the technology world-at-large was with his own company, Interactive Media, based in Virginia. There, he developed multimedia training applications and kiosks, and began training IT professionals in the Microsoft BackOffice suite of products. His passion for training soon won over his time from the app development side of the business, and a new company, Protégé, emerged to provide technical development training to a wide scope of computer and networking professionals. Hank has authored both public and private customized courses that are still in use at many companies today.

Currently, Hank is the director of education for trainAbility in Scottsdale, Arizona, providing consultation, training, and development services to IBM Global Services, HP, Compaq, Lockheed-Martin, Bell South, Mastering Computers, PLATINUM technology, Computer Associates, Framatome Technologies, TRW, and a host of other companies.

**Derek Melber** focuses on technical writing and instructing, as well as computer consultation. Most recently he has been working with Microsoft to develop the Certification Skills and Assessment Program for Windows 2000. He is also contributing to the Windows 2000 certification efforts for many training companies throughout the United States.

Although Derek focuses most of his efforts on certification preparation for both Microsoft and CompTIA, he often finds himself consulting for companies to design and optimize their network infrastructure and server configurations. He leverages his consultations with his experience. He has worked both as a network administrator for the University of Kansas and as a technology manager for a major commodities exchange company.

Derek currently has his Microsoft Certified Systems Engineer (MCSE) and CompTIA A+ certifications. Although a computer guy now, he has a Masters of Civil Engineering from the University of Kansas. Derek also runs his own business, Melber and Associates, which focuses on developing and training certification preparation courseware and tools. When he is not working on a computer, Derek is enjoying KU Jayhawk Basketball, "Rock Chalk Jayhawk!" You can catch up with Derek at **melber@iname.com**.

**Richard Taylor** has been characterized as a "computer geek" since junior high school. His father, a former engineer with Bell Labs, brought home an Apple II computer in 1976 and Richard became fascinated and never looked back.

Since that time, Richard has worked in various capacities in the IT industry. Honeywell, Intel, and MicroAge are among the companies from which Richard has gained and used his experience. He is currently an independent contractor and instructs in various Microsoft technologies. Some of the projects Richard has participated in include providing content for Microsoft Certified Professional exams and designing a Windows 2000 network infrastructure for Computer Education Specialists.

Richard is a gadget freak, whose hobbies include chess, Command & Conquer, and playing the trumpet, guitar, or piano. His wife, Damaris, is the most wonderful person in the world and they have three children: Sariah, Rebecca, and Rachel. He can be reached at **rickt287@yahoo.com**.

# Acknowledgments

Thanks go to those who support my consuming career-hobby without complaint, while still making sure that "Daddy" has his priorities straight. My home is a wonderful place to be thanks to my wife, Michelle, and my children, Henry and Catherine. Your smiles, laughter, and hugs give me joy and strength.

In the world of computers, many have their contribution firmly etched in my accomplishments. Dan Holme, for his guiding vision at trainAbility; Derek and Rick, for their collaboration on this Coriolis project (get some sleep, fellas); and my fellow ConsulTrainers at trainAbility, for contributing their real-life experiences along with their glee in finding that elusive Registry hack that makes something work.

Thanks, also, to The Coriolis Group for being flexible when deadlines and life did not overlap well. The product is an effort, but worth the time.

Technology is a wondrous thing, but not so marvelous as the spirit of the people with whom I have contact every day. Thanks to God for allowing men to make our techno-toys, and for those with whom we play.

*—Hank Carbeck*

I would like to thank my wife and daughter, Yvette and Alexa, for their durable patience. Many thanks to my co-authors, Hank and Rick, for their friendship, knowledge, dedication, and persistence to this book. Thanks go out to Toni, the project editor who was able to bring it all together; to The Coriolis Group for creating such incredible books for the IT industry; and to the entire staff at trainAbility for their dedication to Windows 2000 and the training industry. Last but not least, to the one who allows me to stop, think, and ask the question, WWJD?

*—Derek Melber*

I would like to thank over and above all my dear wife and children for putting up with my absence from my primary duties as husband and father while writing this book. I would also like to thank my co-authors, Hank and Derek, for helping me on and off the field. Special thanks to Andy Barkl, Travis Pera, and especially Alison and Dan Balter, who started me out in this industry.

*—Rick Taylor*

# Contents at a Glance

# Table of Contents

# Introduction

Welcome to *MCSE Windows 2000 Network Exam Cram*! Whether this is your first or your fifteenth *Exam Cram* book, you'll find information here and in Chapter 1 that will help ensure your success as you pursue knowledge, experience, and certification. This book aims to help you get ready to take—and pass—the Microsoft certification Exam 70-216, titled "Implementing and Administering a Microsoft Windows 2000 Network Infrastructure." This Introduction explains Microsoft's certification programs in general and talks about how the *Exam Cram* series can help you prepare for Microsoft's Windows 2000 certification exams.

*Exam Cram* books help you understand and appreciate the subjects and materials you need to pass Microsoft certification exams. *Exam Cram* books are aimed strictly at test preparation and review. They do not teach you everything you need to know about a topic. Instead, we (the authors) present and dissect the questions and problems we've found that you're likely to encounter on a test. We've worked to bring together as much information as possible about Microsoft certification exams.

Nevertheless, to completely prepare yourself for any Microsoft test, we recommend that you begin by taking the Self-Assessment included in this book immediately following this Introduction. This tool will help you evaluate your knowledge base against the requirements for an MCSE under both ideal and real circumstances.

Based on what you learn from that exercise, you might decide to begin your studies with some classroom training or some background reading. On the other hand, you might decide to pick up and read one of the many study guides available from Microsoft or third-party vendors on certain topics, including The Coriolis Group's *Exam Prep* series. We also recommend that you supplement your study program with visits to **ExamCram.com** to receive additional practice questions, get advice, and track the Windows 2000 MCSE program.

We also strongly recommend that you install, configure, and fool around with the software that you'll be tested on, because nothing beats hands-on experience and familiarity when it comes to understanding the questions you're likely to encounter on a certification test. Book learning is essential, but hands-on experience is the best teacher of all!

# The Microsoft Certified Professional (MCP) Program

The MCP program currently includes the following separate tracks, each of which boasts its own special acronym (as a certification candidate, you need to have a high tolerance for alphabet soup of all kinds):

➤ *MCP (Microsoft Certified Professional)*—This is the least prestigious of all the certification tracks from Microsoft. Passing one of the major Microsoft exams qualifies an individual for the MCP credential. Individuals can demonstrate proficiency with additional Microsoft products by passing additional certification exams.

➤ *MCP+SB (Microsoft Certified Professional + Site Building)*—This certification program is designed for individuals who are planning, building, managing, and maintaining Web sites. Individuals with the MCP+SB credential will have demonstrated the ability to develop Web sites that include multimedia and searchable content and Web sites that connect to and communicate with a back-end database. It requires one MCP exam, plus two of these three exams: "70-055: Designing and Implementing Web Sites with Microsoft FrontPage 98," "70-057: Designing and Implementing Commerce Solutions with Microsoft Site Server 3.0, Commerce Edition," and "70-152: Designing and Implementing Web Solutions with Microsoft Visual InterDev 6.0."

➤ *MCSE (Microsoft Certified Systems Engineer)*—Anyone who has a current MCSE is warranted to possess a high level of networking expertise with Microsoft operating systems and products. This credential is designed to prepare individuals to plan, implement, maintain, and support information systems, networks, and internetworks built around Microsoft Windows 2000 and its BackOffice Server 2000 family of products.

To obtain an MCSE, an individual must pass four core operating system exams, one optional core exam, and two elective exams. The operating system exams require individuals to prove their competence with desktop and server operating systems and networking/internetworking components.

For Windows NT 4 MCSEs, the Accelerated exam, "70-240: Microsoft Windows 2000 Accelerated Exam for MCPs Certified on Microsoft Windows NT 4.0," is an option. This free exam covers all of the material tested in the Core Four exams. The hitch in this plan is that you can take the test only once. If you fail, you must take all four core exams to recertify. The Core Four exams are: "70-210: Installing, Configuring and Administering Microsoft Windows 2000 Professional," "70-215: Installing, Configuring and Administering Microsoft

Windows 2000 Server," "70-216: Implementing and Administering a Microsoft Windows 2000 Network Infrastructure," and "70-217: Implementing and Administering a Microsoft Windows 2000 Directory Services Infrastructure."

To fulfill the fifth core exam requirement, you can choose from three design exams: "70-219: Designing a Microsoft Windows 2000 Directory Services Infrastructure," "70-220: Designing Security for a Microsoft Windows 2000 Network," or "70-221: Designing a Microsoft Windows 2000 Network Infrastructure." You are also required to take two elective exams. An elective exam can fall in any number of subject or product areas, primarily BackOffice Server 2000 components. The two design exams that you don't select as your fifth core exam also qualify as electives. If you are on your way to becoming an MCSE and have already taken some exams, visit **www.microsoft.com/ trainingandservices/** for information about how to complete your MCSE certification.

In September 1999, Microsoft announced its Windows 2000 track for MCSE and also announced retirement of Windows NT 4.0 MCSE core exams on 12/31/2000. Individuals who wish to remain certified MCSEs after 12/31/2001 must "upgrade" their certifications on or before 12/31/2001. For more detailed information than is included here, visit **www.microsoft.com/trainingandservices/**.

New MCSE candidates must pass seven tests to meet the MCSE requirements. It's not uncommon for the entire process to take a year or so, and many individuals find that they must take a test more than once to pass. The primary goal of the *Exam Prep* series and the *Exam Cram* series, our test preparation books, is to make it possible, given proper study and preparation, to pass all Microsoft certification tests on the first try. Table 1 shows the required and elective exams for the Windows 2000 MCSE certification.

➤ *MCSD (Microsoft Certified Solution Developer)*—The MCSD credential reflects the skills required to create multi-tier, distributed, and COM-based solutions, in addition to desktop and Internet applications, using new technologies. To obtain an MCSD, an individual must demonstrate the ability to analyze and interpret user requirements; select and integrate products, platforms, tools, and technologies; design and implement code, and customize applications; and perform necessary software tests and quality assurance operations.

To become an MCSD, you must pass a total of four exams: three core exams and one elective exam. Each candidate must choose one of these three desktop application exams—"70-016: Designing and Implementing Desktop Applications with Microsoft Visual C++ 6.0," "70-156: Designing and Implementing Desktop

## Table 1 MCSE Windows 2000 Requirements

### Core

| If you have not passed these 3 Windows NT 4 exams | |
| --- | --- |
| Exam 70-067 | Implementing and Supporting Microsoft Windows NT Server 4.0 |
| Exam 70-068 | Implementing and Supporting Microsoft Windows NT Server 4.0 in the Enterprise |
| Exam 70-073 | Microsoft Windows NT Workstation 4.0 |
| **then you must take these 4 exams** | |
| Exam 70-210 | Installing, Configuring and Administering Microsoft Windows 2000 Professional |
| Exam 70-215 | Installing, Configuring and Administering Microsoft Windows 2000 Server |
| Exam 70-216 | Implementing and Administering a Microsoft Windows 2000 Network Infrastructure |
| Exam 70-217 | Implementing and Administering a Microsoft Windows 2000 Directory Services Infrastructure |
| **If you have already passed exams 70-067, 70-068, and 70-073, you may take this exam** | |
| Exam 70-240 | Microsoft Windows 2000 Accelerated Exam for MCPs Certified on Microsoft Windows NT 4.0 |

### 5th Core Option

| Choose 1 from this group | |
| --- | --- |
| Exam 70-219* | Designing a Microsoft Windows 2000 Directory Services Infrastructure |
| Exam 70-220* | Designing Security for a Microsoft Windows 2000 Network |
| Exam 70-221* | Designing a Microsoft Windows 2000 Network Infrastructure |

### Elective

| Choose 2 from this group | |
| --- | --- |
| Exam 70-019 | Designing and Implementing Data Warehouse with Microsoft SQL Server 7.0 |
| Exam 70-219* | Designing a Microsoft Windows 2000 Directory Services Infrastructure |
| Exam 70-220* | Designing Security for a Microsoft Windows 2000 Network |
| Exam 70-221* | Designing a Microsoft Windows 2000 Network Infrastructure |
| Exam 70-222 | Migrating from Microsoft Windows NT 4.0 to Microsoft Windows 2000 |
| Exam 70-028 | Administering Microsoft SQL Server 7.0 |
| Exam 70-029 | Designing and Implementing Databases on Microsoft SQL Server 7.0 |
| Exam 70-080 | Implementing and Supporting Microsoft Internet Explorer 5.0 by Using the Internet Explorer Administration Kit |
| Exam 70-081 | Implementing and Supporting Microsoft Exchange Server 5.5 |
| Exam 70-085 | Implementing and Supporting Microsoft SNA Server 4.0 |
| Exam 70-086 | Implementing and Supporting Microsoft Systems Management Server 2.0 |
| Exam 70-088 | Implementing and Supporting Microsoft Proxy Server 2.0 |

This is not a complete listing—you can still be tested on some earlier versions of these products. However, we have included mainly the most recent versions so that you may test on these versions and thus be certified longer. We have not included any tests that are scheduled to be retired.

* The 5th Core Option exam does not double as an elective.

Applications with Microsoft Visual FoxPro 6.0," or "70-176: Designing and Implementing Desktop Applications with Microsoft Visual Basic 6.0"—*plus* one of these three distributed application exams—"70-015: Designing and Implementing Distributed Applications with Microsoft Visual C++ 6.0," "70-155: Designing and Implementing Distributed Applications with Microsoft Visual FoxPro 6.0," or "70-175: Designing and Implementing Distributed Applications with Microsoft Visual Basic 6.0." The third core exam is "70-100: Analyzing Requirements and Defining Solution Architectures." Elective exams cover specific Microsoft applications and languages, including Visual Basic, C++, the Microsoft Foundation Classes, Access, SQL Server, Excel, and more.

➤ *MCDBA (Microsoft Certified Database Administrator)*—The MCDBA credential reflects the skills required to implement and administer Microsoft SQL Server databases. To obtain an MCDBA, an individual must demonstrate the ability to derive physical database designs, develop logical data models, create physical databases, create data services by using Transact-SQL, manage and maintain databases, configure and manage security, monitor and optimize databases, and install and configure Microsoft SQL Server.

To become an MCDBA, you must pass a total of three core exams and one elective exam. The required core exams are "70-028: Administering Microsoft SQL Server 7.0," "70-029: Designing and Implementing Databases with Microsoft SQL Server 7.0," and "70-215: Installing, Configuring and Administering Microsoft Windows 2000 Server."

The elective exams that you can choose from cover specific uses of SQL Server and include "70-015: Designing and Implementing Distributed Applications with Microsoft Visual C++ 6.0," "70-019: Designing and Implementing Data Warehouses with Microsoft SQL Server 7.0," "70-155: Designing and Implementing Distributed Applications with Microsoft Visual FoxPro 6.0," "70-175: Designing and Implementing Distributed Applications with Microsoft Visual Basic 6.0," and two exams that relate to Windows 2000: "70-216: Implementing and Administering a Microsoft Windows 2000 Network Infrastructure," and "70-087: Implementing and Supporting Microsoft Internet Information Server 4.0."

If you have taken the three core Windows NT 4 exams on your path to becoming an MCSE, you qualify for the Accelerated exam (it replaces the Network Infrastructure exam requirement). The Accelerated exam covers the objectives of all four of the Windows 2000 core exams. In addition to taking the Accelerated exam, you must take only the two SQL exams—Administering and Database Design.

Note that the exam covered by this book is an elective for the MCDBA certification. Table 2 shows the requirements for the MCDBA certification.

## Table 2    MCDBA Requirements

### Core

| If you have not passed these 3 Windows NT 4 exams | |
|---|---|
| Exam 70-067 | Implementing and Supporting Microsoft Windows NT Server 4.0 |
| Exam 70-068 | Implementing and Supporting Microsoft Windows NT Server 4.0 in the Enterprise |
| Exam 70-073 | Microsoft Windows NT Workstation 4.0 |
| **you must take this exam** | |
| Exam 70-215 | Installing, Configuring and Administering Microsoft Windows 2000 Server |
| **plus these 2 exams** | |
| Exam 70-028 | Administering Microsoft SQL Server 7.0 |
| Exam 70-029 | Designing and Implementing Databases with Microsoft SQL Server 7.0 |

### Elective

| Choose 1 of the following exams | |
|---|---|
| Exam 70-015 | Designing and Implementing Distributed Applications with Microsoft Visual C++ 6.0 |
| Exam 70-019 | Designing and Implementing Data Warehouses with Microsoft SQL Server 7.0 |
| Exam 70-087 | Implementing and Supporting Microsoft Internet Information Server 4.0 |
| Exam 70-155 | Designing and Implementing Distributed Applications with Microsoft Visual FoxPro 6.0 |
| Exam 70-175 | Designing and Implementing Distributed Applications with Microsoft Visual Basic 6.0 |
| ➤ Exam 70-216 | Implementing and Administering a Microsoft Windows 2000 Network Infrastructure |

OR

| If you have already passed exams 70-067, 70-068, and 70-073, you may take this exam | |
|---|---|
| Exam 70-240 | Microsoft Windows 2000 Accelerated Exam for MCPs Certified on Microsoft Windows NT 4.0 |
| **plus these 2 exams** | |
| Exam 70-028 | Administering Microsoft SQL Server 7.0 |
| Exam 70-029 | Designing and Implementing Databases with Microsoft SQL Server 7.0 |

➤ *MCT (Microsoft Certified Trainer)*—Microsoft Certified Trainers are deemed able to deliver elements of the official Microsoft curriculum, based on technical knowledge and instructional ability. Thus, it is necessary for an individual seeking MCT credentials (which are granted on a course-by-course basis) to pass the related certification exam for a course and complete the official Microsoft training in the subject area, and to demonstrate an ability to teach.

This teaching skill criterion may be satisfied by proving that one has already attained training certification from Novell, Banyan, Lotus, the Santa Cruz Operation, or Cisco, or by taking a Microsoft-sanctioned workshop on instruction. Microsoft makes it clear that MCTs are important cogs in the Microsoft training channels. Instructors must be MCTs before Microsoft will allow them to teach in any of its official training channels, including Microsoft's affiliated Certified Technical Education Centers (CTECs) and its online training partner network. As of January 1, 2001, MCT candidates must also possess a current MCSE.

Microsoft has announced that the MCP+I and MCSE+I credentials will not be continued when the MCSE exams for Windows 2000 are in full swing because the skill set for the Internet portion of the program has been included in the new MCSE program. Therefore, details on these tracks are not provided here; go to **www.microsoft.com/trainingandservices/** if you need more information.

Once a Microsoft product becomes obsolete, MCPs typically have to recertify on current versions. (If individuals do not recertify, their certifications become invalid.) Because technology keeps changing and new products continually supplant old ones, this should come as no surprise. This explains why Microsoft has announced that MCSEs have 12 months past the scheduled retirement date for the Windows NT 4 exams to recertify on Windows 2000 topics. (Note that this means taking at least two exams, if not more.)

The best place to keep tabs on the MCP program and its related certifications is on the Web. The URL for the MCP program is **www.microsoft.com/ trainingandservices/**. But Microsoft's Web site changes often, so if this URL doesn't work, try using the Search tool on Microsoft's site with either "MCP" or the quoted phrase "Microsoft Certified Professional" as a search string. This will help you find the latest and most accurate information about Microsoft's certification programs.

# Taking a Certification Exam

Once you've prepared for your exam, you need to register with a testing center. Each computer-based MCP exam costs $100, and if you don't pass, you can retest for an additional $100 for each additional try. In the United States and Canada, tests are administered by Prometric and by Virtual University Enterprises (VUE). Here's how you can contact them:

➤ *Prometric*—You can sign up for a test through the company's Web site at **www.prometric.com**. Or, you can register by phone at 800-755-3926 (within the United States or Canada) or at 410-843-8000 (outside the United States and Canada).

➤ *Virtual University Enterprises*—You can sign up for a test or get the phone numbers for local testing centers through the Web page at **www.vue.com/ms/**.

To sign up for a test, you must possess a valid credit card, or contact either company for mailing instructions to send them a check (in the U.S.). Only when payment is verified, or a check has cleared, can you actually register for a test.

To schedule an exam, call the number or visit either of the Web pages at least one day in advance. To cancel or reschedule an exam, you must call before 7 P.M. pacific standard time the day before the scheduled test time (or you may be charged, even if you don't appear to take the test). When you want to schedule a test, have the following information ready:

➤ Your name, organization, and mailing address.

➤ Your Microsoft Test ID. (Inside the United States, this means your Social Security number; citizens of other nations should call ahead to find out what type of identification number is required to register for a test.)

➤ The name and number of the exam you wish to take.

➤ A method of payment. (As we've already mentioned, a credit card is the most convenient method, but alternate means can be arranged in advance, if necessary.)

Once you sign up for a test, you'll be informed as to when and where the test is scheduled. Try to arrive at least 15 minutes early. You must supply two forms of identification—one of which must be a photo ID—to be admitted into the testing room.

All exams are completely closed-book. In fact, you will not be permitted to take anything with you into the testing area, but you will be furnished with a blank sheet of paper and a pen or, in some cases, an erasable plastic sheet and an erasable pen. We suggest that you immediately write down on that sheet of paper all the information you've memorized for the test. In *Exam Cram* books, this information appears on a tear-out sheet inside the front cover of each book. You will have some time to compose yourself and record this information before you start the exam.

When you complete a Microsoft certification exam, the software will tell you whether you've passed or failed. If you need to retake an exam, you'll have to schedule a new test with Prometric or VUE and pay another $100.

The first time you fail a test, you can retake the test the next day. However, if you fail a second time, you must wait 14 days before retaking that test. The 14-day waiting period remains in effect for all retakes after the second failure.

# Tracking MCP Status

As soon as you pass any Microsoft exam (except Networking Essentials), you'll attain Microsoft Certified Professional (MCP) status. Microsoft also generates transcripts that indicate which exams you have passed. You can view a copy of your transcript at any time by going to the MCP secured site and selecting Transcript Tool. This tool will allow you to print a copy of your current transcript and confirm your certification status.

Once you pass the necessary set of exams, you'll be certified. Official certification normally takes anywhere from six to eight weeks, so don't expect to get your credentials overnight. When the package for a qualified certification arrives, it includes a Welcome Kit that contains a number of elements (see Microsoft's Web site for other benefits of specific certifications):

➤ A certificate suitable for framing, along with a wallet card and lapel pin.

➤ A license to use the MCP logo, thereby allowing you to use the logo in advertisements, promotions, and documents, and on letterhead, business cards, and so on. Along with the license comes an MCP logo sheet, which includes camera-ready artwork. (Note: Before using any of the artwork, individuals must sign and return a licensing agreement that indicates they'll abide by its terms and conditions.)

➤ A subscription to *Microsoft Certified Professional Magazine*, which provides ongoing data about testing and certification activities, requirements, and changes to the program.

Many people believe that the benefits of MCP certification go well beyond the perks that Microsoft provides to newly anointed members of this elite group. We're starting to see more job listings that request or require applicants to have an MCP, MCSE, and so on, and many individuals who complete the program can qualify for increases in pay and/or responsibility. As an official recognition of hard work and broad knowledge, one of the MCP credentials is a badge of honor in many IT organizations.

# How to Prepare for an Exam

Preparing for any Windows 2000 Server-related test (including "Implementing and Administering a Microsoft Windows 2000 Network Infrastructure") requires that you obtain and study materials designed to provide comprehensive information about the product and its capabilities that will appear on the specific exam for which you are preparing. The following list of materials will help you study and prepare:

➤ The Windows 2000 Server product CD includes comprehensive online documentation and related materials; it should be a primary resource when you are preparing for the test.

➤ The exam preparation materials, practice tests, and self-assessment exams on the Microsoft Training & Services page at **www.microsoft.com/ trainingandservices/default.asp?PageID=mcp**. The Testing Innovations link offers samples of the new question types found on the Windows 2000 MCSE exams. Find the materials, download them, and use them!

➤ The exam preparation advice, practice tests, questions of the day, and discussion groups on the **ExamCram.com** e-learning and certification destination Web site (**www.examcram.com**).

In addition, you'll probably find any or all of the following materials useful in your quest for Network Infrastructure expertise:

➤ *Microsoft training kits*—Microsoft Press offers a training kit that specifically targets Exam 70-216. For more information, visit: **http://mspress.microsoft. com/findabook/list/series_ak.htm**. This training kit contains information that you will find useful in preparing for the test.

➤ *Microsoft TechNet CD*—This monthly CD-based publication delivers numerous electronic titles that include coverage of Network Infrastructure and related topics on the Technical Information (TechNet) CD. Its offerings include product facts, technical notes, tools and utilities, and information on how to access the Seminars Online training materials for Network Infrastructure. A subscription to TechNet costs $299 per year, but it is well worth the price. Visit **www.microsoft.com/technet/** and check out the information under the "TechNet Subscription" menu entry for more details.

➤ *Study guides*—Several publishers—including The Coriolis Group—offer Windows 2000 titles. The Coriolis Group series include the following:

➤ *The Exam Cram series*—These books give you information about the material you need to know to pass the tests.

➤ *The Exam Prep series*—These books provide a greater level of detail than the *Exam Cram* books and are designed to teach you everything you need to know from an exam perspective. Each book comes with a CD that contains interactive practice exams in a variety of testing formats.

Together, the two series make a perfect pair.

➤ *Multimedia*—These Coriolis Group materials are designed to support learners of all types—whether you learn best by reading or doing:

➤ *The Exam Cram Personal Trainer*—Offers a unique, personalized self-paced training course based on the exam.

➤ *The Exam Cram Personal Test Center*—Features multiple test options that simulate the actual exam, including Fixed-Length, Random, Review, and Test All. Explanations of correct and incorrect answers reinforce concepts learned.

➤ *Classroom training*—CTECs, online partners, and third-party training companies (like Wave Technologies, Learning Tree, Data-Tech, and others) all offer classroom training on Windows 2000. These companies aim to help you prepare to pass Exam 70-216. Although such training runs upwards of $350 per day in class, most of the individuals lucky enough to partake find it to be quite worthwhile.

➤ *Other publications*—There's no shortage of materials available about Network Infrastructure. The resource sections at the end of each chapter should give you an idea of where we think you should look for further discussion.

By far, this set of required and recommended materials represents a nonpareil collection of sources and resources for Network Infrastructure and related topics. We anticipate that you'll find that this book belongs in this company

# About this Book

Each topical *Exam Cram* chapter follows a regular structure, along with graphical cues about important or useful information. Here's the structure of a typical chapter:

➤ *Opening hotlists*—Each chapter begins with a list of the terms, tools, and techniques that you must learn and understand before you can be fully conversant with that chapter's subject matter. We follow the hotlists with one or two introductory paragraphs to set the stage for the rest of the chapter.

➤ *Topical coverage*—After the opening hotlists, each chapter covers a series of topics related to the chapter's subject title. Throughout this section, we highlight topics or concepts likely to appear on a test using a special Exam Alert layout, like this:

 This is what an Exam Alert looks like. Normally, an Exam Alert stresses concepts, terms, software, or activities that are likely to relate to one or more certification test questions. For that reason, we think any information found offset in Exam Alert format is worthy of unusual attentiveness on your part. Indeed, most of the information that appears on The Cram Sheet appears as Exam Alerts within the text.

Pay close attention to material flagged as an Exam Alert; although all the information in this book pertains to what you need to know to pass the exam, we flag certain items that are really important. You'll find what appears in the meat of each chapter to be worth knowing, too, when preparing for the test. Because this book's material is very condensed, we recommend that you use this book along with other resources to achieve the maximum benefit.

In addition to the Exam Alerts, we have provided tips that will help you build a better foundation for Network Infrastructure knowledge. Although the information may not be on the exam, it is certainly related and will help you become a better test-taker.

> This is how tips are formatted. Keep your eyes open for these, and you'll become a Network Infrastructure guru in no time!

➤ *Practice questions*—Although we talk about test questions and topics throughout the book, a section at the end of each chapter presents a series of mock test questions and explanations of both correct and incorrect answers.

➤ *Details and resources*—Every chapter ends with a section titled "Need to Know More?". This section provides direct pointers to Microsoft and third-party resources offering more details on the chapter's subject. In addition, this section tries to rank or at least rate the quality and thoroughness of the topic's coverage by each resource. If you find a resource you like in this collection, use it, but don't feel compelled to use all the resources. On the other hand, we recommend only resources we use on a regular basis, so none of our recommendations will be a waste of your time or money (but purchasing them all at once probably represents an expense that many network administrators and would-be MCPs and MCSEs might find hard to justify).

The bulk of the book follows this chapter structure slavishly, but there are a few other elements that we'd like to point out. Chapter 10 includes a sample test that provides a good review of the material presented throughout the book to ensure you're ready for the exam. Chapter 11 is an answer key to the sample test that appears in Chapter 10. In addition, you'll find a handy glossary and an index.

Finally, the tear-out Cram Sheet attached next to the inside front cover of this *Exam Cram* book represents a condensed and compiled collection of facts and tips that we think you should memorize before taking the test. Because you can dump this information out of your head onto a piece of paper before taking the exam, you can master this information by brute force—you need to remember it only long enough to write it down when you walk into the test room. You might even want to look at it in the car or in the lobby of the testing center just before you walk in to take the test.

# How to Use this Book

We've structured the topics in this book to build on one another. Therefore, some topics in later chapters make more sense after you've read earlier chapters. That's why we suggest you read this book from front to back for your initial test preparation. If you need to brush up on a topic or you have to bone up for a second try, use the index or table of contents to go straight to the topics and questions that you need to study. Beyond helping you prepare for the test, we think you'll find this book useful as a tightly focused reference to some of the most important aspects of Network Infrastructure.

Given all the book's elements and its specialized focus, we've tried to create a tool that will help you prepare for—and pass—Microsoft Exam 70-216. Please share your feedback on the book with us, especially if you have ideas about how we can improve it for future test-takers. We'll consider everything you say carefully, and we'll respond to all suggestions.

Send your questions or comments to us at **learn@examcram.com**. Please remember to include the title of the book in your message; otherwise, we'll be forced to guess which book you're writing about. And we don't like to guess—we want to *know*! Also, be sure to check out the Web pages at **www.examcram.com**, where you'll find information updates, commentary, and certification information.

Thanks, and enjoy the book!

# Self-Assessment

The reason we included a Self-Assessment in this *Exam Cram* is to help you evaluate your readiness to tackle MCSE certification. It should also help you understand what you need to know to master the topic of this book—namely, Exam 70-216, "Implementing and Administering a Microsoft Windows 2000 Network Infrastructure." But before you tackle this Self-Assessment, let's talk about concerns you may face when pursuing an MCSE for Windows 2000, and what an ideal MCSE candidate might look like.

## MCSEs in the Real World

In the next section, we describe an ideal MCSE candidate, knowing full well that only a few real candidates will meet this ideal. In fact, our description of that ideal candidate might seem downright scary, especially with the changes that have been made to the program to support Windows 2000. But take heart: Although the requirements to obtain an MCSE may seem formidable, they are by no means impossible to meet. However, be keenly aware that it does take time, involve some expense, and require real effort to get through the process.

Increasing numbers of people are attaining Microsoft certifications, so the goal is within reach. You can get all the real-world motivation you need from knowing that many others have gone before, so you will be able to follow in their footsteps. If you're willing to tackle the process seriously and do what it takes to obtain the necessary experience and knowledge, you can take—and pass—all the certification tests involved in obtaining an MCSE. In fact, we've designed *Exam Crams*, the companion *Exam Preps*, *Exam Cram Personal Trainers*, and *Exam Cram Personal Test Centers* to make it as easy on you as possible to prepare for these exams. We've also greatly expanded our Web site, **www.examcram.com**, to provide a host of resources to help you prepare for the complexities of Windows 2000.

Besides MCSE, other Microsoft certifications include:

➤ MCSD, which is aimed at software developers and requires one specific exam, two more exams on client and distributed topics, plus a fourth elective exam drawn from a different, but limited, pool of options.

➤ Other Microsoft certifications, whose requirements range from one test (MCP) to several tests (MCP+SB, MCDBA).

# The Ideal Windows 2000 MCSE Candidate

Just to give you some idea of what an ideal MCSE candidate is like, here are some relevant statistics about the background and experience such an individual might have. Don't worry if you don't meet all of these qualifications, or don't come that close—this is a far from ideal world, and where you fall short is simply where you'll have more work to do.

➤ Academic or professional training in network theory, concepts, and operations. This includes everything from networking media and transmission techniques through network operating systems, services, and applications.

➤ Three-plus years of professional networking experience, including experience with Ethernet, token ring, modems, and other networking media. This must include installation, configuration, upgrade, and troubleshooting experience.

*Note: The Windows 2000 MCSE program is much more rigorous than the previous NT MCSE program; therefore, you'll really need some hands-on experience. Some of the exams require you to solve real-world case studies and network design issues, so the more hands-on experience you have, the better.*

➤ Two-plus years in a networked environment that includes hands-on experience with Windows 2000 Server, Windows 2000 Professional, Windows NT Server, Windows NT Workstation, and Windows 95 or Windows 98. A solid understanding of each system's architecture, installation, configuration, maintenance, and troubleshooting is also essential.

➤ Knowledge of the various methods for installing Windows 2000, including manual and unattended installations.

➤ A thorough understanding of key networking protocols, addressing, and name resolution, including TCP/IP, IPX/SPX, and NetBEUI.

➤ A thorough understanding of NetBIOS naming, browsing, and file and print services.

➤ Familiarity with key Windows 2000-based TCP/IP-based services, including HTTP (Web servers), DHCP, WINS, and DNS, plus familiarity with one or more of the following: Internet Information Server (IIS), Index Server, and Proxy Server.

➤ An understanding of how to implement security for key network data in a Windows 2000 environment.

➤ Working knowledge of NetWare 3.x and 4.x, including IPX/SPX frame formats; NetWare file, print, and directory services; and both Novell and Microsoft client software. Working knowledge of Microsoft's Client Service For NetWare (CSNW), Gateway Service For NetWare (GSNW), the NetWare Migration Tool (NWCONV), and the NetWare Client For Windows (NT, 95, and 98) is essential.

➤ A good working understanding of Active Directory. The more you work with Windows 2000, the more you'll realize that this new operating system is quite different from Windows NT. New technologies like Active Directory have really changed the way that Windows is configured and used. We recommend that you find out as much as you can about Active Directory and acquire as much experience using this technology as possible. The time you take learning about Active Directory will be time very well spent!

Fundamentally, this boils down to a bachelor's degree in computer science, plus three years' experience working in a position involving network design, installation, configuration, and maintenance. We believe that well under half of all certification candidates meet these requirements, and that, in fact, most meet less than half of these requirements—at least, when they begin the certification process. But because all the people who already have been certified have survived this ordeal, you can survive it too—especially if you heed what our Self-Assessment can tell you about what you already know and what you need to learn.

# Put Yourself to the Test

The following series of questions and observations is designed to help you figure out how much work you must do to pursue Microsoft certification and what kinds of resources you may consult on your quest. Be absolutely honest in your answers, or you'll end up wasting money on exams you're not yet ready to take. There are no right or wrong answers, only steps along the path to certification. Only you can decide where you really belong in the broad spectrum of aspiring candidates.

Two things should be clear from the outset, however:

➤ Even a modest background in computer science will be helpful.

➤ Hands-on experience with Microsoft products and technologies is an essential ingredient to certification success.

## Educational Background

1. Have you ever taken any computer-related classes? [Yes or No]

   If Yes, proceed to question 2; if No, proceed to question 4.

2. Have you taken any classes on computer operating systems? [Yes or No]

   If Yes, you will probably be able to handle Microsoft's architecture and system component discussions. If you're rusty, brush up on basic operating system concepts, especially virtual memory, multitasking regimes, user mode versus kernel mode operation, and general computer security topics.

   If No, consider some basic reading in this area. We strongly recommend a good general operating systems book, such as *Operating System Concepts, 5th Edition*, by Abraham Silberschatz and Peter Baer Galvin (John Wiley & Sons, 1998, ISBN 0-471-36414-2). If this title doesn't appeal to you, check out reviews for other, similar titles at your favorite online bookstore.

3. Have you taken any networking concepts or technologies classes? [Yes or No]

   If Yes, you will probably be able to handle Microsoft's networking terminology, concepts, and technologies (brace yourself for frequent departures from normal usage). If you're rusty, brush up on basic networking concepts and terminology, especially networking media, transmission types, the OSI Reference Model, and networking technologies such as Ethernet, token ring, FDDI, and WAN links.

   If No, you might want to read one or two books in this topic area. The two best books that we know of are *Computer Networks, 3rd Edition*, by Andrew S. Tanenbaum (Prentice-Hall, 1996, ISBN 0-13-349945-6) and *Computer Networks and Internets, 2nd Edition*, by Douglas E. Comer (Prentice-Hall, 1998, ISBN 0-130-83617-6).

   Skip to the next section, "Hands-on Experience."

4. Have you done any reading on operating systems or networks? [Yes or No]

   If Yes, review the requirements stated in the first paragraphs after Questions 2 and 3. If you meet those requirements, move on to the next section. If No, consult the recommended reading for both topics. A strong background will help you prepare for the Microsoft exams better than just about anything else.

# Hands-on Experience

The most important key to success on all of the Microsoft tests is hands-on experience, especially with Windows 2000 Server and Professional, plus the many add-on services and BackOffice components around which so many of the Microsoft certification exams revolve. If we leave you with only one realization after taking this Self-Assessment, it should be that there's no substitute for time spent installing, configuring, and using the various Microsoft products upon which you'll be tested repeatedly and in depth.

5. Have you installed, configured, and worked with:

   ➤ Windows 2000 Server? [Yes or No]

   If Yes, make sure you understand basic concepts as covered in Exam 70-215. You should also study the TCP/IP interfaces, utilities, and services for Exam 70-216, plus implementing security features for Exam 70-220.

 You can download objectives, practice exams, and other data about Microsoft exams from the Training and Certification page at **www.Microsoft.com/ trainingandservices/default.asp?PageID=mcp/**. Use the "Exams" link to obtain specific exam information.

   If No, you must obtain one or two machines and a copy of Windows 2000 Server. Then, learn the operating system and whatever other software components on which you'll also be tested.

   In fact, we recommend that you obtain two computers, each with a network interface, and set up a two-node network on which to practice. With decent Windows 2000-capable computers selling for about $500 to $600 apiece these days, this shouldn't be too much of a financial hardship. You may have to scrounge to come up with the necessary software, but if you scour the Microsoft Web site you can usually find low-cost options to obtain evaluation copies of most of the software that you'll need.

   ➤ Windows 2000 Professional? [Yes or No]

   If Yes, make sure you understand the concepts covered in Exam 70-210.

   If No, you will want to obtain a copy of Windows 2000 Professional and learn how to install, configure, and maintain it. You can use *MCSE Windows 2000 Professional Exam Cram* to guide your activities and studies, or work straight from Microsoft's test objectives if you prefer.

For any and all of these Microsoft exams, the Resource Kits for the topics involved are a good study resource. You can purchase softcover Resource Kits from Microsoft Press (search for them at **http://mspress.microsoft.com**), but they also appear on the TechNet CDs (**www.microsoft.com/technet**). Along with *Exam Crams* and *Exam Preps*, we believe that Resource Kits are among the best tools you can use to prepare for Microsoft exams.

6. For any specific Microsoft product that is not itself an operating system (for example, SQL Server), have you installed, configured, used, and upgraded this software? [Yes or No]

If the answer is Yes, skip to the next section. If it's No, you must get some experience. Read on for suggestions on how to do this.

Experience is a must with any Microsoft product exam, be it something as simple as FrontPage 2000 or as challenging as SQL Server 7. For trial copies of other software, search Microsoft's Web site using the name of the product as your search term. Also, search for bundles like "BackOffice" or "Small Business Server."

If you have the funds, or your employer will pay your way, consider taking a class at a Certified Training and Education Center (CTEC) or at an Authorized Academic Training Partner (AATP). In addition to classroom exposure to the topic of your choice, you get a copy of the software that is the focus of your course, along with a trial version of whatever operating system it needs, with the training materials for that class.

Before you even think about taking any Microsoft exam, make sure you've spent enough time with the related software to understand how it may be installed and configured, how to maintain such an installation, and how to troubleshoot that software when things go wrong. This will help you in the exam, and in real life!

## Testing Your Exam-Readiness

Whether you attend a formal class on a specific topic to get ready for an exam or use written materials to study on your own, some preparation for the Microsoft certification exams is essential. At $100 a try, pass or fail, you want to do everything you can to pass on your first try. That's where studying comes in.

We have included a practice exam in this book, so if you don't score that well on the test, you can study more and then tackle the test again. We also have exams that you can take online through the **ExamCram.com** Web site at **www.examcram.com**. If you still don't hit a score of at least 70 percent after these tests, you'll want to investigate the other practice test resources we mention in this section.

For any given subject, consider taking a class if you've tackled self-study materials, taken the test, and failed anyway. The opportunity to interact with an instructor and fellow students can make all the difference in the world, if you can afford that privilege. For information about Microsoft classes, visit the Training and Certification page at **www.microsoft.com/education/partners/ctec.asp** for Microsoft Certified Education Centers or **www.microsoft.com/aatp/default.htm** for Microsoft Authorized Training Providers.

If you can't afford to take a class, visit the Training and Certification page anyway, because it also includes pointers to free practice exams and to Microsoft Certified Professional Approved Study Guides and other self-study tools. And even if you can't afford to spend much at all, you should still invest in some low-cost practice exams from commercial vendors.

7. Have you taken a practice exam on your chosen test subject? [Yes or No]

   If Yes, and you scored 70 percent or better, you're probably ready to tackle the real thing. If your score isn't above that threshold, keep at it until you break that barrier.

   If No, obtain all the free and low-budget practice tests you can find and get to work. Keep at it until you can break the passing threshold comfortably.

When it comes to assessing your test readiness, there is no better way than to take a good-quality practice exam and pass with a score of 70 percent or better. When we're preparing ourselves, we shoot for 80-plus percent, just to leave room for the "weirdness factor" that sometimes shows up on Microsoft exams.

# Assessing Readiness for Exam 70-216

In addition to the general exam-readiness information in the previous section, there are several things you can do to prepare for the Implementing and Administering a Microsoft Windows 2000 Network Infrastructure exam. As you're getting ready for Exam 70-216, visit the Exam Cram Windows 2000 Resource Center at **www.examcram.com/studyresource/w2kresource/**. Another valuable resource is the Exam Cram Insider newsletter. Sign up at **www.examcram.com** or send a blank email message to **subscribe-ec@mars.coriolis.com**. We also suggest that you join an active MCSE mailing list. One of the better ones is managed by Sunbelt Software. Sign up at **www.sunbelt-software.com** (look for the Subscribe button).

You can also cruise the Web looking for "braindumps" (recollections of test topics and experiences recorded by others) to help you anticipate topics you're likely to encounter on the test. The MCSE mailing list is a good place to ask where the useful braindumps are, or you can check Shawn Gamble's list at **www.commandcentral.com**.

You can't be sure that a braindump's author can provide correct answers. Thus, use the questions to guide your studies, but don't rely on the answers in a braindump to lead you to the truth. Double-check everything you find in any braindump.

Microsoft exam mavens also recommend checking the Microsoft Knowledge Base (available on its own CD as part of the TechNet collection, or on the Microsoft Web site at **http://support.microsoft.com/support/**) for "meaningful technical support issues" that relate to your exam's topics. Although we're not sure exactly what the quoted phrase means, we have also noticed some overlap between technical support questions on particular products and troubleshooting questions on the exams for those products.

# Onward, through the Fog!

Once you've assessed your readiness, undertaken the right background studies, obtained the hands-on experience that will help you understand the products and technologies at work, and reviewed the many sources of information to help you prepare for a test, you'll be ready to take a round of practice tests. When your scores come back positive enough to get you through the exam, you're ready to go after the real thing. If you follow our assessment regime, you'll not only know what you need to study, but when you're ready to make a test date at Prometric or VUE. Good luck!

# Microsoft
# Certification Exams

. . . . . . . . . . . . . . . . . . . . . . . . . . . . . . . . . . . . . . . . . . . . .

### Terms you'll need to understand:

✓ Case study

✓ Multiple-choice question formats

✓ Build-list-and-reorder question format

✓ Create-a-tree question format

✓ Drag-and-connect question format

✓ Select-and-place question format

✓ Fixed-length tests

✓ Simulations

✓ Adaptive tests

✓ Short-form tests

### Techniques you'll need to master:

✓ Assessing your exam-readiness

✓ Answering Microsoft's varying question types

✓ Altering your test strategy depending on the exam format

✓ Practicing (to make perfect)

✓ Making the best use of the testing software

✓ Budgeting your time

✓ Guessing (as a last resort)

Exam taking is not something that most people anticipate eagerly, no matter how well prepared they might be. In most cases, familiarity helps offset test anxiety. In plain English, this means you probably won't be as nervous when you take your fourth or fifth Microsoft certification exam as you'll be when you take your first one.

Whether it's your first exam or your tenth, understanding the details of taking the new exams (how much time to spend on questions, the environment you'll be in, and so on) and the new exam software will help you concentrate on the material rather than on the setting. Likewise, mastering a few basic exam-taking skills should help you recognize—and perhaps even outfox—some of the tricks and snares you're bound to find in some exam questions.

This chapter, besides explaining the exam environment and software, describes some proven exam-taking strategies that you should be able to use to your advantage.

# Assessing Exam-Readiness

We strongly recommend that you read through and take the Self-Assessment included with this book. (It appears just before this chapter, in fact.) This will help you compare your knowledge base to the requirements for obtaining an MCSE, and it will also help you identify parts of your background or experience that might be in need of improvement, enhancement, or further learning. If you get the right set of basics under your belt, obtaining Microsoft certification will be that much easier.

Once you've gone through the Self-Assessment, you can remedy those topical areas where your background or experience might not measure up to an ideal certification candidate. But you can also tackle subject matter for individual tests at the same time, so you can continue making progress while you're catching up in some areas.

Once you've worked through an *Exam Cram*, have read the supplementary materials, and have taken the practice test, you'll have a pretty clear idea of when you should be ready to take the real exam. Although we strongly recommend that you keep practicing until your scores top the 75 percent mark, 80 percent is a good goal to give yourself some margin for error in a real exam situation (where stress will play more of a role than when you practice). Once you hit that point, you should be ready to go. But if you get through the practice exam in this book without attaining that score, you should keep taking practice tests and studying the materials until you get there. You'll find more pointers on how to study and prepare in the Self-Assessment. But now, on to the exam itself!

# The Exam Situation

When you arrive at the testing center where you scheduled your exam, you'll need to sign in with an exam coordinator. He or she will ask you to show two forms of identification, one of which must be a photo ID. After you've signed in and your time slot arrives, you'll be asked to deposit any books, bags, or other items you brought with you. Then, you'll be escorted into a closed room.

All exams are completely closed book. In fact, you will not be permitted to take anything with you into the testing area, but you will be furnished with a blank sheet of paper and a pen or, in some cases, an erasable plastic sheet and an erasable pen. Before the exam, you should memorize as much of the important material as you can so you can write that information on the blank sheet as soon as you are seated in front of the computer. You can refer to this piece of paper anytime you like during the test, but you'll have to surrender the sheet when you leave the room.

You will have some time to compose yourself and to record this information, before you start the exam.

Typically, the room will be furnished with anywhere from one to half a dozen computers, and each workstation will be separated from the others by dividers designed to keep you from seeing what's happening on someone else's computer. Most test rooms feature a wall with a large picture window. This permits the exam coordinator to monitor the room, to prevent exam-takers from talking to one another, and to observe anything out of the ordinary that might go on. The exam coordinator will have preloaded the appropriate Microsoft certification exam—for this book, that's Exam 70-216—and you'll be permitted to start as soon as you're seated in front of the computer.

All Microsoft certification exams allow a certain maximum amount of time in which to complete your work. (This time is indicated on the exam by an on-screen counter/clock, so you can check the time remaining whenever you like.) All Microsoft certification exams are computer generated. In addition to multiple choice, you'll encounter select and place (drag and drop), create a tree (categorization and prioritization), drag and connect, and build list and reorder (list prioritization) on most exams. Although this might sound quite simple, not only do the questions check your mastery of basic facts and figures about network infrastructure administration, but they also require you to evaluate one or more sets of circumstances or requirements. Often, you'll be asked to give more than one answer to a question. Likewise, you might be asked to select the best or most effective solution to a problem from a range of choices, all of which technically are correct. Taking the exam is quite an adventure, and it involves real thinking. This book shows you what to expect and how to deal with the potential problems, puzzles, and predicaments.

In the next section, you'll learn more about how Microsoft test questions look and how they must be answered.

# Exam Layout and Design

The format of Microsoft's Windows 2000 exams is different from that of its previous exams. For the design exams (70-219, 70-220, 70-221), each exam consists entirely of a series of case studies, and the questions can be of six types. For the Core Four exams (70-210, 70-215, 70-216, 70-217), the same six types of questions can appear, but you are not likely to encounter complex multiquestion case studies.

For design exams, each case study or "testlet" presents a detailed problem that you must read and analyze. Figure 1.1 shows an example of what a case study looks like. You must select the different tabs in the case study to view the entire case.

Following each case study is a set of questions related to the case study; these questions can be one of six types (which are discussed next). Careful attention to details provided in the case study is the key to success. Be prepared to toggle frequently between the case study and the questions as you work. Some of the case studies also include diagrams, which are called *exhibits*, that you'll need to examine closely to understand how to answer the questions.

Once you complete a case study, you can review all the questions and your answers. However, once you move on to the next case study, you might not be able to return to the previous case study and make any changes.

The six types of question formats are:

➤ Multiple choice, single answer

➤ Multiple choice, multiple answers

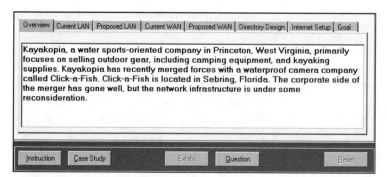

**Figure 1.1** This is how case studies appear.

➤ Build list and reorder (list prioritization)

➤ Create a tree

➤ Drag and connect

➤ Select and place (drag and drop)

*Note: Exam formats may vary by test center location. You might want to call the test center or visit ExamCram.com to see if you can find out which type of test you'll encounter.*

## Multiple-Choice Question Format

Some exam questions require you to select a single answer, whereas others ask you to select multiple correct answers. The following multiple-choice question requires you to select a single correct answer. Following the question is a brief summary of each potential answer and why it is either right or wrong.

## Question 1

You want fault tolerance for your DNS. You are using Active Directory with four Windows 2000 domain controllers, and your primary DNS zone is configured as standalone. How many DNS servers must you configure to ensure fault tolerance for DNS?

○ a.  1

○ b.  2

○ c.  3

○ d.  4

The correct answer is b. A secondary zone will have to be configured to provide fault tolerance for the DNS zone stored on the primary server. Active Directory does provide fault tolerance for DNS if the zone is integrated, but this DNS is a primary zone, thus needing a secondary zone for fault tolerance. Therefore, answer a is incorrect. Configuring additional DNS servers (beyond 2) would provide additional fault tolerance but is not required, making answers c and d incorrect.

This sample question format corresponds closely to the Microsoft certification exam format; the only difference on the exam is that questions are not followed by answer keys. To select an answer, you position the cursor over the radio button next to the answer. Then, click the mouse button to select the answer.

Let's examine a question where one or more answers are possible. This type of question provides checkboxes rather than radio buttons for marking all appropriate selections.

## Question 2

---

> How can host computers have their DNS records automatically updated?
> [Choose all correct answers]
>
> ❑ a. Using the **ipconfig** command
>
> ❑ b. From the DHCP server
>
> ❑ c. Through the DNS client
>
> ❑ d. Through the computer properties setting in Active Directory Users
> and Computers

Answers a, b, and c are correct. The DNS client is registered automatically when the computer running the client is booted, and it can be manually refreshed or initiated from that client using the **ipconfig** command. You can also configure a DHCP server to update client information in DNS. Active Directory Users and Computers contains no such setting for the computer or facility to update DNS. Therefore, answer d is incorrect.

For this particular question, three answers are required. Microsoft sometimes gives partial credit for partially correct answers. For Question 2, you have to check the boxes next to items a, b, and c to obtain credit for a correct answer. Notice that picking the right answers also means knowing why the other answers are wrong!

## Build-List-and-Reorder Question Format

Questions in the build-list-and-reorder format present two lists of items—one on the left and one on the right. To answer the question, you must move items from the list on the right to the list on the left. The final list must then be reordered into a specific order.

These questions can best be characterized as "From the following list of choices, pick the choices that answer the question. Arrange the list in a certain order." To give you practice with this type of question, some questions of this type are included in this study guide. Question 3 shows an example of how they appear in this book; for a sample of how they appear on the test, see Figure 1.2.

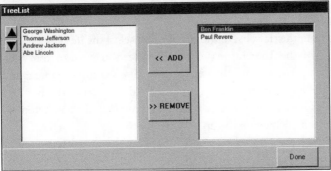

**Figure 1.2** This is how build-list-and-reorder questions appear.

## Question 3

From the following list of famous people, pick those who have been elected President of the United States. Arrange the list in the order that they served.

Thomas Jefferson

Ben Franklin

Abe Lincoln

George Washington

Andrew Jackson

Paul Revere

The correct answer is:

> George Washington
>
> Thomas Jefferson
>
> Andrew Jackson
>
> Abe Lincoln

On an actual exam, the entire list of famous people would initially appear in the list on the right. You would move the four correct answers to the list on the left and then reorder the list on the left. Notice that the answer to the question did not include all items from the initial list. However, this may not always be the case.

To move an item from the right list to the left list, first select the item by clicking on it and then click on the Add button (left arrow). Once you move an item from one list to the other, you can move the item back by first selecting the item and then clicking on the appropriate button (either the Add button or the Remove button). Once items have been moved to the left list, you can reorder an item by selecting the item and clicking on the up or down button.

## Create-a-Tree Question Format

Questions in the create-a-tree format also present two lists—one on the left side of the screen and one on the right side of the screen. The list on the right consists of individual items, and the list on the left consists of nodes in a tree. To answer the question, you must move items from the list on the right to the appropriate node in the tree.

These questions can best be characterized as simply a matching exercise. Items from the list on the right are placed under the appropriate category in the list on the left. Here's an example of how they appear in this book; for a sample of how they appear on the test, see Figure 1.3.

# Question 4

The calendar year is divided into four seasons:

Winter

Spring

Summer

Fall

Identify the season when each of the following holidays occurs:

Christmas

Fourth of July

Labor Day

Flag Day

Memorial Day

Washington's Birthday

Thanksgiving

Easter

The correct answer is:

Winter

Christmas

Washington's Birthday

Spring

Flag Day

Memorial Day

Easter

Summer

Fourth of July

Labor Day

Fall

Thanksgiving

In this case, all the items in the list were used. However, this may not always be the case.

To move an item from the right list to its appropriate location in the tree, you must first select the appropriate tree node by clicking on it. Then, you select the item to be moved and click on the Add button. If one or more items have been added to a tree node, the node will be displayed with a "+" icon to the left of the node name. You can click on this icon to expand the node and view the item(s) that have been added. If you accidentally add an item to the wrong tree node, you can remove it by selecting it and clicking on the Remove button.

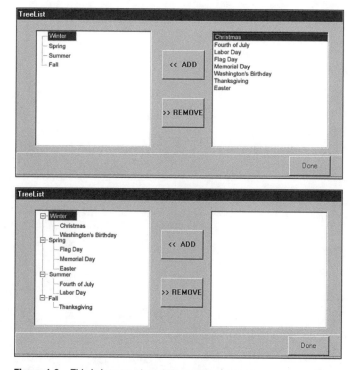

**Figure 1.3**   This is how create-a-tree questions appear.

## Drag-and-Connect Question Format

Questions in the drag-and-connect format present a group of objects and a list of "connections." To answer the question, you must move the appropriate connections between the objects.

This type of question is best described using graphics. Here's an example.

## Question 5

The following objects represent the different states of water:

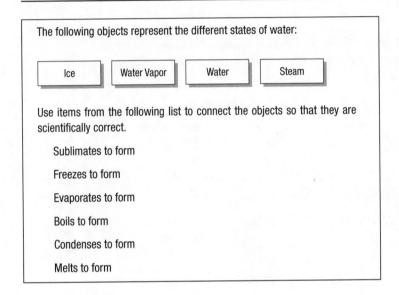

Ice    Water Vapor    Water    Steam

Use items from the following list to connect the objects so that they are scientifically correct.

Sublimates to form

Freezes to form

Evaporates to form

Boils to form

Condenses to form

Melts to form

The correct answer is:

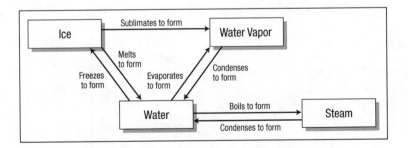

For this type of question, it's not necessary to use every object, and each connection can be used multiple times.

# Select-and-Place Question Format

Questions in the select-and-place (drag-and-drop) format present a diagram with blank boxes and a list of labels that you drag to correctly fill in the blank boxes. To answer the question, you must move the labels to their appropriate positions on the diagram.

This type of question is best described using graphics. Here's an example.

## Question 6

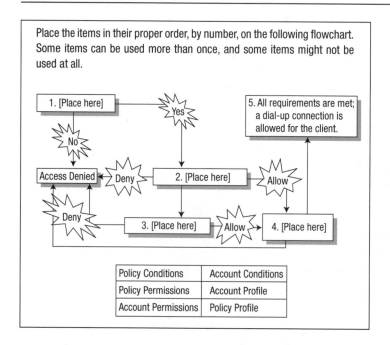

The correct answer is:

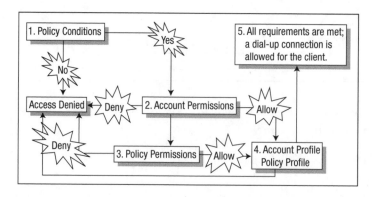

# Microsoft's Testing Formats

Currently, Microsoft uses four different testing formats:

➤ Case study

➤ Fixed length

➤ Adaptive

➤ Short form

As we mentioned earlier, the case-study approach is used with Microsoft's design exams. These exams consist of a set of case studies that you must analyze to answer questions related to the case studies. Such exams include one or more case studies (tabbed topic areas), each of which is followed by 4 to 10 questions. The question types for design exams and for Core Four Windows 2000 exams are multiple choice, build list and reorder, create a tree, drag and connect, and select and place. Depending on the test topic, some exams are totally case-based, whereas others are not.

Other Microsoft exams employ advanced testing capabilities that might not be immediately apparent. Although the questions that appear are primarily multiple choice, the logic that drives them is more complex than older Microsoft tests, which use a fixed sequence of questions, called a *fixed-length test*. Some questions employ a sophisticated user interface, which Microsoft calls a *simulation*, to test your knowledge of the software and systems under consideration in a more or less "live" environment that behaves just like the original. The Testing Innovations link at **www.microsoft.com/trainingandservices/default.asp?PageID=mcp** includes a downloadable practice simulation.

For some exams, Microsoft has turned to a well-known technique, called *adaptive testing*, to establish a test-taker's level of knowledge and product competence. Adaptive exams look the same as fixed-length exams, but they discover the level of difficulty at which an individual test-taker can correctly answer questions. Test-takers with differing levels of knowledge or ability therefore see different sets of questions; individuals with high levels of knowledge or ability are presented with a smaller set of more difficult questions, whereas individuals with lower levels of knowledge are presented with a larger set of easier questions. Two individuals might answer the same percentage of questions correctly, but the test-taker with a higher knowledge or ability level will score higher because his or her questions are worth more.

Also, the lower-level test-taker will probably answer more questions than his or her more-knowledgeable colleague. This explains why adaptive tests use ranges of values to define the number of questions and the amount of time it takes to complete the test.

Adaptive tests work by evaluating the test-taker's most recent answer. A correct answer leads to a more difficult question (and the test software's estimate of the test-taker's knowledge and ability level is raised). An incorrect answer leads to a less difficult question (and the test software's estimate of the test-taker's knowledge and ability level is lowered). This process continues until the test targets the test-taker's true ability level. The exam ends when the test-taker's level of accuracy meets a statistically acceptable value (in other words, when his or her performance demonstrates an acceptable level of knowledge and ability) or when the maximum number of items has been presented (in which case, the test-taker is almost certain to fail).

Microsoft also introduced a short-form test for its most popular tests. This test delivers 25 to 30 questions to its takers, giving them exactly 60 minutes to complete the exam. This type of exam is similar to a fixed-length test, in that it allows readers to jump ahead or return to earlier questions and to cycle through the questions until the test is done. Microsoft does not use adaptive logic in this test, but claims that statistical analysis of the question pool is such that the 25 to 30 questions delivered during a short-form exam conclusively measure a test-taker's knowledge of the subject matter in much the same way as an adaptive test. You can think of the short-form test as a kind of "greatest hits exam" (that is, the most important questions are covered) version of an adaptive exam on the same topic.

*Note: Some of the Microsoft exams can contain a combination of adaptive and fixed-length questions.*

Microsoft tests can come in any one of these forms. Whatever you encounter, you must take the test in whichever form it appears; you can't choose one form over another. If anything, it pays more to prepare thoroughly for an adaptive exam than for a fixed-length or a short-form exam: The penalties for answering incorrectly are built into the test itself on an adaptive exam, whereas the layout remains the same for a fixed-length or short-form test, no matter how many questions you answer incorrectly.

 The biggest difference between an adaptive test and a fixed-length or short-form test is that on a fixed-length or short-form test, you can revisit questions after you've read them over one or more times. On an adaptive test, you must answer the question when it's presented, and you have no opportunities to revisit that question thereafter.

# Strategies for Different Testing Formats

Before you choose a test-taking strategy, you must know whether your test is case-study based, fixed length, short form, or adaptive. When you begin your exam, you'll know right away whether the test is based on case studies. The interface will consist of a tabbed window that allows you to easily navigate through the sections of the case.

If you are taking a test that is not based on case studies, the software will tell you that the test is adaptive, if in fact the version you're taking is an adaptive test. If your introductory materials fail to mention this, you're probably taking a fixed-length test (50 to 70 questions). If the total number of questions involved is 25 to 30, you're taking a short-form test. Some tests announce themselves by indicating that they will start with a set of adaptive questions, followed by fixed-length questions.

You'll be able to tell for sure whether you are taking an adaptive, fixed-length, or short-form test by the first question. If it includes a checkbox that lets you mark the question for later review, you're taking a fixed-length or short-form test. If the total number of questions is 25 to 30, it's a short-form test; if more than 30, it's a fixed-length test. Adaptive test questions can be visited (and answered) only once, and they include no such checkbox.

## The Case-Study Exam Strategy

Most test-takers find that the case-study type of test used for the design exams (70-219, 70-220, and 70-221) is the most difficult to master. When it comes to studying for a case-study test, your best bet is to approach each case study as a standalone test. The biggest challenge you'll encounter is that you'll feel you won't have enough time to get through all of the cases that are presented.

Each case provides a lot of material that you need to read and study before you can effectively answer the questions that follow. The trick to taking a case-study exam is to first scan the case study to get the highlights. Make sure you read the overview section of the case so that you understand the context of the problem at hand. Then, quickly move on and scan the questions.

As you are scanning the questions, make mental notes to yourself so that you'll remember which sections of the case study you should focus on. Some case studies provide a fair amount of extra information that you don't really need to answer the questions. The goal with our scanning approach is to avoid having to study and analyze material that is not completely relevant.

When studying a case, carefully read the tabbed information. It is important to answer each and every question. You will be able to toggle back and forth from case to questions and from question to question within a case testlet. However, once you leave the case and move on, you might not be able to return to it. You might want to take notes while reading useful information so you can refer to them when you tackle the test questions. It's hard to go wrong with this strategy when taking any kind of Microsoft certification test.

## The Fixed-Length and Short-Form Exam Strategy

A well-known principle when taking fixed-length or short-form exams is to first read over the entire exam from start to finish while answering only those questions you feel absolutely sure of. On subsequent passes, you can dive into more complex questions more deeply, knowing how many such questions you have left.

Fortunately, the Microsoft exam software for fixed-length and short-form tests makes the multiple-visit approach easy to implement. At the top-left corner of each question is a checkbox that permits you to mark that question for a later visit.

*Note: Marking questions makes review easier, but you can return to any question by clicking the Forward or Back button repeatedly.*

As you read each question, if you answer only those you're sure of and mark for review those that you're not sure of, you can keep working through a decreasing list of questions as you answer the trickier ones in order.

 There's at least one potential benefit to reading the exam over completely before answering the trickier questions: Sometimes, information supplied in later questions sheds more light on earlier questions. At other times, information you read in later questions might jog your memory about network infrastructure administration facts, figures, or behavior that helps you answer earlier questions. Either way, you'll come out ahead if you defer those questions about which you're not absolutely sure.

Here are some question-handling strategies that apply to fixed-length and short-form tests. Use them if you have the chance:

➤ When returning to a question after your initial read-through, read every word again—otherwise, your mind can fall quickly into a rut. Sometimes, revisiting a question after turning your attention elsewhere lets you see something you missed, but the strong tendency is to see what you've seen before. Try to avoid that tendency at all costs.

➤ If you return to a question more than twice, try to articulate to yourself what you don't understand about the question, why answers don't appear to make sense, or what appears to be missing. If you chew on the subject awhile, your subconscious might provide the details you lack, or you might notice a "trick" that points to the right answer.

As you work your way through the exam, another counter that Microsoft provides will come in handy—the number of questions completed and questions outstanding. For fixed-length and short-form tests, it's wise to budget your time by making sure that you've completed one-quarter of the questions one-quarter of the way through the exam period and three-quarters of the questions three-quarters of the way through.

If you're not finished when only five minutes remain, use that time to guess your way through any remaining questions. Remember, guessing is potentially more valuable than not answering because blank answers are always wrong, but a guess can turn out to be right. If you don't have a clue about any of the remaining questions, pick answers at random, or choose all a's, b's, and so on. The important thing is to submit an exam for scoring that has an answer for every question.

At the very end of your exam period, you're better off guessing than leaving questions unanswered.

## The Adaptive Exam Strategy

If one principle applies to taking an adaptive test, it could be summed up as "Get it right the first time." You cannot elect to skip a question and move on to the next one when taking an adaptive test, because the testing software uses your answer to the current question to select whatever question it plans to present next. Nor can you return to a question once you've moved on, because the software gives you only one chance to answer the question. You can, however, take notes, because sometimes information supplied in earlier questions will shed more light on later questions.

Also, when you answer a question correctly, you are presented with a more difficult question next, to help the software gauge your level of skill and ability. When you answer a question incorrectly, you are presented with a less difficult question, and the software lowers its current estimate of your skill and ability. This continues until the program settles into a reasonably accurate estimate of what you know and can do and takes you on average through somewhere between 15 and 30 questions as you complete the test.

The good news is that if you know your stuff, you'll probably finish most adaptive tests in 30 minutes or so. The bad news is that you must really, really know your stuff to do your best on an adaptive test. That's because some questions are so convoluted, complex, or hard to follow that you're bound to miss one or two, at a minimum, even if you do know your stuff. So the more you know, the better you'll do on an adaptive test, even accounting for the occasionally weird or un-fathomable questions that appear on these exams.

Because you can't always tell in advance whether a test is fixed length, short form, or adaptive, you are best served by preparing for the exam as if it were adaptive. That way, you should be prepared to pass no matter what kind of test you take. But if you do take a fixed-length or short-form test, remember our tips from the preceding section. They should help you improve on what you could do on an adaptive test.

If you encounter a question on an adaptive test that you can't answer, you must guess an answer immediately. Because of how the software works, you might suffer for your guess on the next question if you guess right, because you'll get a more difficult question next!

# Question-Handling Strategies

For those questions that take only a single answer, usually two or three of the answers will be obviously incorrect, and two of the answers will be plausible; of course, only one can be correct. Unless the answer leaps out at you (if it does, reread the question to look for a trick; sometimes those are the ones you're most likely to get wrong), begin the process of answering by eliminating those answers that are most obviously wrong.

Almost always, at least one answer out of the possible choices for a question can be eliminated immediately because it matches one of these conditions:

➤ The answer does not apply to the situation.

➤ The answer describes a nonexistent issue, an invalid option, or an imaginary state.

After you eliminate all answers that are obviously wrong, you can apply your retained knowledge to eliminate further answers. Look for items that sound cor-rect but refer to actions, commands, or features that are not present or not avail-able in the situation that the question describes.

If you're still faced with a blind guess among two or more potentially correct an-swers, reread the question. Try to picture how each of the possible remaining an-swers would alter the situation. Be especially sensitive to terminology; sometimes the choice of words ("remove" instead of "disable") can make the difference between a right answer and a wrong one.

Only when you've exhausted your ability to eliminate answers, but remain unclear about which of the remaining possibilities is correct, should you guess at an answer. An unanswered question offers you no points, but guessing gives you at least some chance of getting a question right; just don't be too hasty when making a blind guess.

*Note: If you're taking a fixed-length or a short-form test, you can wait until the last round of reviewing marked questions (just as you're about to run out of time or out of unanswered questions) before you start making guesses. You have the same option within each case–study testlet (but once you leave a testlet, you might not be allowed to return to it). If you're taking an adaptive test, you have to guess to move on to the next question if you can't figure out an answer some other way. Either way, guessing should be your technique of last resort!*

Numerous questions assume that the default behavior of a particular utility is in effect. If you know the defaults and understand what they mean, this knowledge will help you cut through many Gordian knots.

# Mastering the Inner Game

In the final analysis, knowledge breeds confidence, and confidence breeds success. If you study the materials in this book carefully and review all the practice questions at the end of each chapter, you should become aware of those areas where additional learning and study are required.

After you've worked your way through the book, take the practice exam in the back of the book. Taking this test will provide a reality check and help you identify areas to study further. Make sure you follow up and review materials related to the questions you miss on the practice exam before scheduling a real exam. Only when you've covered that ground and feel comfortable with the whole scope of the practice exam should you set an exam appointment. Only if you score 80 percent or better should you proceed to the real thing (otherwise, obtain some additional practice tests so you can keep trying until you hit this magic number).

If you take a practice exam and don't score at least 80 to 85 percent correct, you'll want to practice further. Microsoft provides links to practice exam providers and also offers self-assessment exams at **www.microsoft.com/trainingandservices/**. You should also check out **ExamCram.com** for downloadable practice questions.

Armed with the information in this book and with the determination to augment your knowledge, you should be able to pass the certification exam. However, you need to work at it, or you'll spend the exam fee more than once before you finally pass. If you prepare seriously, you should do well. We are confident that you can do it!

The next section covers other sources you can use to prepare for the Microsoft certification exams.

# Additional Resources

A good source of information about Microsoft certification exams comes from Microsoft itself. Because its products and technologies—and the exams that go with them—change frequently, the best place to go for exam-related information is online.

If you haven't already visited the Microsoft Certified Professional site, do so right now. The MCP home page resides at **www.microsoft.com/trainingandservices/** (see Figure 1.4).

*Note: This page might not be there by the time you read this, or it may be replaced by something new and different, because things change regularly on the Microsoft site. Should this happen, please read the sidebar titled "Coping with Change on the Web."*

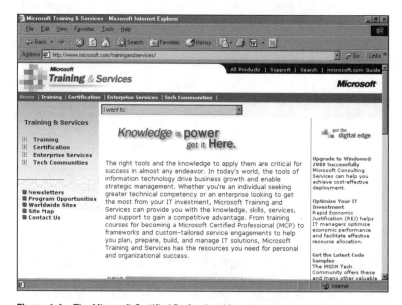

**Figure 1.4**   The Microsoft Certified Professional home page.

## Coping with Change on the Web

Sooner or later, all the information we've shared with you about the Microsoft Certified Professional pages and the other Web-based resources mentioned throughout the rest of this book will go stale or be replaced by newer information. In some cases, the URLs you find here might lead you to their replacements; in other cases, the URLs will go nowhere, leaving you with the dreaded "404 File not found" error message. When that happens, don't give up.

There's always a way to find what you want on the Web if you're willing to invest some time and energy. Most large or complex Web sites—and Microsoft's qualifies on both counts—offer a search engine. On all of Microsoft's Web pages, a Search button appears along the top edge of the page. As long as you can get to Microsoft's site (it should stay at **www.microsoft.com** for a long time), use this tool to help you find what you need.

The more focused you can make a search request, the more likely the results will include information you can use. For example, you can search for the string

```
"training and certification"
```

to produce a lot of data about the subject in general, but if you're looking for the preparation guide for Exam 70-216, "Implementing and Administering a Microsoft Windows 2000 Network Infrastructure," you'll be more likely to get there quickly if you use a search string similar to the following:

```
"Exam 70-216" AND "preparation guide"
```

Likewise, if you want to find the Training and Certification downloads, try a search string such as this:

```
"training and certification" AND "download page"
```

Finally, feel free to use general search tools—such as **www.search.com**, **www.altavista.com**, and **www.excite.com**—to look for related information. Although Microsoft offers great information about its certification exams online, there are plenty of third-party sources of information and assistance that need not follow Microsoft's party line. Therefore, if you can't find something where the book says it lives, intensify your search.

# Network Protocols

### Terms you'll need to understand:

✓ Protocol

✓ OSI reference model

✓ Subnet mask

✓ Packet filtering

### Techniques you'll need to master:

✓ Knowing the differences between routable and nonroutable protocols

✓ Implementing and configuring multiple network protocols

✓ Installing and managing TCP/IP packet filters

Protocols are the language of computers. If computers want to talk to one another, they must speak the same language, or in other words, use the same protocol. If they don't use the same protocol, they cannot exchange information. The good thing about Windows 2000 is that it supports many of the common network protocols in use today, which makes it a good choice of operating system to use in different types of networks.

Protocols are sets of rules that define how computers and components interact with one another. They are developed either by a single entity or by an organization made up of a group of entities. The International Organization for Standardization (ISO), located in Geneva, Switzerland, is responsible for developing and publishing standards. This group designed a standard that is used as a model for network communication, the Open Systems Interconnection (OSI) reference model.

# The OSI Reference Model

Network communication is a complex process, requiring that participating parties all be "on the same page." Having a set of rules to follow increases the chance that information will be exchanged, which is why the OSI reference model was designed. The model is a guide for developers to follow when creating or implementing a protocol.

The OSI model is divided into seven layers. Each layer defines a part of the network communication process, by specifying the layer's function in transmitting data on the network. *Network communication* is information passed between the layers. Each layer is directly related to the layer above it and the layer below it. The following are the OSI reference model layers:

➤ *Physical layer*—Responsible for putting the data on the medium.

➤ *Data Link layer*—Defines how the data is accessed from the medium and how it is put on the medium.

➤ *Network layer*—Makes sure the information has the address of where it needs to go.

➤ *Transport layer*—Provides error-checking and makes sure the information arrives.

➤ *Session layer*—Establishes communication channels between hosts.

➤ *Presentation layer*—Formats the information.

➤ *Application layer*—Defines the way applications interact with the network.

To understand how the OSI model works, imagine the following illustration: You have just received information about airplanes and airlines. Your friend Joe is excited about his new position with a major airline, and you want to communicate this new information to him. To communicate with Joe, you can use various methods, one of which is a telephone.

The first thing you need is a telephone, a piece of hardware you can buy at the store. After you purchase a telephone, it does you no good (meaning you can't communicate with Joe) until you take the next step, which is plugging it into the wall jack. Even after plugging it into the wall, you can't communicate with Joe until you pick up the phone and ensure you have a dial tone. You have to dial his phone number, you have to make sure the person who answers the phone speaks your language, and you have to make sure that Joe eventually gets on the line. After you have done all this, you then need to explain the information to Joe in a way that he can understand it. After this is done, Joe can then apply the information you have communicated to him.

Let's see how this illustrates the OSI model.

➤ *Physical layer*—The telephone

➤ *Data Link layer*—The dial tone

➤ *Network layer*—The phone number

➤ *Transport layer*—The correct language

➤ *Session layer*—Joe getting on the line

➤ *Presentation layer*—The format for the information that Joe understands

➤ *Application layer*—Joe using the information you communicated to him

Many other everyday scenarios can illustrate the OSI reference model. The purpose here is to help you see how the layers work with each other to pass on information.

*Note: It is important to note that different protocols can work at different layers of the OSI model. Some protocols only work at one layer, but others work at more than one layer.*

Network connectivity devices also function at different levels of the OSI model. Hubs, media, repeaters, and network interface cards all function at the Physical layer. Switches and bridges function at the Data Link layer. Routers (default gateways) function at the Network layer, and gateways (protocol translators) typically function at the Application layer.

# Protocols Supported by Windows 2000

Just as there are many different languages in the world, there are many different types of protocols. In Windows 2000, the protocols supported are:

➤ NetBIOS Enhanced User Interface (NetBEUI)

➤ NWLink Internetwork Packet Exchange/Sequenced Packet Exchange (IPX/SPX)

➤ AppleTalk

➤ Data Link Control (DLC)

➤ Transmission Control Protocol/Internet Protocol (TCP/IP)

Let's discuss each of these protocols and how Windows 2000 uses them in network communication.

## NetBIOS Enhanced User Interface (NetBEUI)

NetBEUI is a small and fast protocol used by Microsoft operating systems. Some of the documentation you see concerning NetBEUI also mentions the word *efficient*. That is debatable. If efficient means getting to where it needs to go with no regard for network traffic, then yes, it is efficient. However, if efficient takes into account network traffic, then no, it is not.

NetBEUI works at the Transport layer; therefore, it has a reliable delivery aspect. NetBEUI was designed for smaller networks because the protocol has a tendency to be chatty. *Chatty* means it is broadcast based, and you don't want a lot of chat happening in a network.

In Windows 2000, NetBEUI is in version 3 and is known as NetBIOS Frame (NBF). NBF is Microsoft's implementation of the NetBEUI protocol on Windows 2000 computers. If you have a network of 20 or fewer Windows 2000 computers, NetBEUI is a good choice, unless you need to segment your network or get to the Internet. The minute you start putting routers in your network, all bets are off concerning NetBEUI. NetBEUI is not routable, and therefore you cannot use it as the protocol of choice for large networks that are segmented by routers.

*Note: NBF does support routing on an IBM Token-Ring network.*

The Windows 2000 version of NetBEUI has fewer limitations on it, such as the 254-session connection limitation that existed with the original NetBEUI protocol.

When NetBEUI is installed on a Windows 2000-based computer, you do not need to configure the protocol. If you really want to, however, you can change the default values for NetBEUI in the Registry. The NetBEUI startup entries appear under the following subkey:

```
HKEY_LOCAL_MACHINE\SYSTEM\Services\NBF\Parameters
```

Only make changes to the Registry if you cannot find the appropriate tool in the Microsoft Management Console (MMC).

If you have multiple network interface cards (NICs) in your computer, do not bind NetBEUI to more than one card on the same physical network or on bridged Ethernet segments. The reason is that NetBEUI tries to register the name from all NICs, and you get a duplicate name error.

Another funny thing about NetBEUI is that if you have a Windows 2000 computer running only NetBEUI, it receives the master browser list from the master browser running NetBEUI. Browsing on a computer running Windows 2000 happens per protocol. The client uses one protocol at a time. It first tries one, and then uses another if it doesn't receive a response. This might cause problems with Windows 2000 computers running only TCP/IP or some other network protocol, where the computer does not receive a completely accurate browse list.

## NWLink Internetwork Packet Exchange/Sequenced Packet Exchange (IPX/SPX)

NWLink is Microsoft's implementation of the IPX/SPX protocol developed by Novell. As the name indicates, it is really two different protocols that operate at different levels of the OSI model. IPX functions at the Network layer, defining addressing on a NetWare network. SPX functions at the Transport layer, providing reliability.

Unlike NetBEUI, NWLink is routable. Because of this capability, this protocol is better suited for larger networks that use routers. Although this protocol is included with Windows 2000, it is usually only used in networks that include NetWare servers. NWLink assists with NetWare client/server applications running Winsock. Windows 2000 clients that need access to files and print services on NetWare servers must install Client Services for NetWare or Gateway Services for NetWare. NWLink installs automatically when you install Client Services for NetWare or Gateway Services for NetWare. For NetWare clients that need to access files and print services on Windows 2000 servers, there is File and Print Services for NetWare.

## AppleTalk

Windows 2000 supports the AppleTalk protocol, which was developed by Apple. The AppleTalk protocol is not used as a communications protocol between Windows 2000 computers. It is only used to accommodate Macintosh computers. AppleTalk is routable and therefore can be implemented in larger networks. There is a caveat: Windows 2000 Server uses the AppleTalk protocol to allow Macintosh clients to access file and print services that are installed if the Windows 2000 server is also running File Services for Macintosh and Print Services for Macintosh.

## Data Link Control (DLC)

Data Link Control is a protocol used primarily to connect Windows 2000 computers to IBM mainframe computers or to access Hewlett-Packard JetDirect printers. DLC is not used for network communication between Windows 2000 computers or any Microsoft operating systems.

## TCP/IP

Volumes have been written on the subject of TCP/IP, its history, its uses, and its possible future. This chapter will not contain a complete discussion of TCP/IP. The purpose of this section is to give a basic background and to examine TCP/IP in relation to the Windows 2000 exam objectives.

TCP/IP is really a suite of protocols. In other words, it consists of a number of protocols that together effect network communication. It is the most open of all the protocol stacks, and for this reason, it is the most utilized. *Open* in this sense means that no single vendor controls it, unlike IPX/SPX or AppleTalk, which are owned by Novell and Apple, respectively. Almost every operating system supports TCP/IP, and Windows 2000 is no exception.

The TCP/IP reference model is an example of how protocols work together to effect network communications. Microsoft uses a four-layer model for its TCP/IP stack that maps nicely to the OSI reference model. All the protocols in the TCP/IP suite are contained in the following four layers:

➤ Application layer

➤ Transport layer

➤ Internet layer

➤ Network Interface layer

These layers are an implementation of the OSI reference model specifically used in the TCP/IP protocol stack.

Remember, a protocol stack is a bunch of protocols, so the TCP/IP protocol stack consists of many protocols.

At the top of the stack is the Application layer. This is where (surprise, surprise) the applications reside. Two of the protocols that reside at this layer are File Transfer Protocol (FTP) and Hypertext Transfer Protocol (HTTP).

The next layer is the Transport layer. This is where data is either passed up to a specific application in the Application layer or passed down to the Internet layer for delivery. The two main protocols at this layer are User Datagram Protocol (UDP) and TCP. UDP provides fast, connectionless (non-guaranteed) delivery, whereas TCP provides connection-oriented (guaranteed) delivery.

The next layer is the Internet layer. This layer is responsible for addressing and routing network communications. Some of the protocols in this layer are IP, Internet Control Message Protocol (ICMP), Internet Group Management Protocol (IGMP), and Address Resolution Protocol (ARP).

The last and lowest-level layer in the protocol stack is the Network Interface layer. The Network Interface layer is responsible for taking data off of the medium and also for putting data onto the medium. Ethernet and Token Ring are two common protocols that reside in this layer. These protocols are concerned with how data is transmitted on the medium.

## IP Addresses

In a network, every host must know how to communicate with other hosts. Through protocols, hosts are able to address other hosts on a network. If they use TCP/IP, they use an IP address. Each host has a unique IP address.

An IP address is a 32-bit number represented in dotted decimal notation, such as 131.107.2.200. Each number that precedes a dot represents eight bits of the address called an *octet*. Because a bit is a binary digit (0 or 1), there are 256 possible combinations for each octet ($2^8$ equals 256). This translates to a range from 0 through 255.

Part of the IP address represents the host, and part of it represents the network. It's similar to a street address. If I live at 123 Redmond Way, Redmond Way represents my street and 123 represents my house. Think of the house as the host and the street as the network. If my IP address was 131.107.2.200, part of that address represents the network I am on, and part of it represents my computer. So how do I know what part?

IP addresses are divided into classes. This chapter covers four classes: A, B, C, and D.

If a host has a class A IP address, the first octet determines what network it is on. If the host has a class B IP address, the first two octets are used, and for a class C address, the first three octets determine the network. The remaining octets that are not used to determine the network indicate which host it is on the network.

The first octet of Class A addresses ranges from 1 through 126. There are two reserved numbers in Class A networks: the number 127 is reserved for diagnostic purposes and the number 10 is reserved for private internal addresses.

The first octet of Class B addresses ranges from 128 through 191, and the first octet for class C addresses ranges from 192 through 223.

Class D addresses are reserved for IP multicasting. This address class is used for applications to multicast data to multicast-capable hosts on an internetwork. A classic example would be hosts on a private company network waiting to receive a company multicast. The first octet of Class D addresses ranges from 224 through 239.

An IP address actually has two parts. The address itself consists of the network ID and the host ID, which is defined by the subnet mask. The subnet mask "masks" a portion of the IP address so you can determine the network ID. You might be saying, "Wait! Didn't you say that if I have a class A address, the first octet tells me what network I am on?" The answer is yes, if there is only one network. What if you have many networks (subnetworks)? You then need a way for other hosts to find you. The subnet mask helps hosts determine exactly where you are on the network. It does this through a process called *ANDing*. I don't discuss the process in this text because it is discussed in detail in *MCSE TCP/IP Exam Cram, 3rd Edition* (The Coriolis Group, 2000). Let's talk about how TCP/IP installation and configuration is done in Windows 2000.

## TCP/IP Installation

TCP/IP is the default protocol in Windows 2000, meaning if you choose all the defaults during setup, TCP/IP is the protocol installed. In the next chapter, a new feature concerning IP address allocation in Windows 2000, Automatic private IP addressing, will be discussed.

## Installing Network Protocols

Installing network protocols is an easy task in Windows 2000. To install a network protocol, follow these steps:

1. From the Start menu, choose Settings|Control Panel.

2. Double-click Network And Dial-up Connections.

3. Double-click Local Area Connections, and then select Properties (see Figure 2.1).

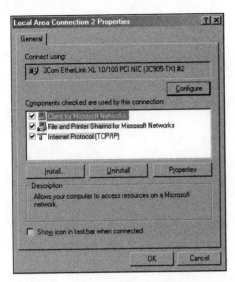

**Figure 2.1**    The Local Area Connection Properties dialog box.

4. Click Install, select Protocol, and then click Add (see Figure 2.2).

5. Choose the protocol you want to install and then click OK (see Figure 2.3).

## Configuring Network Bindings

Configuring network bindings for network protocols is just as easy a task:

1. From the Start menu, choose Settings|Control Panel.

2. Double-click Network And Dial-up Connections.

3. Select Advanced|Advanced Settings from the menu bar.

4. In the Connections area of the Advanced Settings dialog box, select Local Area Connection (see Figure 2.4).

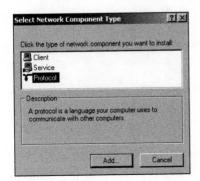

**Figure 2.2**    The Select Network Component Type dialog box.

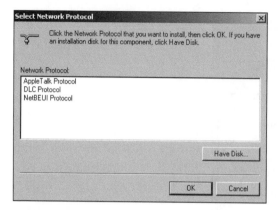

**Figure 2.3**   The Select Network Protocol dialog box.

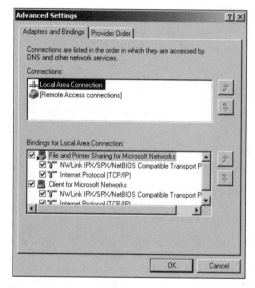

**Figure 2.4**   You can configure bindings on different types of network connections from this dialog box.

5. In the Bindings For Local Area Connection area, select the appropriate binding.

6. Use the arrows next to the Bindings For Local Area Connection list to adjust the priority.

## Packet Filters

Windows 2000 allows you to set up TCP/IP packet filters for three protocols: TCP, UDP, and IP. Packet filtering lets you decide what type of incoming network traffic you want. This feature is really best used in conjunction with IP packet filtering through Routing and Remote Access.

TCP/IP filtering can be enabled and disabled for all adapters through a single checkbox. If the port to which the incoming packet is directed is in the list in the dialog box, the packet gets processed. The only exception is if the packet is an ICMP packet. ICMP packets cannot be filtered using this feature; you must use IP packet filtering through Routing and Remote Access.

*Note: Filtering is applied to incoming packets only.*

To configure TCP/IP packet filtering, follow these steps:

1. From the Start menu, choose Settings|Control Panel.

2. Double-click Network And Dial-up Connections.

3. Right-click Local Area Connection and click Properties.

4. Highlight Internet Protocol (TCP/IP) and click Properties.

5. Click the Advanced button, and then click the Options tab (see Figure 2.5).

6. In the Optional Settings area, select TCP/IP Filtering and click Properties.

7. Choose the appropriate ports on the appropriate protocols you want to allow (see Figure 2.6).

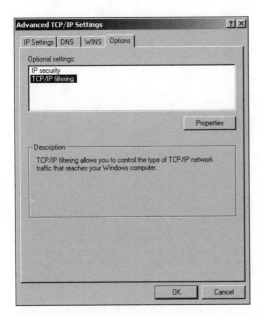

**Figure 2.5**    From the Options tab of the Advanced TCP/IP Settings dialog box, you can configure IPSec and TCP/IP filtering.

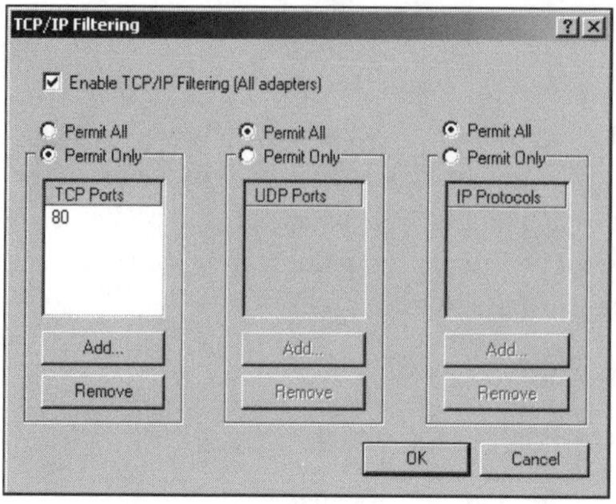

**Figure 2.6** From this dialog box, you can configure the port numbers of the protocols you want to filter.

If you want to monitor the traffic that comes in or you want to configure protocol security, refer to Chapter 8 in this book.

# Practice Questions

## Question 1

A router is or can be which of the following? [Check all correct answers]

❑  a.  A multihomed computer

❑  b.  An information service

❑  c.  A default gateway

❑  d.  A standalone device

The correct answers are a, c, and d. A router is or can be a multihomed computer, a default gateway, and a standalone device. A router is not an information service. Therefore, answer b is incorrect.

## Question 2

What organization developed the Open Systems Interconnection (OSI) reference model?

○  a.  IEEE

○  b.  ISO

○  c.  IETF

○  d.  ODI

The correct answer is b. The International Organization for Standardization (ISO) designed the OSI reference model as a standard for network communication. The Institute of Electrical and Electronics Engineers (IEEE) advances the theory and application of electrotechnology and allied sciences. The Internet Engineering Task Force (IETF) is a large, open, international community concerned with the evolution of the Internet architecture and the smooth operation of the Internet. Therefore, answers a and c are incorrect. ODI stands for Open Data Link Interface and actually is part of a protocol stack. Therefore, answer d is incorrect.

## Question 3

Which layer of the OSI model is responsible for establishing communication channels between hosts?

○ a.  Application

○ b.  Network

○ c.  Session

○ d.  Hardware

The correct answer is c. If you draw from the OSI scenario, establishing communication is necessary for information to be exchanged between two hosts. The Session layer is responsible for doing this. The Application layer serves as the window for users and application processes to access network services. The Network layer determines what physical path the data takes. Therefore, answers a and b are incorrect. There is no such thing as the Hardware layer in the OSI model. Therefore, answer d is incorrect.

## Question 4

What protocols does Windows 2000 support? [Check all correct answers]

❑ a.  TCP/IP

❑ b.  NetBEUI

❑ c.  AppleTalk

❑ d.  DLC

❑ e.  NWLink (IPX/SPX)

The correct answers are a, b, c, d, and e. Windows 2000 supports TCP/IP, NetBEUI, AppleTalk, DLC, and NWLink (IPX/SPX). Therefore, all the answers are correct.

# Question 5

Which of the following protocols are nonroutable on an Ethernet network?
[Check all correct answers]

❑ a. TCP/IP

❑ b. DLC

❑ c. NetBEUI

❑ d. AppleTalk

❑ e. NWLink

The correct answer is c. All the protocols that Windows 2000 supports, including TCP/IP, DLC, AppleTalk, and NWLink are routable on an Ethernet network with the exception of NetBEUI. Therefore, answers a, b, d, and e are incorrect.

# Question 6

The IP address 131.107.2.200 is what class of IP address?

○ a. Class A

○ b. Class B

○ c. Class C

○ d. Class D

The correct answer is b. The number in the first octet is 131, which falls into the range of class B (128 through 191). The range of the first octet for class A addresses is from 1 through 126. The range for the first octet of a class C address is from 192 through 223 and the range for the first octet of a class D address is from 224 through 239.

## Question 7

Which layers belong to the TCP/IP suite of protocols? [Check all correct answers]

❏ a. Application

❏ b. Session

❏ c. Transport

❏ d. Network

The correct answers are a and c. The four layers are Application, Transport, Internet, and Network Interface. The Session and Network layers belong to the OSI model; therefore, answers b and d are incorrect.

## Question 8

By default, NWLink gets installed on Windows 2000.

○ a. True

○ b. False

The correct answer is b. TCP/IP is the default protocol. You must install NWLink on the computer.

## Question 9

If I can't use static IP addressing and I don't have a DHCP server on my private network, I cannot use TCP/IP.

○ a. True

○ b. False

The correct answer is b. Windows 2000 uses a new feature called Automatic Private IP Addressing (APIPA) configuration, which automatically assigns an IP address if no DHCP server is available.

# Need to Know More?

 Berg, Glenn. *MCSE: Networking Essentials, 2nd Edition*. Indianapolis, Ind.: New Riders Publishing, 1998. ISBN 1-56205-919-X. Chapter 7, "Transport Protocols," contains information regarding protocols that reside in the Transport layer.

 Lammle, Todd, Monica Lammle, and James Chellis. *MSCE: TCP/IP Study Guide, 3rd Edition*. San Francisco: Sybex Network Press, 1998. ISBN 0-7821-2224-8. Chapter 3, "Implementing IP Routing," contains information regarding routing with IP.

 Novosel, Gary, Kurt Hudson, and James Michael Stewart, *MCSE TCP/IP Exam Cram, 3rd Edition*. Scottsdale, AZ: The Coriolis Group, 2000. ISBN 1-57610-677-2. this book contains a wealth of information on TCP/IP.

 Search the TechNet CD (or its online version through **www.microsoft. com**) and the *Windows 2000 Server Resource Kit* CD using the keywords "TCP/IP", "OSI", and "routing".

 The following RFCs relate to TCP/IP: 768, 791, 792, 793, 826, 894, 919, 922, 950, 959, and 1001/1002. You can find them at **www.rfc-editor.org/rfcsearch.html**.

# Dynamic Host Configuration Protocol (DHCP)

**Terms you'll need to understand:**

✓ Lease

✓ Scope

✓ Scope option

✓ Authorize

✓ BOOTP client

✓ DHCP relay agent

**Techniques you'll need to master:**

✓ Understanding the lease process

✓ Configuring a scope

✓ Understanding the difference between a scope and a superscope

✓ Knowing when to configure a DHCP relay agent

✓ Knowing how and why DHCP communicates with DNS

Because Windows 2000 requires that TCP/IP be implemented on all Active Directory networks, every computer needs to have an IP address. The assignment of the addresses can be either manual or dynamic. If your network has 20,000 nodes, manually assigning those IP addresses and all IP configurations can be overwhelming. A *Dynamic Host Configuration Protocol (DHCP)* server can assign an IP address and other necessary options to each and every node on your network, including all of the other IP-related configurations that are required.

# Why Use DHCP?

Even though it is clear that DHCP servers dynamically assign IP addresses to clients that request them, why is this such a great concept? The reasons are multifold. First, consider configuring those 20,000 nodes manually. This would take a tremendous amount of time and effort. Every computer would need to be configured by a person, sitting at a computer console. Second, to correctly configure 20,000 computers, every computer would need a unique IP address. This would require some serious documentation and overhead. Finally, if any parameter changed for the IP configuration, all 20,000 computers would have to be "touched" again, to make the change.

DHCP eliminates all of these factors by allowing network hosts to obtain their IP addresses and all other necessary IP information from a centrally managed service. IP addresses are grouped into scopes that help control the assignment of IP addresses to different subnets. The DHCP server is responsible for keeping track of the IP addresses that have been assigned, to eliminate duplicate addresses. DHCP options are the additional IP-related configurations, which are either linked to the IP scopes or configured for the entire DHCP server. When the client computer receives the IP address, it also receives the additional IP options.

# Installing the DHCP Service

Installing DHCP on a Windows 2000 server is a simple process. The service can be installed along with the initial Windows 2000 server install, or after the server is running. DHCP is installed only if the specific DHCP service is selected. This is not the default configuration, so additional work must be completed.

If the DHCP server is running when the Windows 2000 server is first started, the DHCP service will be configured using the installation wizard. When the installation wizard prompts for the configuration of additional Windows components, select the Networking Services option. Once you investigate the Details for this group of services, the DHCP service can be selected.

If the DHCP server needs to be installed after the Windows 2000 server is already running, the service needs to be installed through the installation wizard. To access the installation wizard for the DHCP server, select the Add/Remove Programs option in Control Panel. In the Add/Remove Programs utility, select Add/Remove Windows Components. The Windows Components wizard will start. Follow the same steps as listed above to install the DHCP server.

# The DHCP Lease Process

A client can be either DHCP-enabled or statically configured. Only clients that are DHCP-enabled are eligible to lease an IP address from a DHCP server. A new client follows four steps to obtain a new lease from the DHCP server:

1. The client must request an IP address from a DHCP server.

2. A DHCP server offers an IP address to the client.

3. The client selects the desired IP address and notifies the appropriate DHCP server.

4. The appropriate DHCP server responds to the client confirming the lease.

These four steps are referred to as request, offer, selection, and acknowledgement. Each step has a DHCP message that enables communication between the client and the server. Table 3.1 lists the pertinent DHCP messages.

| Table 3.1 DHCP messages. | |
|---|---|
| **Message** | **Description** |
| DHCPDISCOVER | Initial broadcast message sent from client to obtain IP address. |
| DHCPOFFER | Message from DHCP server that contains a possible IP address for the client. |
| DHCPREQUEST | Message from client to DHCP server indicating that the client would like to receive the offered IP address. |
| DHCPACK | Final message from server to client in initial lease process, where the server acknowledges that the IP address is assigned to the client. |
| DHCPNAK | A negative acknowledgement message sent from the DHCP server to the client indicating that the IP address requested is no longer valid. |
| DHCPRELEASE | A message from the client to the server requesting that the current IP address be canceled and the lease expired. |
| DHCPINFORM | A new message type for Windows 2000. This message is used for clients to obtain IP information (typically options) for their local configuration. The client might have an IP address for the network, which was not received by DHCP, but needs the options from the DHCP server to function on the network. |

# IP Request

When a DHCP-enabled client starts for the first time, it broadcasts to obtain an IP address. This broadcast is a DHCPDISCOVER message that is destined for a DHCP server. The message contains the Media Access Control (MAC) address and the NetBIOS name of the client. The broadcast packet has the source address 0.0.0.0 and the destination address 255.255.255.255. If the client does not receive a response from a DHCP server, it immediately retries four times. The interval of the retries is 2, 4, 8, and 16 seconds. If after the four attempts the server still does not respond, the client continues to broadcast at intervals of five minutes.

# IP Offer

When the DHCP server or servers receive the request for an IP address, they return an offer message, DHCPOFFER, to the client. The offer packet contains the following information:

➤ DHCP MAC address

➤ DHCP IP address

➤ Offered IP address

➤ Subnet mask of offered IP address

➤ Lease time

➤ Client MAC address

The offered IP address is temporarily reserved on the DHCP server to prevent it from being offered to other DHCP clients.

# IP Selection

The client receives and replies to the first DHCPOFFER. Subsequent offers from other DHCP servers are discarded. The client replies to the DHCPOFFER with another message, known as the DHCPREQUEST packet. This packet must be broadcast back on the network because the client does not have an IP address yet. The packet does, however, contain the destination DHCP server IP address, which allows all other DHCP servers to withdraw their offers.

# IP Acknowledgement

The DHCP server that initially offered the IP address responds to the client request with a DHCPACK packet using an IP broadcast. The packet contains the original IP information as well as any additional DHCP options. The server reserves the IP address for the client. The lease is valid until it expires, the client renews the lease, or the client releases the address. When the client receives the acknowledgement packet, the IP configuration is bound to the TCP/IP stack. This finalizes the binding of the IP address to the client.

In rare instances, the server responds with a DHCPNAK message. This usually occurs when the original IP address is no longer valid or has been assigned to another computer. If the client receives a DHCPNAK message in this final stage of the process, the client must begin the lease process again.

# Automatic Private IP Address

Historically, when a client attempted to obtain an IP address from the DHCP server, it successfully bound the address or received an error indicating that the DHCP server was not available. A new feature in Windows 2000 eliminates the errors that occur when a DHCP server is not available. Automatic Private IP Addressing (APIPA) is a client-side feature for Windows 98 and Windows 2000 DHCP clients. If the client's attempt to negotiate with a DHCP server fails, the client automatically receives an IP address from the range 169.254.0.0 to 169.254.255.255, with a subnet mask of 255.255.0.0.

Be aware of the new APIPA scheme for troubleshooting client issues. Clients no longer receive an error message indicating that a DHCP server is not available. Now, a client will simply receive an APIPA address. To determine the IP configuration for the client use the following command from the client computer:

```
ipconfig /all
```

The client checks for the DHCP server every five minutes. The client is not able to communicate on the network until it successfully negotiates an IP address with the DHCP server.

# Managing Scopes

The DHCP server allocates IP addresses based on the configuration of scopes. A *scope* is a range of IP addresses that has a beginning and ending IP address. A DHCP server must have a scope configured for each subnet in which it will allocate IP addresses to DHCP clients. Figure 3.1 shows the standard scope configuration window from the New Scope Wizard.

Creating a scope is relatively easy. While in the DHCP manager, right-click on the server for which the scope will be configured, and then specify New Scope. This starts the New Scope Wizard, which walks you through the configuration of the scope. The different configurations for a new scope include an IP address range, including the subnet mask, exclusions, reservations, client type, and lease

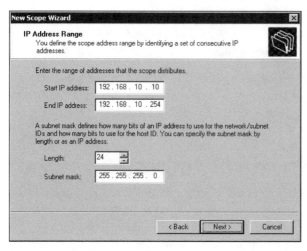

**Figure 3.1** New Scope Wizard showing the IP address range.

duration. You can configure DHCP options for scopes, as well as the server and reserved clients. Different types of scopes include the "basic" scope, superscopes, and multicast scopes (discussed later in the chapter). After any scope is created and configured, it must be activated to start allocating addresses to clients.

## IP Address Range

The IP address range sets the available IP addresses that the DHCP server can allocate to clients. The range has a starting and ending IP address, as indicated in Figure 3.1. When specifying the range, it is mandatory to configure the subnet mask for the range. Windows 2000 offers the new feature of allowing you to specify either the number of bits or the subnet mask itself, also shown in Figure 3.1.

 The IP address ranges should never overlap in different scopes. DHCP does not keep track of other scopes and will duplicate IP addresses for clients if the address ranges overlap.

## Exclusions

Sometimes, a portion of the IP address scope should not be distributed to clients. At times, this situation is planned for devices like routers, printers, and servers. Other times, an exclusion is required due to a device having a static IP address in the middle of the scope. In either case, you can exclude part of the IP address range from the other IP addresses that are distributed to clients. Figure 3.2 shows the exclusion page from the New Scope Wizard.

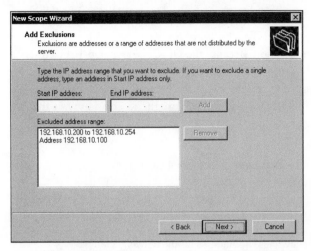

**Figure 3.2**   The Add Exclusions page of the New Scope Wizard.

An exclusion can be either a single IP address or a range of IP addresses. Numerous devices on the network should have static IP addresses, including servers, printers, firewalls, and routers. All of these IP addresses should fall outside the scope or be excluded from the scope.

*Note: It is a best practice to have exclusions when creating a fault-tolerant DHCP server scenario.*

## Reservations

Although reservations are not part of the standard setup or wizard, they are an important feature of a DHCP server. A reservation allows the administrator to reserve an IP address specifically for a client computer. You do this by configuring the reservation settings shown in Figure 3.3.

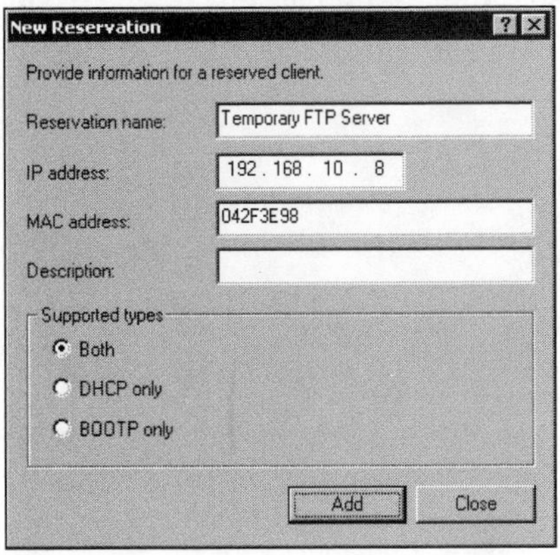

**Figure 3.3**   A new reservation configuration.

The reservation name does not have to be the client NetBIOS name; it is only a reference name inside of DHCP. The DHCP client MAC address is the key configuration for the reservation. Because the DHCP server associates a reservation with the DHCP client MAC address, this number cannot change during the extent of the reservation. Therefore, if the network card is changed in the client computer, you must delete and reconfigure the reservation with the new DHCP client MAC address.

To obtain the MAC address for a client computer, use the following command:

ipconfig /all

This will show the MAC address for the network adapter.

## Client Types

A scope can support two types of clients: BOOTP and DHCP. BOOTP (boot-strap protocol) is the host configuration that precedes DHCP. BOOTP was origi-nally designed for client computers that did not have disks. Configuring BOOTP support consists of setting up the BOOTP table and enabling the scope to sup-port BOOTP clients.

Configuring the BOOTP table, as shown in Figure 3.4, includes indicating the boot image file name, the full server path to the boot image, and the Trivial File Transfer Protocol (TFTP) file server. To configure a new BOOTP table, open the DHCP snap-in and right-click on the BOOTP Table folder under the cor-rect DHCP server. The menu option for configuring the BOOTP table is New Boot Image.

Windows 2000 DHCP server also provides support for dynamic BOOTP. This feature gives the BOOTP client a lease duration, similar to the DHCP clients.

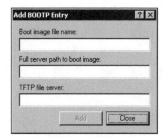

**Figure 3.4** BOOTP table configurations.

The support for dynamic BOOTP IP addresses for clients is new with Windows 2000, so be prepared to know all of the details because it is common to see "new features" on the exam.

DHCP is more sophisticated than BOOTP, to support advanced client computers. DHCP was the first dynamic version of BOOTP, designed for clients that did not need an image from the TFTP server.

*Note: You can configure reservations for DHCP clients, BOOTP clients, or both. If you configure both types for the reservation, you should be careful when configuring the scope options. BOOTP clients cannot support the same options that DHCP clients can. Be certain that both clients in this configuration support the scope options.*

# DHCP Lease

When a DHCP server leases an IP address to a client, it must give the client a time limit for the IP address. This time limit is known as a *lease duration* and is eight days by default. This time limit is longer than it was in Windows NT 4, which had a lease duration of three days. The additional days allow for an entire week, including the weekend, to pass before the client loses the lease. Figure 3.5 shows where you set the lease duration on the Scope Properties page.

## Determining the Lease Duration

The lease duration depends on the network design and implementation. You can set the lease duration very low, such as one minute, to very high, unlimited. It is

```
Scope [192.168.10.0] LAN-15 Properties                    ? X

General │ DNS │ Advanced │

    ▢      Scope


Scope name:      │LAN-15                                    │

Start IP address:  │ 192 . 168 .  10 .  10 │

End IP address:   │ 192 . 168 .  10 . 254 │

Subnet mask:     │ 255 . 255 . 255 .  0 │   Length: 24

┌ Lease duration for DHCP clients ──────────────────
│  ⊙ Limited to:
│     Days:      Hours:   Minutes:
│     │8  ⬍│   │0 ⬍│   │0 ⬍│
│
│  ○ Unlimited

Description:   │                                        │


                 │   OK   │   Cancel   │   Apply   │
```

**Figure 3.5**   Scope Properties page showing the lease duration setting.

best to customize the lease for the network environment. Some network environment considerations include the following:

➤ If the number of IP addresses available is considerably higher than the number of client computers, then a higher lease time is satisfactory. This might be a subnet of 254 addresses for 50 computers. You can set the lease duration to three months.

➤ If the number of IP addresses available is near the number of computers, the lease duration should be low, possibly three days.

➤ If the configuration for the network rarely changes, or if the clients rarely move around, then you can set the lease duration to a higher number, such as two months.

➤ If the configurations for the network change often or the clients are mobile, then you should set the lease duration lower, such as three to eight days.

➤ Unlimited leases are available but should be used sparingly. An unlimited lease is hard to administer if you want to control the number of IP addresses for the network. If you want a long lease, it is best to set the lease duration to a high number, such as eight months, instead of an unlimited lease.

### Renewing the Lease

After receiving an IP address from the DHCP server, the client still needs to communicate with the DHCP server. The client needs to establish communications with the DHCP server at some point during the lease to renew the lease. This communication is first attempted at 50 percent of the lease time. At this time, the client broadcasts a DHCPREQUEST message to renew the lease to the full duration. If the server is available, it responds with a DHCPACK message, renewing the lease and updating any DHCP options.

If the server is not available, the client continues to hold the lease. The client makes a final attempt to renew the lease at 87.5 percent of the lease. If the server is available, the lease is renewed. If the server is not available, the client loses the lease at the end of the duration and performs the lease process again.

*Note: Previous versions of Microsoft DHCP referred to the 50 percent and 87.5 percent renewal times as T1 and T2.*

## DHCP Options

A DHCP server can configure several types of options. You must understand the following list of DHCP options both to work in the real world and to pass the exam:

➤ *Server* options, including user and vendor class options

➤ *Scope* options, including user and vendor class options

➤ *Reserved client* options, including user and vendor class options

These options appear in order of precedence. The server options apply first and are overridden by specific user and vendor class options set for the server option. The scope options then apply, again overridden by the user and vendor class options specific to the scope. The final option applied is the reserved client option followed by any user and vendor class options for the reserved client option.

 If the client has any "hard-coded" IP configurations, they will take precedence over the options delegated by the DHCP server.

Even though you can configure approximately 60 options, most clients do not support these settings. The DHCP options typically used for any of the different levels of options include those listed in Table 3.2.

## Server Options

Server options are applied to all clients who lease addresses from a DHCP server. The server options are a default folder located directly off the server tree in the DHCP manager. To implement server options, right-click on the Server Options folder and select Configure Options.

 Server options are sometimes referred to as *global options*. This is confusing because Windows NT DHCP servers have global options. There should not be any confusion on the exam, but just in case, now you're prepared.

| Table 3.2 | Standard DHCP options. | |
|---|---|---|
| Number | Name | Description |
| 003 | Router | Also known as the default gateway. Contains a list of IP addresses for routers on the client subnet. |
| 006 | DNS Servers | Contains a list of IP addresses for DNS servers available for the client. |
| 015 | DNS Domain Name | Specifies the domain name the client should use for DNS locator services. |
| 044 | WINS Servers | Contains a list of IP addresses for WINS servers for NetBIOS name resolution. |
| 046 | WINS Node Type | Specifies the type of NetBIOS name resolution, either broadcast or WINS. There are four options: 1 = B-node, 2 = P-node, 4 = M-node, and 8 = H-node. 8 is the most efficient and should be used most often. |

## Scope Options

Scope options are additional configurations that go beyond the required scope settings. Scope options are applied to any client that receives an IP address from a scope on the DHCP server that has scope options configured. Class or reserved client settings for the option type can override scope options.

Figure 3.6 shows the interface used to configure the different scope options. If you use the wizard to configure the scope options, the wizard prompts you to configure the standard scope options.

*Note: If a client needs an updated option, run the following command from the client computer:*

```
ipconfig /renew
```

## Reserved Client Options

If a DHCP client has a reservation, there is a good chance the client needs special IP configurations. The reserved client options are the most granular of the three DHCP options, excluding the user and vendor class options. Accessing the specific reservation under the Reservations folder configures the reserved client options.

## Vendor and User Class Options

A new feature of Windows 2000 DHCP server is the ability to recognize particular vendor- and client- (user-) specific features. These features comply with

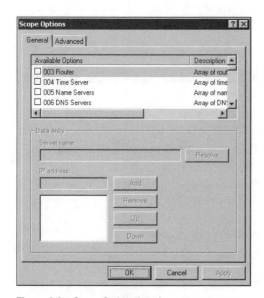

**Figure 3.6** Scope Options interface.

RFC 2132, which defines DHCP options and BOOTP vendor extensions. You apply vendor and user class options at any of the three option levels: server, scope, or reserved client. Figure 3.7 shows the typical window where you configure vendor and user class options.

The vendor class option allows for unique identification for different vendor devices. First, you set up a different vendor class with a unique pattern of data bits. Then, when the device comes online, it is either a standard vendor class or a newly configured vendor class.

User classes are similar in function, but not in detail. The goal with a user class is to differentiate clients from one another by type. Different types can include laptops, desktops, and servers.

## Superscopes

A *superscope* is a grouping of individual scopes. The individual, member scopes are responsible for allocating IP addresses to different IP logical subnets functioning on the same network.

*Note: Mulitiple logical IP subnets on a single physical network segment are often called multinets.*

A superscope is required for a multinet DHCP environment. If the superscope is not present on a multinet network, the DHCP server is not able to allocate IP addresses from two scopes to clients on the same physical network. A superscope

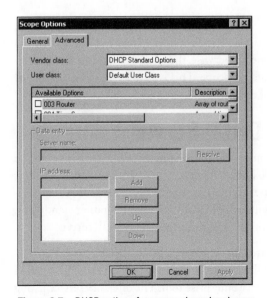

**Figure 3.7**  DHCP options for user and vendor classes.

is also a valuable configuration if the DHCP server is servicing a network on the other side of a BOOTP/DHCP relay agent that is using a multinet. The superscope allocates an IP address from either of the superscope member scopes to the remote network, which gains access to the DHCP server via the relay agent.

## Multicast Scopes

*Multicasting* is a directed transmission from a single point to many points. The multicast address range is Class D, which uses the addresses from 224.0.0.0 to 239.255.255.255. When you configure a multicast scope, the range of addresses must fall within these parameters. Multicast scopes are supported through a proposed standard protocol, Multicast Address Dynamic Client Allocation Protocol (MADCAP). MADCAP controls how the multicast addresses are allocated to the MADCAP clients on the network.

*Note: To prevent multicast traffic from being copied to the adjoining host, usually the Internet interface, it is best to use the IP address range from 239.0.0.0 to 239.255.255.255.*

Multicast scopes do not use scope options because they do not support any of the configurations. Instead, multicast scopes have a configuration for the multicast scope lifetime, which determines when the multicast scope expires on the client. The default is such that the lifetime is set to infinite. This setting does not expire the scope and must be manually removed.

## Activating the Scope

After all of the IP configurations are complete for the scope, you must activate it. Depending on which configurations you select in the New Scope Wizard, you are prompted to activate the scope. Otherwise, the wizard reminds you to configure the scope options and activate the scope. This is a tricky point because many users don't read the fine print of the wizard.

# Authorizing the DHCP Server

Gone are the days when the junior admin brought up a DHCP server in the middle of the day, giving out 100 bogus addresses and creating a sea of IP address conflicts. Windows 2000 now uses Active Directory to authorize DHCP servers. The authorization process is quite simple from the administration standpoint. Figure 3.8 displays the menu option that authorizes the DHCP server.

You authorize the server through a special DHCP packet, called the *DHCPINFORM packet*. The DHCP server broadcasts the DHCPINFORM packet to locate the directory service enterprise root. The directory service listing

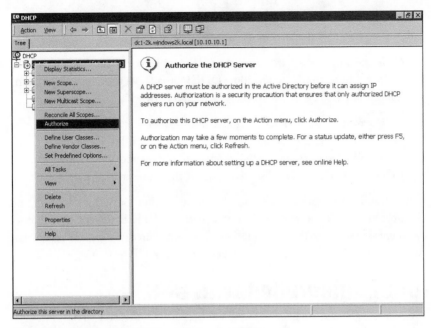

**Figure 3.8**   Authorizing the DHCP server from the DHCP menu.

is in the Active Directory. This is where DHCP servers are configured and listed as authenticated or not authenticated.

It is best to have DHCP servers installed on Windows 2000 domain controllers and domain member servers. The importance of this step is due to membership in the Active Directory domain. Standalone Windows 2000 and Windows NT servers (not joined to the domain) can easily go undetected on the network and could hand out unauthorized IP addresses. Windows 2000 DHCP servers in a workgroup have built-in guards against this, but the possibility is still there.

# Relay Agent

When a DHCP-enabled client starts, it relies on a network broadcast to find a DHCP server. If the network has multiple segments, it is configured with one or multiple routers. For most of these routing environments, the router is not config-ured to forward broadcasts. In this case, the broadcast from the DHCP client is not successful if the DHCP server is on another segment. This is why a relay agent is used, to pass along the communication from the client to the DHCP server.

For a router to support the forwarding of DHCP/BOOTP broadcast messages, it must be RFC 2131-compliant. Each network is different, and the location of the DHCP server and the type of router are no exceptions.

There are two methods of providing DHCP/BOOTP clients with access to a DHCP server located on a remote subnet:

➤ If the network uses hardware-based RFC 2131-compliant routers, an "IP Helper" can be configured to allow DHCP broadcasts to be forwarded to the appropriate DHCP server(s) across a routed network.

➤ If your routers are non-RFC 2131-compliant, or you are using a Windows NT or Windows 2000 router, you can configure a DHCP relay agent on a Windows 2000 server, which will receive DHCP broadcasts and forward them to the appropriate DHCP server(s) across the routed network.

The DHCP relay agent is now an IP routing option located in Routing and Remote Access Services. As indicated above, the DHCP servers on the other segments are added to the configuration. Once configured, the DHCP relay agent will forward all DHCP broadcast packets to the DHCP servers.

# DHCP Integration with DNS

Windows 2000 relies on DNS to locate servers, clients, and server services throughout the enterprise. Typically, you must manually enter the client computer name and IP address into DNS. This manual procedure has been eliminated with Windows 2000 DHCP and DNS. A Windows 2000 DHCP server can dynamically update DNS on behalf of the DHCP client. This powerful feature can support the dynamic updating of DNS for clients running Windows 2000, Windows NT, Windows 9x, and Windows for Workgroups. The configuration that supports the dynamic updating of DNS appears in Figure 3.9.

The DHCP server is, by default, configured to automatically update DHCP clients in DNS. DHCP is also configured to delete the forward lookup zone record when the lease for the client expires. Other configurations for the DHCP server can serve your enterprise well. The following sections take a look at the different options and how they impact your network.

## Automatically Updating Client Information to DNS

You must investigate different scenarios when looking at the DHCP server automatically updating client information to the DNS server. Table 3.3 outlines the different scenarios.

The reason that Windows 2000 clients and non-Windows 2000 clients are separated with regard to the DNS update is due to the new capability of the Windows 2000 clients. Windows 2000 supports an additional DHCP option, the client fully qualified domain name (FQDN) option (option 81). This client option is responsible for instructing the DHCP server on how it wants the server to process the

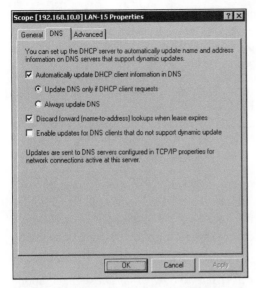

**Figure 3.9**   DNS configuration for the DHCP server.

| Table 3.3   **DHCP updating DNS scenarios.** | | |
|---|---|---|
| **DHCP Configuration** | **Windows 2000 Client** | **Non-Windows 2000 Client** |
| Automatically update DHCP client information in DNS. | X | |
| Update DNS only if DHCP client requests. | X | |
| Always update DNS. | X | |
| Enable updates for DNS clients that do not support dynamic updates. | | X |

DNS update. Non-Windows 2000 DHCP clients do not support this feature. With the different options that are available in the DHCP DNS configuration, a multitude of scenarios can be developed from the different combinations. The following is a list of the possible combinations and the results of the configuration:

➤ *Disabling dynamic DNS update with Windows 2000 DHCP clients*—If the option Automatically Update DHCP Client Information In DNS is disabled and the client is a Windows 2000 machine, the DHCP server does not perform any update to the DNS server for the client. In this case, the client is responsible for updating both the forward lookup record (the host A resource record) and the reverse lookup record (the pointer PTR resource record) on the DNS server.

Knowing which settings are the default and how the default DHCP server communicates with DNS for the client is a must for the exam. The client also has communications with DNS, so be certain to know that the client also updates the DNS server resource records.

➤ *Client-requested DNS updates with Windows 2000 DHCP clients*—If the option Update DNS Only If DHCP Client Requests is selected and the client is a Windows 2000 machine, the DHCP server handles only part of the DNS update. The client, by default, updates the A record on the DNS server and the DHCP server updates the PTR record on the DNS server for the client.

➤ *Always updating DNS with Windows 2000 DHCP clients*—If the option Always Update DNS is selected and the client is a Windows 2000 machine, the DHCP server always updates the A record and the PTR record for the DHCP client. This occurs regardless of how the client machine is configured to perform these tasks.

➤ *Updating DNS for clients that don't support dynamic updates*—If the option Update DNS Only If DHCP Client Requests is selected and the client is a non-Windows 2000 DHCP client, the DHCP server relies on another setting on the DNS tab for the DNS update. Figure 3.9 shows an additional setting for non-Windows 2000 clients, Enable Updates For DNS Clients That Do Not Support Dynamic Update. If this setting is cleared, neither the DHCP client nor the DHCP server updates the appropriate DNS entries. If the setting is selected, the DHCP server updates DNS for both the A and the PTR records on behalf of the client.

Non-Windows 2000 clients *do not* support dynamic updates to DNS. The use of DHCP in this case is powerful for a mixed-mode environment. Even though the client cannot update DNS, the DHCP server does on its behalf, if configured properly.

## DNSUpdateProxy Group

The DNSUpdateProxy group is a default security group responsible for handling the ownership of the DNS entry for both A and PTR records. The members of this group do not take ownership of the files created in DNS. This is important when considering the ability for the DHCP server to make updates in DNS for the client. There are two different scenarios where the DNS entries can become locked due to ownership:

➤ DHCP ServerA updates the A record for clientZ. ServerA is now the owner of the A record in DNS. If ServerA becomes unavailable and DHCP ServerB is going to help the client update DNS, the update will fail. The failure is not that ServerB cannot update DNS. The failure is that there is already an entry in DNS for clientZ.

➤ The Windows 2000 DHCP server updates the A record for clientY, which is a non-Windows 2000 client. After clientY is upgraded to a Windows 2000 machine, it is capable of updating DNS itself. When the client attempts to update its own A record, it will fail. The DHCP server is the owner, not the client.

The DNSUpdateProxy group eliminates these problems. When a member of the DNSUpdateProxy group updates DNS, the member does not take ownership of the entry. Ownership is established when the first security principal, which is not a member of the DNSUpdateProxy group, accesses the entry.

### Security Issues with the DNSUpdateProxy Group

Because no member of the DNSUpdateProxy group becomes the owner of the DNS entry it performs, you might face a security problem. Note the following three distinct issues with a domain controller being placed into the DNSUpdate-Proxy group:

➤ The server that is part of this group does not own any records it places into DNS, including its own. If the DHCP server that is part of this group is also a domain controller, the domain controller DNS entry is not secure.

➤ Any resource records registered by the Netlogon service from the domain controller are not secure. These entries include all service location (SRV), host (A), and alias (CNAME) resource records.

➤ Because the DHCP server is installed on a domain controller, the DHCP server has full control over all DNS objects stored in the Active Directory.

The solution to all of these issues is straightforward and simple. Do not place any domain controller in the DNSUpdateProxy group. This stipulation applies to any domain controller, whether it has DHCP running or not.

# DHCP Administration

DHCP relies on the knowledge of the administrator. DHCP is not integrated between different DHCP servers, so you must handle the administration of each DHCP server with all of the other DHCP servers in the enterprise. Because a client is limited in its mechanism to contact a DHCP server to receive the IP information, you must ensure that all clients can successfully obtain an IP address. When a client cannot receive an IP address, you can implement common commands and practices to determine the root of the problem.

## Administering the IP Address Allocation

When configuring all of the DHCP servers in the enterprise, it is important to consider what would happen if two DHCP servers handed out the same IP address.

The alternative is to consider what would happen if there were no DHCP server to give out IP addresses because the DHCP server is down. To resolve both of these issues, it is best to design your IP scopes with the following points in mind:

➤ Document the IP address scopes in a single location. This should include dial-up and virtual private networking (VPN) static scopes, too. Never let a scope overlap among any of these IP address pools.

➤ Use the 80/20 rule to configure IP address ranges on different servers. This lets you configure the complete scope of IP addresses among two DHCP servers. If one server is offline, then the other DHCP server is still servicing the client requests. Table 3.4 gives an example of the 80/20 rule on two DHCP servers.

The configuration of including the entire IP address range, and then excluding a portion of the range, is important to note here. This is the correct format for configuring the 80/20 rule on two different DHCP servers. This format also applies to creating an 80/20 rule between two superscopes.

## Placing DHCP Servers in a Routed Environment

The placement of the DHCP servers in a routed environment is critical to ensure that all clients receive an IP address. The ideal configuration is to have at least one DHCP server in each segment. If fault tolerance is critical, you should place two DHCP servers in each segment. This involves finance issues because each DHCP server must run on a Windows 2000 server. If money is an issue or if you want to consolidate services on servers, the DHCP relay agent might be required in a routed environment. If you have few DHCP servers, but numerous segments, some client segments will not have a DHCP server. The DHCP relay agent or BOOTP router will assist in those clients receiving an IP address.

# Monitoring and Troubleshooting DHCP

Once the DHCP servers are up and running, they need to be monitored to ensure that there are enough addresses for the DHCP clients and that the servers are running without defect. The DHCP manager is the main tool for monitoring

| Table 3.4 | The DHCP 80/20 rule across two DHCP servers. | |
|---|---|---|
| **DHCP Server** | **IP Address Range** | **Exclusion Range** |
| DHCP1 | 192.168.10.10 to 192.168.10.254 | 192.168.10.200 to 192.168.10.254 |
| DHCP1 | 192.168.20.10 to 192.168.20.254 | 192.168.20.10 to 192.168.20.200 |
| DHCP2 | 192.168.10.10 to 192.168.10.254 | 192.168.10.10 to 192.168.10.200 |
| DHCP2 | 192.168.20.10 to 192.168.20.254 | 192.168.20.200 to 192.168.20.254 |

the DHCP servers. Other tools that will help with the monitoring and trouble-shooting of DHCP include the Event Viewer, Network Monitor, and Performance System Monitor. To help troubleshoot client issues with DHCP, the **ipconfig** command and associated switches will be the tool of choice.

## Tools for Monitoring and Troubleshooting DHCP

There are built in tools to help monitor the entire Windows 2000 server. These tools should not be unfamiliar to anyone that is taking this exam, but be aware of how the tools can help monitor DHCP services:

➤ *DHCP manager*—The DHCP manager allows the administrator to view the DHCP server status (authorized and active), active leases, and scope reconciliation. Reconciling the DHCP server can fix inconsistencies with missing or incorrect client IP address leases. Enhanced monitoring has been added to the DHCP server for Windows 2000. For example, an icon can be triggered and changed to yellow when 90 percent of the IP addresses for a particular scope have been assigned. A second alert can be triggered, changing the icon to red, when the pool of IP addresses is exhausted.

➤ *Event Viewer*—The Event Viewer logs the critical information for system services and Active Directory. The starting and stopping of the DHCP service will be logged as a system service in the Event Viewer. As a DHCP server is authorized or activated, the Event Viewer will also log this information.

➤ *Network Monitor*—Network Monitor is an invaluable tool for tracking the lease process or other DHCP-related network messages and packets. This "sniffer" can capture and display packets that are transferred to and from the DHCP server.

➤ *Performance System Monitor*—To track DHCP traffic such as the lease process, duplicate IP addresses that were dropped, and network bandwidth, the Performance System Monitor counters will help. There is a specific performance object for the DHCP server to track all of the details related to the DHCP service.

## Troubleshooting DHCP with ipconfig

When clients are not receiving IP addresses or the correct DHCP options, it is difficult to determine where the problem lies. **ipconfig** can help track down some of these problems. If you use **ipconfig** with no switch, it provides the IP bindings for each adapter on the computer. The result is a list of the IP address, subnet mask, and default gateway for the adapters. You can use numerous switches with **ipconfig**, each with a specific use in tracking down DHCP-related issues. The following are the most common switches used with **ipconfig**:

➤ /release—The /release switch is important when the client has an IP address but needs to clean the IP stack of all of the DHCP-provided IP configurations. The /release switch forces the client to release the IP address back to the server.

➤ /renew—The /renew switch is useful in two different scenarios. One instance is when the client needs to get new DHCP options from the DHCP server. The other reason to use the /renew switch is to obtain a new IP address. The /renew switch only sends out the DHCPDISCOVER message to the DHCP server when the client has no configurations. If the client already has IP information from a DHCP server, it sends a DHCPREQUEST message.

*Note: For a client to receive a new IP address with the new options, it must first run the ipconfig command with the /release switch. After the client has relinquished the IP address and information, it can run the ipconfig /renew command to receive all new information.*

➤ /all—The /all switch is critical in determining what settings the client obtained from the DHCP server. The /all switch displays all of the IP settings that the client has for each adapter interface bound to IP. Figure 3.10 shows the output from the **ipconfig /all** command.

Using the **ipconfig** command and all of the switches is critical in the real world, as well as for success on the exam.

```
C:\WINNT\System32\cmd.exe

C:\>ipconfig /all

Windows 2000 IP Configuration

        Host Name . . . . . . . . . . . . : dc1-2k
        Primary DNS Suffix . . . . . . . : windows2k.local
        Node Type . . . . . . . . . . . . : Hybrid
        IP Routing Enabled. . . . . . . . : Yes
        WINS Proxy Enabled. . . . . . . . : No
        DNS Suffix Search List. . . . . . : windows2k.local

Ethernet adapter Local Area Connection:

        Connection-specific DNS Suffix  . :
        Description . . . . . . . . . . . : 3Com EtherLink XL 10/100 PCI TX NIC
(3C905B-TX)
        Physical Address. . . . . . . . . : 00-50-DA-5E-94-94
        DHCP Enabled. . . . . . . . . . . : No
        IP Address. . . . . . . . . . . . : 10.10.10.1
        Subnet Mask . . . . . . . . . . . : 255.255.255.0
        Default Gateway . . . . . . . . . :
        DNS Servers . . . . . . . . . . . : 10.10.10.1

C:\>_
```

**Figure 3.10**   IP settings as a result of the **ipconfig /all** command.

# Practice Questions

## Question 1

> To ensure that the DHCP server functions properly with the Active Directory
> and the enterprise network, on which type of Windows server should you
> install the DHCP server? [Check all correct answers]
>
> ❏  a.  Windows 2000 standalone server in a workgroup
>
> ❏  b.  Windows 2000 domain member server
>
> ❏  c.  Windows 2000 domain controller
>
> ❏  d.  Windows NT 4 domain member server

The correct answers are b and c. It is important to remember that the DHCP
server must be authorized in a Windows 2000 environment. Answers b and c are
correct because they are authorized from the Active Directory. Answers a and d
are incorrect because if the DHCP server is located on a standalone or NT 4
server, the registration and verification of the authorization can fail. If the authorization fails and the DHCP server starts to allocate IP addresses to the clients,
IP duplication can occur. This causes serious network problems, and it might
take days to fully recover from such a problem.

## Question 2

> The DHCP server in the Logistics domain has two scopes configured in a
> superscope. The first scope is called LAN1 and contains the IP addresses
> 10.10.5.10 to 10.10.5.254. The second scope is called LAN2 and contains
> the IP addresses 10.10.6.10 to 10.10.6.254. The Cisco firewall has a reser-
> vation for the IP address 10.10.6.100. From the following list of DHCP op-
> tions configured for the DHCP server, select those that apply to the client
> that receives the IP address 10.10.6.100. Arrange the list in the order in
> which they are applied:
>
> Server options
>
> Cisco vendor option under the server option
>
> Scope option for LAN1
>
> Scope option for LAN2
>
> Reservation client option for 10.10.6.100
>
> Cisco vendor option under the reservation client option

The correct answer is:

Server options

Scope option for LAN2

It is important to first understand the way options are applied to DHCP-enabled clients. First, the server options are applied, followed by user and vendor class options. Next, the scope options are applied, followed by user and vendor class options. Finally, reservation client options are applied, followed by user and vendor class options. The client does not have a reservation and does not belong to any user or vendor classes. Therefore, the Cisco vendor options and the scope option for LAN1 do not apply to this client.

# Question 3

---

If a client does not have an IP lease from any DHCP server, what type of DHCP message does it first send on the network after booting?

○ a.  DHCPINFORM

○ b.  DHCPREQUEST

○ c.  DHCPOFFER

○ d.  DHCPDISCOVER

The correct answer is d. If a DHCP-enabled client does not have an IP address or lease, it immediately sends a DHCPDISCOVER message attempting to find a DHCP server. Answer a is incorrect because it is not even part of the lease process. Answers b and c are incorrect because they are the second and third steps in the lease process.

# Question 4

The Windows 2000 DHCP server has just been installed and configured as a member of the domain. The scope has been created correctly for the network. The DHCP clients on the network cannot gain access to the network resources. You run the command **ipconfig /all** and determine that the DHCP clients are all receiving an IP address from the 169.254.0.0 network. What should you do to fix the problem?

○ a.  Run **ipconfig /renew** from the client computer.

○ b.  Run **ipconfig /release** from the client computer.

○ c.  Create a superscope to include the DHCP scope.

○ d.  Authorize the DHCP server.

The correct answer is d. The DHCP server must be authorized to start allocating addresses to clients on the network. Answers a and b are incorrect because any **ipconfig** command at this point will be unsuccessful because the DHCP server is not functioning. Answer c is incorrect because it does not provide any assistance with the authorization of the DHCP server; it only places the scope under a different configuration.

## Question 5

> The scope for the network computers has been configured properly and the clients are functioning properly. You must make reservations for some computers on the network. To make the reservations for these DHCP and BOOTP client computers, you must configure information for these computers specifically. The following are the types of reserved clients needed:
>
> Both (DHCP and BOOTP)
>
> DHCP only
>
> BOOTP only
>
> Identify which of the following information is required to make a reservation for the different reserved client types. (Not all information must be used. Each client type must have at least one piece of information.)
>
> MAC address
>
> Lease duration for BOOTP clients
>
> Lease duration for DHCP clients
>
> IP address
>
> Default gateway
>
> Subnet mask
>
> DNS server
>
> WINS server

The correct answer is:

Both (DHCP and BOOTP)

  MAC address

  IP address

DHCP only

  MAC address

  IP address

BOOTP only

  MAC address

  IP address

The only answers possible are MAC address and IP address. These are the only two configurations in the reservation window. The other answers are incorrect because they are configured for the entire scope, not the reservation. The scenario also indicated the clients were functioning properly before the reservations were needed, so the other answers are also wrong for this reason.

## Question 6

There is a mixture of Windows 2000 Professional and Windows NT 4 Workstation clients on the network. All clients are DHCP-enabled to obtain an IP address and all options from the DHCP server. When configuring the DHCP server for DNS updates, you want to ensure that the DHCP server updates the forward and reverse lookup zone resource record for all clients. Which items should you select to ensure that all clients are updated correctly? [Check all correct answers]

- ❑ a.  Automatically Update DHCP Client Information In DNS

- ❑ b.  Update DNS Only If DHCP Client Requests

- ❑ c.  Always Update DNS

- ❑ d.  Enable Updates For DNS Clients That Do Not Support Dynamic Update

The correct answers are a, c, and d. Answers a and c are required to update the Windows 2000 clients properly in DNS. Answer d is required for the Windows NT 4 Workstations. DHCP can only update Windows NT 4 Workstations if this option is selected because these clients do not support option 81, which is the DNS dynamic update message. Answer b is incorrect because this option only updates the reverse lookup zone resource record. However, the DHCP server can be configured to update both the A and PTR records at the Windows 2000 client's request.

# Question 7

> Two DHCP servers are configured on the network. One is a Windows NT 4 server and the other is a Windows 2000 server. They are both part of the same workgroup called ServerFarm. Some of the clients are having trouble resolving names and accessing resources on the network, but other clients are having no problems. After investigating DNS, you notice that the clients having trouble do not have a forward or reverse lookup zone resource record entry. What must you do to resolve this problem?
>
> ○ a.  Authorize the Windows NT 4 server.
>
> ○ b.  Authorize the Windows 2000 server.
>
> ○ c.  Upgrade the Windows NT 4 server to a Windows 2000 server.
>
> ○ d.  Configure the DHCP scope option 81, which enables dynamic DNS updates.

The correct answer is c. The problem is that the Windows NT 4 server does not support dynamic updates for the clients. The NT 4 server must be upgraded to function properly with DNS. Answers a and b are incorrect because neither of the servers can be authorized because they are not part of the domain. Even if the NT 4 server were part of the domain, it could not be authorized. Answer d is incorrect because the client, not the server, does option 81.

# Question 8

> The network is being upgraded to include multiple DHCP servers instead of static IP addresses for the clients. You want to ensure that the DHCP servers do not allocate IP addresses without first being authorized and that the security of the dynamic updates is managed. Select the servers where you will locate the DHCP servers. [Check all correct answers]
>
> ❑ a.  Windows 2000 domain controllers
>
> ❑ b.  Windows 2000 member servers
>
> ❑ c.  Windows 2000 standalone servers
>
> ❑ d.  Windows NT backup domain controllers
>
> ❑ e.  Windows NT member servers
>
> ❑ f.  Windows NT standalone servers

The correct answer is b. The only answer is b because only the Windows 2000 member servers can be authenticated as well as secure the dynamic update properly. Answer a is incorrect because of the security implications of a domain controller and the dynamic updates. The domain controller could be jeopardized because the domain controller does not own the resource records. Answer c is incorrect because a standalone server cannot be authorized. Answers d, e, and f are incorrect because NT servers cannot be authorized.

## Question 9

Your network has remote clients that need access to local network resources. To track which user is accessing the resources, you decide to create static address pools for both the dial-up server and the VPN server, which reside on different Windows 2000 servers. A special subnet of 192.168.10.0 has been configured for all remote clients. The main network is the 192.168.20.0 subnet. Fifty VPN clients and 25 dial-up clients need to gain access at any one time. How should you configure the two static address pools?

○ a. Dial-up pool    192.168.10.200 to 192.168.10.225

      VPN pool    192.168.10.200 to 192.168.10.250

○ b. Dial-up pool    192.168.10.200 to 192.168.10.225

      VPN pool    192.168.20.200 to 192.168.20.250

○ c. Dial-up pool    192.168.10.100 to 192.168.10.125

      VPN pool    192.168.10.200 to 192.168.10.250

○ d. Dial-up pool    192.168.10.100 to 192.168.10.125

      VPN pool    192.168.20.200 to 192.168.20.250

The correct answer is c. The only subnet that the IP address pools should be configured for is 192.168.10.0. The other consideration is that the two address pools should not overlap IP address ranges. Answer a is incorrect because the address ranges overlap. Answers b and d are incorrect because the VPN pools are configured for the local address subnet, not the remote address subnet.

## Question 10

A group of clients were configured with incorrect IP addresses. You have since corrected the problem on the DHCP server. The clients now need to be configured to obtain the correct IP address information, without being rebooted. From the following list of commands, select those required to help the client obtain the IP address information. Arrange the list in the order in which they need to be run.

**ipconfig /all**

**ipconfig /renew**

**ipconfig /release**

**ipconfig**

The correct answer is:

ipconfig /release

ipconfig /renew

The client first needs to release the IP address that it currently has, which is done with the **/release** switch. Then, the client needs to get a new address, which is done with the **/renew** switch. **ipconfig** and **ipconfig /all** do not accomplish anything as far as updating any information. These commands are for information only. If you have selected these items, you are not wrong in the sense that they don't work, only in the sense that they do nothing to help the client receive the correct information.

# Need to Know More?

 Hunt, Craig, and Gigi Estabrook (Editor). *TCP/IP Network Administration.* Cambridge, Mass.: O'Reilly & Associates, 1998. ISBN 1565923227. Chapter 9, "Configuring Network Servers," contains information about the roots of BOOTP and DHCP.

 Lemon, Ted, and Ralph E. Droms. *The DHCP Handbook: Understanding, Deploying, and Managing Automated Configuration Services.* Indianapolis, Ind.: Macmillan Technical Publishing, 1999. ISBN 1578701376. This book covers DHCP configuration, deployment, and troubleshooting.

 Search the DHCP help file within the Windows 2000 server operating system. The help file provides details for configuring, implementing, and troubleshooting.

 Search the TechNet CD (or its online version through **www.microsoft. com**) and the *Windows 2000 Server Resource Kit* CD using the keywords "DHCP", "dynamic IP", "DNS update", "RFC 951", "RFC 2131", "RFC 2132", and "MADCAP".

# Domain Name System (DNS)

**Terms you'll need to understand:**

✓ Resource records

✓ Zone types

✓ Zone transfers

✓ Active Directory integrated zone

✓ Dynamic updates

✓ WINS

✓ Caching

**Techniques you'll need to master:**

✓ Configuring resource records within a zone

✓ Designing zone replication strategies

✓ Integrating DNS and WINS

✓ Integrating an existing DNS with Active Directory

Although Domain Name System (DNS) servers have controlled the navigation of the Internet and Unix-based networks via hostnames for many years, Microsoft operating systems have relied upon NetBIOS names to define the location of resources on the network. NetBIOS names were typically resolved to network client addresses through a Windows Internet Naming Service (WINS) server. With Window 2000's change in directory services to Active Directory, DNS is now the defined name resolution and locator service. Knowledge of how to configure the new DNS and to ensure continued functionality with legacy systems on your network is crucial to your success with Windows 2000.

# DNS Overview

The Domain Name System is a hierarchical, distributed database and an associated set of protocols that define:

➤ *The schema of the database that dictates what types of items (resource records) are available and how these records are stored.* Hostnames (A records), aliases (CNAME records), and service resource (SRV) records are among those stored in this database. These entries are categorized and organized by zones.

➤ *Mechanisms for querying and updating the database.* Requests for information from client computers are processed by the DNS server (or servers), with the resulting information passed back to the client.

➤ *Mechanisms for replicating the information in the database among servers.* Copies of the database can be organized to provide both fault tolerance and optimized performance.

# DNS Names

Each computer, or host, on a network is identifiable by several means:

➤ Network card, physical, or Media Access Control (MAC) address (such as 00-E0-98-07-10-7A)

➤ TCP/IP address (such as 192.101.81.3)

➤ NetBIOS name (such as \\computer1)

➤ Hostname (such as computer1)

➤ Fully Qualified Domain Name (such as computer1.domain.com)

DNS organizes hosts by fully qualified domain name (FQDN), which appends the hostname with a computer's domain suffix. For example, if a record for computer1 exists in the domain.com domain portion of the DNS database, the FQDN for computer1 is computer1.domain.com. See Figure 4.1.

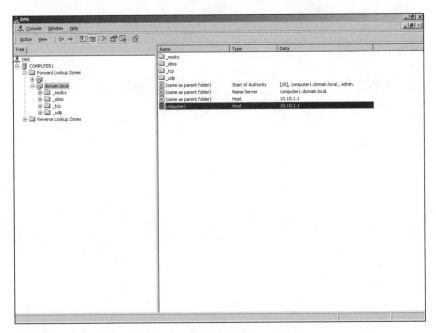

**Figure 4.1**    A sample DNS table for computer1.domain.com.

# DNS Name Resolution

When an FQDN query is issued to the DNS, both the client and the server begin performing specific duties. Proper configuration of both client and server is essential because the DNS database is searched using the queried name for an IP address match.

## At the DNS Server

A DNS database consists of resource records (RRs). Each RR identifies a particular resource within the database. There are various types of RRs in DNS. Table 4.1 provides information on the structure of common RRs.

When a name request (a query) is received by the DNS server, the database is searched for a matching entry. If a host record match is found, the IP address is returned to the client. If the query is in the form of an IP address, then the reverse lookup database (or zone) is checked for matching entries. If a match is found, the name is returned to the client. Both of these query response types are then cached for a specific time (TTL, or time to live) for faster access to often-queried resources. For longer cache times, the Registry setting governing the TTL can be increased using a Registry editor (on each machine) or through Group Policy (multiple machines).Figure 4.2 illustrates the appearance of resource records in DNS.

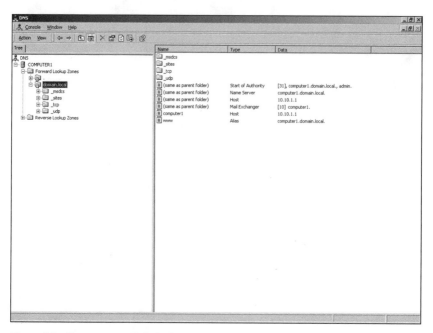

**Figure 4.2** Resource records in DNS.

| Table 4.1 | Common types of resource records. | |
|---|---|---|
| **Description** | **Type** | **Data** |
| Start of Authority | SOA | Owner name, primary name server DNS name, serial number, refresh interval, retry interval, expire time, minimum TTL (time to live) |
| Host | A | Owner name (host DNS name), host IP address |
| Name Server | NS | Owner name, name server DNS name |
| Mail Exchanger | MX | Owner name, mail exchange server DNS name, preference number |
| Canonical Name (alias) | CNAME | Owner name (alias), host DNS name |
| Service | SRV | Service name, host DNS name |

# At the DNS Client

A user, through an application (word processor, command prompt, file dialog box, and so on), requests communication with a resource server computer by name. This resource computer must then be found on the network. The process of finding the resource computer requires that the requested name be resolved (the computer initiating the request for resources is termed the *resolver*) to a TCP/IP address for correct routing on the network, then to the MAC address of the network card of the resource computer. Once the MAC address is known, the client connects and establishes a session. To locate a host computer on a network by name, queries are performed using either a local HOSTS file or a centralized name server (DNS). A HOSTS file will rarely be used on a Windows 2000 network due to the requirement of DNS for Active Directory.

*Note: Legacy clients (Windows 95, Windows 98, and Windows NT 4) use NetBIOS names, thus requiring NetBIOS name-resolution (NBNS) services. These services can be provided centrally by a WINS server or through an LMHOSTS file. An LMHOSTS file is a static file residing on the client machine that contains NetBIOS name to TCP/IP address mappings. When a WINS server is used for centralized name-resolution services, LMHOSTS files are not required but can be used for fault tolerance. Windows 2000 computers only use NetBIOS name-resolution services if DNS services are not present or fail.*

When DNS name resolution begins, the client first checks what kind of name was submitted. Three types of names can be submitted:

➤ Fully qualified domain names, terminated with a period (such as computer1. domain.com.)

➤ Single-label, unqualified domain names (such as computer1)

➤ Multiple-label, unqualified domain names (such as computer1.domain.com or computer1.domain)

When a user enters an FQDN, the client queries DNS using that name. Similarly, when a user enters a multiple-label, unqualified (not terminated with a period) name, the DNS client adds a terminating period and queries DNS using that name.

However, if the user enters a multiple-label, unqualified name and it fails to resolve as an FQDN, or if the user enters a single-label, unqualified name, the client systematically appends different DNS suffixes to the name that the user entered, adding periods to make them FQDNs and resubmitting them to DNS. How this appending proceeds depends on the client configuration:

➤ If the client does not have a domain suffix search list configured, the queries are progressively modified as follows:

1. The primary DNS suffix of the client is appended, which is specified on the Network Identification tab of the System Properties dialog box in the properties for My Computer, as shown in Figure 4.3.

2. If resolution is not successful, the client appends each connection-specific DNS suffix. This suffix can be dynamically assigned by the Dynamic Host Configuration Protocol (DHCP) server or specified on the DNS

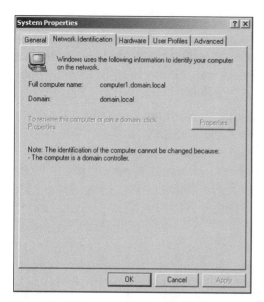

**Figure 4.3** The Network Identification tab in My Computer.

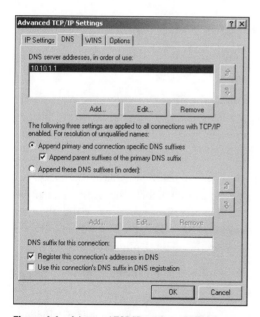

**Figure 4.4** Advanced TCP/IP settings, DNS tab.

tab in the Advanced TCP/IP Settings dialog box for each connection, as shown in Figure 4.4.

3. If resolution is still not successful, the client devolves the FQDN by appending the parent suffix of the primary DNS suffix name, the parent

of that suffix, and so on, until only two labels are left. For example, if the user enters the name computer1 and the primary DNS suffix is sales.domain.com, the client tries computer1.sales.domain.com and then computer1.domain.com.

➤ On the other hand, if the client has a domain suffix search list entered on the DNS tab:

1. Both the primary DNS suffix and the connection-specific domain name are ignored, and neither is appended to the hostname before the FQDN is submitted to DNS.

2. Instead, the client appends each suffix from the search list in order and submits it to the DNS server until it finds a match or reaches the end of the list.

 By statically configuring any resolution method settings on the client, you override any dynamically delivered (DHCP) settings.

When the query is resolved, the result is saved in the DNS cache on the client for a specific period of time (TTL setting on the client) for faster access to often-needed resources.

# What's in a Zone?

DNS database resource records are stored on and loaded from disk at startup, as well as refreshed periodically. These files, and their represented data in the interface, are called *zones*. Zone files, either copied or partitioned, can be stored on multiple servers for load balancing and fault tolerance.

In addition to providing access to zone data, a DNS can also be a caching-only server, which means that no zone or copy of a zone is stored at that computer. Caching-only servers forward queries they cannot resolve to other, zone-holding servers and then cache the results. The caching-only server resolves later queries for the same data as long as the records are available (that is, the records' TTL is greater than 0). This caching also includes *negative* resolutions for names not found in the authoritative zone, assuming that the **NegativeTimeCache** for the caching-only server is greater than 0.

If the DNS database resides on one server only, performance suffers as the network traffic and associated number of queries to the server increase. Additionally, if this lone server fails, there is no mechanism for continued name services on the network. It is advisable to configure your network in such a way as to provide both optimized service and fault tolerance for your DNS.

## Server Types

The two, standard types of servers are primary and secondary. The primary server is where all changes to the DNS database partition for that zone are made. Secondary servers receive copies of the primary zone sent via a zone transfer. A server could function as both a primary server for one zone and a secondary server for another zone, but common practice is to keep the number of different zones on a server to a minimum. In any construct, one server must host the authoritative changes to a zone. The SOA and NS records in a zone file define which server is the master server for the zone, that is, from where authoritative changes to zone information should be drawn.

*Note: Windows 2000 brings support for incremental zone transfers (IXFR) that replicate only the changes to zone information under normal circumstances. Earlier versions of DNS, including that of NT 4, do not support IXFR, only full zone transfers (AXFR), which is a complete data conveyance at each zone transfer.*

The master server can be primary or secondary. If the master is primary, the zone transfer comes directly from the source. If the master server is secondary, the file received from the master server by means of a zone transfer is a copy of the read-only zone file. Usually, the master server for the zone is also a primary server.

Incremental zone transfer works much the same as full zone transfer. The secondary server for the zone still uses the SOA resource record to determine when to poll the master server for the zone, when to retry, and so on. However, if it needs to perform a zone transfer, it sends an IXFR query instead of an AXFR query, requesting that the master server for the zone perform an incremental zone transfer.

The master server for the zone, meanwhile, maintains a recent version history of the zone, which observes any record changes that occurred in the most recent version updates of the zone. Then, if the master server for the zone has a newer version of the zone, it can forward only those record changes that have occurred between the two different versions of the zone (the current versions on the master and secondary servers) to the secondary server for the zone. The master server sends the oldest updates first and the newest updates last.

When the secondary server receives an incremental zone transfer, it creates a new version of the zone and begins replacing its resource records with the updated resource records, starting with the oldest updates and ending with the newest. When all of the updates have been made, the secondary server replaces its old version of the zone with the new version of the zone.

The master server for the zone is not required to perform an incremental transfer. It can perform a full zone transfer if it does not support incremental zone transfer, if it does not have all the necessary data for performing an incremental zone transfer, or if an incremental zone transfer takes more bandwidth than a full zone transfer.

## Reverse Lookup Zones

*Reverse lookup zones* provide, as the name suggests, the opposite type of name resolution from *forward lookup zones*. Whereas forward lookup zones provide name-to-IP address resolution, reverse lookup zones provide IP address-to-name resolution.

During the installation of Active Directory, the Active Directory Installation Wizard can automatically configure a forward lookup zone, but does not automatically add a reverse lookup zone and pointer (PTR) resource records. This is because it is possible that another server, such as the parent server, controls the reverse lookup zone. Generally, you should only add a reverse lookup zone to your server if no other server controls the reverse lookup zone for the hosts listed in your forward lookup zone. Reverse lookup zones and PTR resource records are not necessary for Active Directory to work, but you need them if you want clients to be able to resolve FQDNs from IP addresses. Also, PTR resource records are commonly used by some applications to verify the identities of clients. Figure 4.5 illustrates records found as PTR records in a reverse lookup zone.

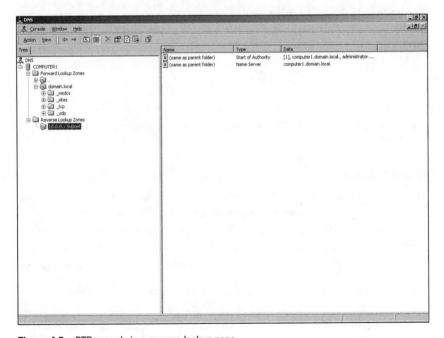

**Figure 4.5**    PTR records in a reverse lookup zone.

To simplify administration, create as few reverse lookup zones as possible. For example, if you have only one Class C network identifier (even if you have subnetted your network), it is simplest to organize your reverse lookup zones along Class C boundaries. You can add the reverse lookup zone and all the PTR resource records on an existing DNS server on your network.

 Subdomains do not need to have their own reverse lookup zones.

# Integrating Zones with Active Directory

Previous to Windows 2000, secondary zone transfer was the only method for getting zone information from one DNS server to another. In Windows 2000, you can integrate DNS zones into Active Directory, providing increased fault tolerance and security. Every Active Directory integrated zone is replicated among all domain controllers within the Active Directory domain. All DNS servers running on these domain controllers can act as primary servers for the zone, accepting dynamic updates. As with other Active Directory objects, changes replicate on a per-property basis, propagating only relevant changes.

With standard DNS, only the primary server for a zone can modify the zone. With Active Directory replication, all domain controllers for the domain can modify the zone and then replicate the changes to other domain controllers. This replication process is called *multimaster replication* because multiple domain controllers, or masters, can update the zone.

*Note: Although using Active Directory replication transfers Active Directory integrated zones, you can also perform standard zone transfers to secondary servers as you can with standard DNS zones.*

## Name Collisions

Because all domain controllers in the domain can make changes to the same zone, it is possible for several individuals connected to various domain controllers to make nearly simultaneous changes. When a property change made on a second (or third, or fourth) domain controller begins replicating before a change from the first domain controller has been fully propagated, a replication collision occurs.

Suppose that the same name is simultaneously created within the same domain and on two different domain controllers. The changes replicate, and Active Directory determines that there are two different DNS objects that have the same name. To solve the problem, the replication subsystem of Active Directory changes the name of the object that was created first by adding to the name a special character and a globally unique identifier (GUID). This makes the object names unique. The next time that the DNS server receives changes from Active Directory, the DNS server deletes the copy of the host object with the GUID. Practically speaking, the last one to write to the database wins.

Likewise, if you simultaneously modify a name object on two different server replicas, Active Directory must decide which change (attribute value) will be accepted and which will be discarded. To do so, Active Directory selects the attribute value that has the highest version number. If the version numbers are the same, Active Directory selects the attribute value that has the latest timestamp. Thus, DNS accepts the second change.

## Converting Zone Types

You can convert a standard primary or secondary zone to an Active Directory integrated zone, or an Active Directory integrated zone to a primary zone. If you plan to create an Active Directory integrated zone either from scratch or through conversion, the limitations are the same:

➤ For a DNS server to use an Active Directory integrated zone, that server must be running on a domain controller.

➤ You cannot load Active Directory integrated zones from other domains. If you want your DNS server to be authoritative for an Active Directory integrated zone from another domain, the server can only be a secondary server for that zone.

➤ There is no such thing as an Active Directory integrated secondary zone. When you store a zone in Active Directory, all domain controllers can update the zone.

➤ You cannot have an Active Directory integrated zone and a standard primary copy of the same zone on the same server.

If you decide to convert an Active Directory integrated zone to either a standard primary or standard secondary zone, some additional considerations depend on previous environment configuration:

➤ *Zone integrity might be compromised*—If you convert an Active Directory integrated zone to a standard secondary zone, the zone is copied to the name server on which you converted the zone. That server no longer loads the zone from Active Directory, but it has its own secondary copy of the zone. It requests zone transfers from whatever server you specified as the primary server for the zone.

➤ *Zone information in Active Directory will be deleted*—If you convert an Active Directory integrated zone to a standard primary zone, the zone is copied to a standard file on that server and is deleted from Active Directory. The zone no longer appears on other Active Directory integrated DNS servers.

## Give Me a Hint

DNS can be preferentially configured as to how zone file and root hint information should be initially obtained. The root hints file allows querying of authoritative servers outside the domain hosted in the Windows 2000 DNS. *Root hints* specify the name locations of authoritative servers for external networks, commonly the Internet. The options for zone and root hint loading are:

➤ Boot from file

➤ Boot from Registry

➤ Boot from Active Directory and Registry

Table 4.2 explains how the zone and root hints file can be processed on a Windows 2000 DNS.

*Note: If you change the setting of Load Data On Startup, the DNS server first writes the root hints file, zones, and parameters to the locations specified in the original setting of Load Data On Startup and then reads them from the new setting.*

The DNS server can modify all appropriate information if an administrator makes a change to the zone, or if the server is configured to accept dynamic updates and a dynamic update occurs. These boot files can add records of different types to the DNS table through the use of specific commands within the file:

➤ **primary**—Specifies the zone for which this server will be authoritative and the name of the file from which the records for this zone should be loaded.

**Table 4.2   Root hints configuration.**

| File and Function | Boot from File | Boot from Registry | Boot from Active Directory and Registry |
|---|---|---|---|
| Read root hints | Root hints file | Root hints file if available; otherwise, the Directory | The Directory; otherwise, the root hints file |
| Write root hints | Root hints file | Root hints file | The Directory, if available |
| Read zones | Boot file | Registry | The Directory |
| Write zones | Boot file and Registry | Registry and the Directory (if AD integrated) | The Directory and the Registry |

➤ **secondary**—Specifies the zone for which this server will request/receive information and the primary server from which this information should be retrieved.

➤ **cache**—Specifies the file containing host information that is needed to resolve names outside the authoritative domains and names and addresses of root name servers.

# Dynamic Updating of DNS

In Windows 2000, clients can send dynamic updates for three different types of network adapters: DHCP adapters, statically configured adapters, and remote access adapters. Regardless of which adapter is used, the DHCP client service sends dynamic updates to the authoritative DNS server. Unlike Windows NT 4, the DHCP client service runs on all Windows 2000 computers regardless of whether they are configured as DHCP clients.

## Dynamic Update Behavior

By default, the dynamic update client dynamically registers its A resource records and all of its PTR resource records (if the DNS is configured with a reverse lookup zone) every 24 hours or whenever any of the following events occur:

➤ The TCP/IP configuration is changed.

➤ The DHCP address is renewed or a new lease is obtained.

➤ A plug-and-play event occurs involving the network interface.

➤ An IP address is added or removed from the computer when the user changes or adds an IP address for a static adapter. (The user does not need to restart the computer for the dynamic update client to register the name-to-IP address mappings.)

## Dynamic Update Process

There are two steps in the dynamic update process:

1. The client queries its local DNS to find the primary name server and the zone that is authoritative for the name it is updating. The local name server then performs the standard name-resolution process to discover the primary name server that is authoritative for the name. A response is sent with the name of the authoritative server and zone.

2. The client then sends a dynamic update request to the primary server that is authoritative for the zone. If any specified prerequisites at the client are fulfilled, the authoritative server begins the dynamic update process. The authoritative

server then checks whether any specified prerequisites at the server have been fulfilled. If they have, the server performs the update and replies to the client.

*Note: When using the **dcpromo** command to install a domain controller into an existing forest, dynamic updating must be enabled for that upcoming domain controller's authoritative zone. Otherwise, the Active Directory Wizard will attempt to install DNS on the computer being promoted.*

## DHCP Servers, Clients, and Dynamic Updates

Windows 2000 DHCP clients can initiate the dynamic update process. A DHCP client negotiates the process of dynamic updates with the DHCP server when the client leases an IP address or renews the lease, determining which computer will update the A and PTR resource records. The DHCP client, DHCP server, or both update the records by sending a dynamic update request to a primary DNS server that is authoritative for the name that is to be updated.

Clients and servers that are running versions of Windows earlier than Windows 2000 do not support dynamic updates. However, Windows 2000 DHCP servers can perform dynamic updates on behalf of clients that do not support the FQDN option. For example, clients that are running Windows 95, Windows 98, or Windows NT do not support the FQDN option. To enable this functionality, select the option Enable Updates For DNS Clients That Do Not Support Dynamic Update on the DNS tab of the Properties page on the DHCP server. See Figure 4.6.

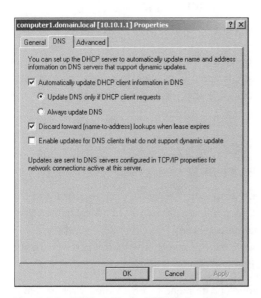

**Figure 4.6** DHCP update for DNS client option.

The DHCP server first obtains the names of legacy clients from the DHCP-REQUEST packet. It then appends the domain name given for that scope and registers the A and PTR resource records.

For enhanced fault tolerance, integrate with Active Directory any zones that accept dynamic updates from Windows 2000 clients.

In some cases, stale PTR or A resource records can appear on DNS servers when the lease of a DHCP client expires. For example, when a Windows 2000 DHCP client tries to negotiate a dynamic update procedure with a Windows NT 4 DHCP server, the Windows 2000 DHCP client must register both A and PTR resource records itself. Later, if the Windows 2000 DHCP client is improperly removed from the network, the client cannot unregister its A and PTR resource records; thus, they become stale.

If a stale A resource record appears in a zone that allows only secure dynamic updates, no person or computer is able to use the name in that A resource record.

## The Rules for Dynamic Updates

Whether the client requests dynamic updates depends on whether the client is running Windows 2000 or some other version of Windows. It also depends on how the client is configured.

Clients can take any of the following actions:

➤ By default, the Windows 2000 DHCP client sends the FQDN option with the Flags field set to 0 to request that the client update the A resource record, and the DHCP server updates the PTR resource record. After the client requests the update, it waits for a response from the DHCP server. Unless the DHCP server sets the Flags field to 3, the client initiates an update for the A resource record. If the DHCP server does not support or is not configured to perform registration of the DNS record, the client attempts registration of the A and PTR resource records.

➤ DHCP clients that are running Windows operating systems of a version earlier than Windows 2000 and Windows 2000 DHCP clients configured not to register DNS resource records do not send the FQDN option. In this case, the client does not try to update either record.

Depending on what the client requests, the server can take different actions. If the DHCP client sends a DHCPREQUEST message without the FQDN option, what happens depends on the type of server and how the server is configured. The server can update both records and does so if it is configured to update records on behalf of clients.

However, in the following cases, the DHCP server does nothing:

➤ The server does not support dynamic updates (for example, a Windows NT 4 server).

➤ The server is running Windows 2000 and is configured not to do dynamic updates for clients that do not support the FQDN option.

➤ The server is running Windows 2000 and configured not to register DNS resource records.

If the Windows 2000–based DHCP client requests that the server updates the PTR resource record but not the A resource record, what happens depends on the type of server and how it is configured:

➤ If the server is running either Windows NT 4 or Windows 2000 and is configured not to perform dynamic updates, the server does not reply using the FQDN option and does not update either record. If this happens, the DHCP client attempts to update both the A and PTR resource records.

➤ If the server is running Windows 2000 and is configured to update according to the request of the client, the server attempts to update the PTR resource record. The server sends a DHCPACK (positive acknowledgement) message to the client. The client then attempts to update the A resource record.

➤ If the server is running Windows 2000 and is configured to always update both records, the server attempts to update both resource records. It sends a DHCPACK message to the client. If the client requested that the server update the PTR resource record but not the A resource record, the server also sets the Flags field to 3. In this case, the client does not attempt to update either resource record.

*Note: Legacy clients can use the Active Directory client software patch to view objects in Active Directory. However, this software does not perform dynamic updating of DNS.*

## Secure Dynamic Updates

You can configure any Active Directory integrated zone for secure dynamic updates and then use the Access Control List (ACL) to specify which users and groups have authority to modify the zone and records in the zone.

*Note: Secure dynamic updates are available only on Active Directory integrated zones.*

## Configuring Secure Dynamic Updates

When you create an Active Directory integrated zone, its default configuration is to allow only secure dynamic updates. If you created the zone as a standard primary zone and then converted it to an Active Directory integrated zone, it is configured for non-secure dynamic updates or for no dynamic updates, depending on how the primary zone was previously configured.

With secure dynamic updates, only the computers and users you specify in an ACL can create or modify dnsNode objects—their host records—within the zone. By default, the ACL gives Create permission to all members of the Authenticated User group. This means that any authenticated user or computer can create a new object in the zone and that the creator owns the new object and is given full control of it.

 You can reserve FQDNs so that only certain users can use them. To do so, create the FQDN in the DNS console and then modify its ACL so that only particular computers or users can change it.

### Secure Dynamic Update Process

To initiate a secure dynamic update:

1. The client determines the underlying security mechanism and begins a secure session with the DNS.

2. The client sends the dynamic update request containing resource records to add, delete, or modify to the server, and the server sends an acknowledgement.

3. The server attempts to update Active Directory on behalf of the client.

# DHCP and Secure Dynamic Updates

You do not want the DHCP server to perform secure dynamic updates on behalf of DHCP clients that do not support the FQDN option. If a DHCP server performs a secure dynamic update on a name, the DHCP server becomes the owner of that name, and only that DHCP server can update the name. Therefore, if you have enabled secure dynamic update, place the server in a special security group called DNSUpdateProxy. Objects created by members of the DNSUpdateProxy group have no security; therefore, any authenticated user can take ownership of the objects. Windows 2000 DHCP clients register their own A resource records; therefore, putting a DHCP server in the DNSUpdateProxy group does not affect the security of the A resource records for Windows 2000 DHCP clients. The A resource record corresponding to the DHCP server has no security if the server is placed in the DNSUpdateProxy group.

If you have installed the DHCP service on a domain controller, be absolutely certain not to make that server a member of the DNSUpdateProxy group. Doing so gives any user or computer full control of the DNS records corresponding to the domain controllers, unless you manually modify the corresponding ACL. Moreover, if a DHCP server running on a domain controller is configured to perform dynamic updates on behalf of its clients, that DHCP server is able to take ownership of any record, even in the zones that are configured to allow only secure dynamic updates. This is because a DHCP server runs under the computer account, so if it is installed on a domain controller, it has full control over DNS objects stored in the Active Directory.

# Integration with WINS

Windows Internet Name Service (WINS) provides dynamic name resolution for the NetBIOS namespace. Before Windows 2000, WINS was required on all clients and servers. The Windows NT 4 DNS server provided a feature called *WINS lookup*. With WINS lookup, you can direct DNS to query WINS for name resolution so that DNS clients can look up the names and IP addresses of WINS clients. Windows 2000 still supports WINS lookup, although for DHCP clients, you can use dynamic updates instead, provided that the DHCP server is running Windows 2000.

*Note: WINS is not required in a purely Windows 2000 environment.*

To use WINS lookup integration, you add two special resource records—the WINS and WINS-R resource records—to your forward and reverse lookup zones, respectively. When a DNS server that is authoritative for that zone is queried for a name it does not find in the authoritative zone, and the zone is configured to use WINS resolution, the DNS server queries the WINS server. If the name is registered with WINS, the WINS server returns the associated record to the DNS server.

Reverse lookups work differently than forward lookups in that when an authoritative DNS server is queried for a nonexistent PTR record, and the authoritative zone contains the WINS-R record, the DNS server uses a NetBIOS node adapter status lookup.

In any case, the DNS server returns the name or IP address in response to the original DNS request.

# Interoperability with Other DNS Servers

Although Windows 2000 has a sufficient suite of DNS services, Windows 2000 is not the only option. Existing environments may have other forms of DNS,

Microsoft-based or otherwise, in operation at the time Windows 2000 is brought into the environment. Correct upgrading of or co-existence with these DNS servers is essential to ensure smooth transition from the old environment to the new.

## Configuring NT 4 DNS Servers for Active Directory Support

For the domain controller locator to work properly, the primary DNS server that is authoritative for the Netlogon service names must support the service resource record (SRV RR). Support of the dynamic update protocol, although beneficial, is not required.

*Note: If the primary DNS server for a zone does not support dynamic update protocol, you have to enter and update all SRV records manually.*

## Configuring Non-Microsoft DNS Servers for Active Directory Support

The following DNS server types support SRV records:

➤ Windows 2000

➤ Windows NT 4 Service Pack 4 and later

➤ BIND 4.9.6 and later

The following DNS server types support dynamic updates:

➤ Windows 2000

➤ BIND 8.1.3 and later (8.1.2 supports SRV records, but the format is incorrect for Active Directory)

If you use a third-party server, however, you cannot use the Microsoft DNS management tools (DNS console, Dnscmd.exe, and so on), Active Directory integration, secure dynamic updates, aging and scavenging of stale records, or remote administration.

The DNS database must include locator resource records (SRV, CNAME, and A) to support each domain controller.

## Name Consistency

Difficulties could arise with nonstandard DNS names. Standard DNS names follow several broad but strict conventions. Table 4.3 enumerates the restrictions. Non-Windows 2000 DNS and NetBIOS names (NT 4, non-DNS) have levels of flexibility that can cause difficulty with third-party DNS servers.

According to RFC 1123, the only characters that can be used in DNS labels are A to Z, a to z, 0 to 9, and the hyphen (-). (The period [.] is also used in DNS names, but only between DNS labels and at the end of an FQDN.) However, adherence to RFC 1123 can be problematic on Windows 2000 networks that still use NetBIOS names.

To simplify the migration process to Windows 2000 from Windows NT 4, Windows 2000 supports a wider character set. RFC 2181, "Clarifications to the DNS Specification," enlarges the character set allowed in DNS names because it removes the restriction that all DNS names must be interpreted as ASCII. This Unicode Translation Format (UTF) character encoding, as described in RFC 2044, includes traditional ASCII and a translation of the UCS-character encoding (also known as Unicode).

Before you get excited about using all those extra characters you have available, consider the following:

➤ Some third-party client software supports only the characters listed in RFC 1123. If you have any third-party client software, that software is probably not able to look up computers with names that have nonstandard characters.

➤ A DNS server that does not support UTF-8 encoding might accept a zone transfer of a zone containing UTF-8 names, but it cannot write back those names to a zone file or reload those names from a zone file. Therefore, you must not transfer a zone that contains UTF-8 characters to a DNS server that does not support them.

You can configure the Windows 2000 DNS server to allow or disallow the use of UTF-8 characters on your Windows 2000 server. You can do so on a per-server basis from within the DNS console. The available choices for allowed characters are as follows:

| Table 4.3 DNS naming restrictions. | | | |
| --- | --- | --- | --- |
| **Restrictions** | **Standard DNS** | **Windows 2000 DNS** | **NetBIOS** |
| Characters | Supports RFC 1123, which permits A to Z, a to z, 0 to 9, and the hyphen | Several different configurations are possible: See the rest of this section for details | Unicode characters, numbers, white space, and the symbols ! @ # $ % ^ & ' ) ( . - _ { } ~ |
| FQDN length | 63 bytes per label and 255 bytes for an FQDN | 63 bytes per label and 255 bytes for an FQDN; domain controllers are limited to 155 bytes for an FQDN | 15 bytes |

➤ *Strict RFC (ANSI)*—Allows A to Z, a to z, the hyphen (-), and the asterisk (*) as a first label, and the underscore (_) as the first character in a label.

➤ *Non RFC (ANSI)*—Allows all characters allowed when you select Strict RFC (ANSI), and allows the underscore (_) anywhere in a name.

➤ *Multibyte (UTF)*—Allows all characters allowed when you select Non RFC (ANSI), and allows UTF-8 characters.

➤ *Any character*—Allows any character, including UTF-8 characters.

*Note: If you enter a DNS name that includes UTF-8 or underscore characters that are not listed in RFC 1123 when you are modifying a hostname or DNS suffix or creating an Active Directory domain, a warning message appears explaining that "some DNS server implementations might not support these characters."*

# Troubleshooting DNS

Windows 2000 provides many tools that can help you diagnose and solve problems with DNS. Familiarity with the tool name, function, and appropriate situational use is needed for the exam:

➤ **nslookup**—You can use **nslookup** to perform DNS queries and to examine the contents of zone files on local and remote servers. Use **nslookup** to verify contact with DNS servers and the validity of entries in the zone database. If a forward lookup zone is unavailable, **nslookup** will fail to connect to the DNS server. If a reverse lookup zone is not available, **nslookup** will timeout. Figure 4.7 illustrates the use of **nslookup**.

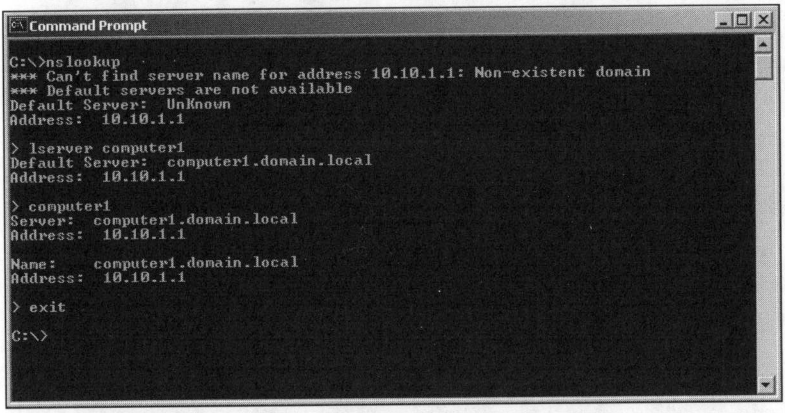

```
C:\>nslookup
*** Can't find server name for address 10.10.1.1: Non-existent domain
*** Default servers are not available
Default Server:  UnKnown
Address:  10.10.1.1

> lserver computer1
Default Server:  computer1.domain.local
Address:  10.10.1.1

> computer1
Server:  computer1.domain.local
Address:  10.10.1.1

Name:    computer1.domain.local
Address:  10.10.1.1

> exit

C:\>
```

**Figure 4.7**  The **nslookup** command resolving computer1.domain.local.

➤ **netdiag**—Provides for more extensive testing than **nslookup**, including Kerberos and LDAP analysis. **netdiage** can also repair minor problems and inconsistencies.

➤ **ipconfig**—You can use **ipconfig** to view DNS client settings, display and flush the client cache, and force a dynamic update client to register its DNS records. Figure 4.8 illustrates the use of **ipconfig**.

**ipconfig** has three new switches in Windows 2000:

➤ **\displaydns**—Allows you to view the client-cached DNS client entries on the client

➤ **\flushdns**—Clears the client cache

➤ **\registerdns**—Attempts to register the client name and IP address in DNS.

**Figure 4.8** The **ipconfig** command options.

➤ *Event Viewer*—You can use Event Viewer to view DNS client and server error messages.

➤ *DNS log*—You can configure the DNS server to monitor certain events and log them in the DNS log for your examination.

➤ *Network redirector command*—Although **ipconfig** is the preferred method of flushing the DNS client cache, the **net stop** and **net start** command perform the same function.

You can perform test queries by using options on the Monitoring tab in the DNS console.

# Practice Questions

## Question 1

> You are configuring your network for Active Directory. You must ensure fault tolerance for your DNS without adding more replication or administration process overhead. Which of the following accomplishes your goal? [Check all correct answers]
>
> ❑ a.  Configure the first domain controller in your domain to host a DNS server.
>
> ❑ b.  Configure all replica domain controllers in your domain to host a DNS server.
>
> ❑ c.  Configure the DNS zone on the first domain controller as standard primary.
>
> ❑ d.  Configure the DNS zones on all replica domain controllers to be standard secondary.
>
> ❑ e.  Configure all DNS zones to be Active Directory integrated.

The correct answers are a, b, and e. Active Directory integrated zones combine the DNS zone replication with that of Active Directory. This requires no additional administrative or replication overhead beyond the volume of the data itself. Although configuring one zone as primary and the remaining zones as secondary provides the fault tolerance for DNS, these zones also require additional replication and administrative maintenance. Therefore, answers c and d are incorrect.

# Question 2

> Your network client base consists of many varieties of Microsoft operating systems, including Windows 95, Windows 98, Windows NT 4 Workstation, and Windows 2000 Professional. You need to have dynamic updating of DNS records for all clients.
>
> The Active Directory client is installed on each non-Windows 2000 client machine. All client computers are configured to use DHCP.
>
> All DNS zones are either standard primary or standard secondary. The highest level of DNS security is desired.
>
> Which additional steps, if any, are required? [Check all correct answers]
>
> ❏ a. Configure DNS to accept only secure dynamic updates.
>
> ❏ b. Configure DHCP to enable updates for the legacy clients.
>
> ❏ c. Install the Active Directory client software on all legacy client computers.
>
> ❏ d. Remove DHCP client configuration. Statically assign TCP/IP configuration on all clients.

The correct answers are a and b. Allowing only secure dynamic updates is the highest level of security possible for DNS, and the non-Windows 2000 client computers on your network need a Windows 2000 DHCP server to update the DNS on their behalf. Even though the Active Directory client software gives some functionality to legacy clients in the Active Directory, dynamically updating DNS is not one of them. Therefore, answer c is incorrect. Statically configuring IP on the clients does not enable dynamic updating. Therefore, answer d is incorrect.

## Question 3

> Your Windows 2000 network consists of three locations: Denver, Miami, and New York. Each of the locations is configured as a site in a single domain, Acme.com. Each site contains two domain controllers: DenverDC1 and DenverDC2; MiamiDC1 and MiamiDC2; and NewYorkDC1 and NewYorkDC2.
>
> DNS is currently configured with an Active Directory integrated zone for Acme.com on DenverDC1.
>
> You want to enable complete, fault-tolerant behavior for your network DNS. Which of the following is necessary to accomplish this?
>
> O a. Use the Active Directory Sites and Services snap-in to configure each site to allow DNS replication.
>
> O b. Install DNS on each domain controller.
>
> O c. Convert the zone on DenverDC1 to standard primary.
>
> O d. Configure DHCP to dynamically update client configuration information in DNS.

The correct answer is b. With an Active Directory integrated zone, the DNS service is all that is required on each domain controller, because the DNS zone information is already replicated. The DNS service then uses the zone information already present. There is no need for special configuration of site replication to allow this. Therefore, answer a is incorrect. Converting the zone on DenverDC1 to standard primary actually removes the zone information from all domain controllers. This would require setting up all domain controllers other than DenverDC1 as standard secondary zones. Therefore, answer c is incorrect. Fault tolerance of DNS is in no way affected by the update method, be it directly from a client or through DHCP. Therefore, answer d is incorrect.

# Question 4

You have been tasked with designing the DNS plan for your network. The proposed domain structure is shown in Figure 4.9. You will install DNS on the computers Asia-DC1 and North America-DC1, given the following objectives:

- No DNS-related replication can cross the site link.

- Name resolution must function for users in both the Asia and North America sites.

You plan the following actions:

1. Install DNS on Asia-DC1 as an Active Directory integrated zone.

2. Install DNS on North America-DC1 as an Active Directory integrated zone.

What objectives do your actions achieve? [Check all correct answers]

❏  a.  No DNS-related replication crosses the site link.

❏  b.  Name resolution functions for users in both the Asia and North America sites.

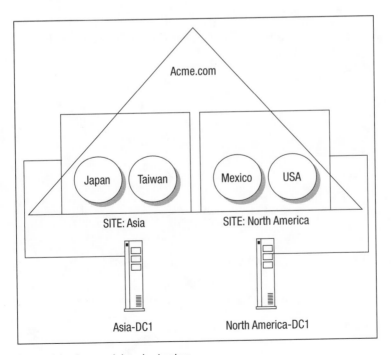

**Figure 4.9**   Proposed domain structure.

The correct answer is b. With an Active Directory integrated zone, all DNS traffic is replicated along with Active Directory information across the site link.

## Question 5

You have been tasked with the DNS plan for your network. Refer to Figure 4.9 for the proposed domain structure. You will install DNS on the computers Asia-DC1 and North America-DC1, given the following objectives:

- No DNS-related replication must cross the site link.

- Name resolution must function for users in both the Asia and North America sites.

You plan the following actions:

1. Install DNS on Asia-DC1 as a standard primary zone.

2. Install DNS on North America-DC1 as a caching-only server.

What objectives do your actions achieve? [Check all correct answers]

❏ a. No DNS-related replication crosses the site link.

❏ b. Name resolution functions for users in both the Asia and North America sites.

The correct answers are a and b. Only name-resolution traffic crosses the link, and name resolution functions properly.

# Question 6

Currently, Unix DNS servers perform the function of name resolution in your NT 4 network. You will continue to use the Unix DNS for Internet name-resolution services but will establish a separate namespace and DNS structure for your Active Directory using Windows 2000 DNS.

Order the steps as appropriate. Use only necessary steps.

Install Windows 2000 DNS on all Windows 2000 domain controllers.

Configure the Unix DNS for dynamic updates.

Configure the Windows 2000 DNS for dynamic updates.

Manually add the SRV records to the Unix DNS.

Manually add the SRV records to the Windows 2000 DNS.

Configure the Windows 2000 DNS as a forwarder to the Unix DNS.

Configure the Windows 2000 DNS with a secondary zone to the Unix DNS primary zone.

Configure the Unix DNS with a secondary zone to the Windows 2000 DNS primary zone.

Configure the Unix DNS as a forwarder to the Windows 2000 DNS.

The correct answer is:

Install Windows 2000 DNS on all Windows 2000 domain controllers.

Configure the Windows 2000 DNS for dynamic updates.

Configure the Windows 2000 DNS as a forwarder to the Unix DNS.

Because the Active Directory is to be separately maintained on the Windows 2000 DNS, installation and dynamic updating is appropriate only on those Windows 2000 DNS servers. The Unix DNS should then be configured as a forwarder for the Windows 2000 DNS for resolution of non-AD machine queries (from the Internet).

## Question 7

> Currently, Unix DNS servers perform the function of name resolution in your NT 4 network. You will continue to use the Unix DNS for Internet name-resolution services as well as for namespace and DNS structure for your Windows 2000 DNS Active Directory. TCP/IP configuration will continue to be assigned through the BOOTP/DHCP process. Dynamic updating of DNS will not be supported.
>
> Order the steps as appropriate. Use only necessary steps.
>
> Install Windows 2000 DNS on all Windows 2000 domain controllers.
>
> Configure the Windows 2000 DNS for dynamic updates.
>
> Manually add the SRV records to the Unix DNS.
>
> Manually add the SRV records to the Windows 2000 DNS.
>
> Configure the Windows 2000 DNS as a forwarder to the Unix DNS.
>
> Configure the Windows 2000 DNS with a secondary zone to the Unix DNS primary zone.
>
> Configure the Unix DNS with a secondary zone to the Windows 2000 DNS primary zone.
>
> Configure the Unix DNS as a forwarder to the Windows 2000 DNS.

The correct answer is:

Manually add the SRV records to the Unix DNS.

The only requirement for using a Unix DNS for Active Directory is the availability of SRV RR (resource records). Windows 2000 DNS could be installed, but the existing structure is best, given that dynamic updates will not be supported. If dynamic updates were supported, then the better choice would be to configure Windows 2000 DNS, forwarding queries to the Unix DNS as appropriate.

# Question 8

> Client computers are running either Windows 2000 Professional or Windows NT 4 Workstation. The Windows NT 4 Workstations will be upgraded within six months.
>
> You want to ensure that only clients that are members of your network update DNS with their configuration information. You intend to do this through setting Allow Only Secured Dynamic Updates on the Windows 2000 DNS servers.
>
> What else must be true in order to accomplish the secure updating of records in DNS? [Check all correct answers]
>
> ❑ a. Dynamic updates must be disabled on the Windows 2000 client computers.
>
> ❑ b. The DHCP must be placed in the DNSUpdateProxy group.
>
> ❑ c. The DHCP server must be configured to dynamically update DNS.
>
> ❑ d. The Active Directory client software must be installed on the NT 4 Workstations.
>
> ❑ e. The Windows 2000 DNS must be configured as an Active Directory integrated zone.

The correct answers are b, c, and e. Dynamic updates from Windows 2000 clients are secure, and with the DNS server configured as given, the client updates would fail with this feature disabled. Therefore, answer a is incorrect.

Windows NT 4 Workstations are the only client computers that need DNS updating via DHCP because Windows 2000 clients update DNS themselves. The DHCP server should be placed in the DNSUpdateProxy group so that when the Windows NT 4 Workstations are upgraded, they will be able to update their own configuration information in DNS. If this option is not enabled, DHCP will own the records, which is fine while the client computer remains NT 4 but not thereafter. The Active Directory client software does not interact with the updating of DNS. Therefore, answer d is incorrect.

# Need to Know More?

 Albitz, Paul and Cricket Liu. *DNS and BIND, 3rd ed.* Sebastopol, CA: O'Reilly & Associates, 1998. This book offers definitive information concerning the DNS namespace and hierarchy development and infrastructure.

 See the Internet Engineering Task Force (IETF) site at **http://windows. microsoft.com/windows2000/reskit/webresources**. Request for Comments (RFC) documents and IETF Internet drafts offer in-depth technical information on the evolving world of DNS and TCP/IP.

**5**

# WINS

. . . . . . . . . . . . . . . . . . . . . . . . . . . . . . . . . . . . . . . . . . .

### Terms you'll need to understand:

✓ NetBIOS

✓ Host

✓ Domain Name System

✓ Name resolution

✓ LMHOSTS

✓ WINS database

✓ WINS proxy

✓ WINS replication

✓ Persistent connection

✓ Manual tombstoning

✓ Burst handling

### Techniques you'll need to master:

✓ Knowing the NetBIOS name-resolution process

✓ Installing and configuring a WINS client and server

✓ Configuring WINS replication

✓ Maintaining, managing, and monitoring the WINS database

The native protocol in Windows 2000 is TCP/IP, and, as discussed earlier, Windows 2000 uses the Domain Name System (DNS) to find other computers (hosts). However, the clients on a Windows 2000 network use NetBIOS (network basic input/output system) to find and communicate with other computers (unless, of course, the entire network is Windows 2000 and nothing else). One of the ways NetBIOS name resolution happens in Windows 2000 is via the Windows Internet Name Service (WINS).

WINS registers a computer name and resolves it to an IP address, much in the same way as DNS resolves hostnames to IP addresses.

# NetBIOS Name Resolution Overview

To understand WINS, you must understand NetBIOS. NetBIOS is what gives computers the ability to communicate on a network. Windows 3.x, Windows 9x, and Windows NT all rely on NetBIOS names to request network services, exchange information, and make and break sessions with each other.

A NetBIOS name identifies a single host on a network and belongs to one and only one host. A NetBIOS name is 16 bytes in length, 15 characters plus an additional character to identify the service or application that is registering the name. The name is also *flat,* which means there is no hierarchal structure to the name. Contrast this with a DNS name, which is hierarchal and uses a fully qualified domain name (FQDN).

## Standard NetBIOS Name Resolution Methods

In a network that is running versions of Windows previous to Windows 2000, applications that use NetBIOS names must have a way to resolve those names to IP addresses. As mentioned before, one way is to use WINS. Another way computers resolve a NetBIOS name is by using a database called LMHOSTS.

There are three standard resolution methods for NetBIOS names:

➤ Local broadcast

➤ NetBIOS name cache

➤ NetBIOS name server

### Local Broadcast Method

A local broadcast is a request sent out by a host to the network in search of the name it seeks and its corresponding IP address. NetBIOS uses User Datagram Protocol (UDP) to query every host on the local network—*every* host. As you can see, this process can eat up a lot of your bandwidth if you choose this method to resolve your NetBIOS names. You can configure this broadcast in an effort to optimize it. Two Registry entries can either alter the number of times the host repeats its broadcast or change the amount of time to wait before sending out another broadcast. These Registry entries appear under the following Registry key:

```
HKEY_LOCAL_MACHINE\SYSTEM\CurrentControlSet\Services\NetBT\
  Parameters
```

The Registry entries are **BcastQueryTimeout** (the default is 750 ms before it tries again) and **BcastQueryCount** (the default is that the system tries three times). If the values for these entries are set too high, your network could be flooded with broadcasts (a bad thing).

## NetBIOS Name Cache Method

Another method that NetBIOS uses to resolve names to IP addresses is the NetBIOS name cache, which is a list of names that have already been resolved. The names on the list remain there for a short period of time (10 minutes by default), and the cache holds only 16 names by default. You can change the number of names that are kept in the cache by modifying the following Registry key:

```
HKEY_LOCAL_MACHINE\SYSTEM\CurrentControlSet\Services\NetBT\
  Parameters
```

The Registry entries are **Size/Small/Medium/Large** (the default is 0x1, which is small) and **CacheTimeout**, which specifies how long a name will remain in the cache (the default is 0x927c0, which is 600,000 ms or 10 minutes).

To view what is in the cache, type **nbtstat -c** at the command prompt.

## NetBIOS Name Server Method

The third method that NetBIOS uses to resolve names to IP addresses is a NetBIOS name server. A NetBIOS name server is a computer that maintains a centralized database of NetBIOS names and IP addresses. Hosts can register their names and IP addresses with the NetBIOS name server. In Windows 2000, the NetBIOS name server is WINS.

WINS is the service that runs on a computer that performs name resolution. It complies with RFC 1001 and RFC 1002. It is a dynamic service, meaning it registers the names of clients when a client makes the request.

# Microsoft NetBIOS Name Resolution Methods

As expected, Microsoft has its own way of resolving names to IP addresses in addition to standard methods. Microsoft implements name resolution in a number of different ways. One way is through DNS; another way is through the

HOSTS file. Both of these methods were discussed in Chapter 4. Another method Microsoft uses is called the LMHOSTS file, which is discussed later in this chapter.

## Name Resolution Using NetBIOS over TCP/IP

Until now, we've discussed the different methods you can use to resolve NetBIOS names to IP addresses. You can use them individually or use them in conjunction with another method. All node types check the NetBIOS name cache first. Then, depending on the node type that the system is configured as, the system will use various means for name resolution, which include the LMHOSTS file, the HOSTS file, and DNS. For example, one of the methods for resolving NetBIOS names to IP addresses is via local broadcast on the network. This particular method is called *B-node* (broadcast). The system configured as a B-node first checks the local NetBIOS name cache; if it doesn't receive resolution, it then broadcasts to the local network. Next, it checks the LMHOSTS file, then the HOSTS file, and then DNS. A system that uses a NetBIOS name server is said to be employing *P-node* (peer-to-peer) name resolution.

Windows 2000 uses the following different methods:

➤ *B-node (broadcast)*—Uses a broadcast for name registration and resolution.

➤ *P-node (peer-to-peer)*—Uses a NetBIOS name server for name registration and resolution.

➤ *M-node (mixed)*—Combines B-node and P-node. If the system cannot first resolve the name via broadcast, it then uses the NetBIOS name server.

➤ *H-node (hybrid)*—Also combines B-node and P-node, but reverses the order; if the system cannot first resolve the name via NetBIOS name server, the system then uses a broadcast.

➤ *Microsoft enhanced B-node*—Checks the NetBIOS name cache for the mapping of the NetBIOS name to IP address. If the mapping is not found, the system initiates a broadcast. If a broadcast is unsuccessful, the system then looks for the mapping in the LMHOSTS file.

If the system is a Windows 2000 computer and it is not configured to use WINS, the system defaults to Microsoft enhanced B-node for name resolution.

To check the node type your system is currently using, at the command prompt type **ipconfig /all**. The node type is configured to broadcast if no WINS server is specified because Windows 2000 defaults to enhanced B-node resolution. Once a WINS server is specified, however, the node type changes to H-node. If you want to change the node type your system is currently using, you have to go to the following Registry subkey:

```
HKEY_LOCAL_MACHINE\SYSTEM\CurrentControlSet\Services\NetBT\
    Parameters\NodeType
```

The values to use (in hex) are:

➤ 0x1 for B-node

➤ 0x2 for P-node

➤ 0x4 for M-node

➤ 0x8 for H-node

# LMHOSTS File

The LMHOSTS file is a text file that resides on the local machine and contains mappings of NetBIOS names to IP addresses. Windows 2000 uses the LMHOSTS file in the same manner as Windows NT did. It loads the entries from the file into the NetBIOS name cache when the system starts up. When the system cannot resolve a name to an IP address by other methods, it searches the LMHOSTS file for the mapping. Computers that do not employ the services of a NetBIOS name server can use the LMHOSTS file to resolve NetBIOS names.

The text file has no extension and appears in the %systemroot%\system32\ drivers\etc directory. The file can also contain tags that add functionality to it. Tags are preceded by a # and let the system know to pay attention to the information immediately following. Table 5.1 defines the tags available in the LMHOSTS file.

| Table 5.1    Predefined keywords for the LMHOSTS file. | |
| --- | --- |
| Tag | Purpose |
| #PRE | An entry followed by this tag is preloaded into the NetBIOS name cache and remains in the cache. |
| #DOM:*<domain_name>* | An entry followed by this tag is considered a domain controller. |
| #INCLUDE *<path to file>* | This tag means there is a centrally located LMHOSTS file that all the systems use. It loads the entry that follows it and directs resolution queries to the location the entry specifies. The entry that follows this tag must also have a name-to-IP-address mapping in the LMHOSTS file (or Windows 2000 won't know how to get to the computer with the centrally located LMHOSTS file). |

*(continued)*

| Table 5.1    Predefined keywords for the LMHOSTS file *(continued)*. | |
| --- | --- |
| Tag | Purpose |
| **#BEGIN_ALTERNATE** | If the system listed in the **#INCLUDE** tag cannot be contacted, this tag allows you to put in more **#INCLUDE** statements and specify other locations for an LMHOSTS file. The system stops reading other **#INCLUDE** statements once one of the entries works. |
| **#END_ALTERNATE** | This tag follows the last **#INCLUDE** statement after the **#BEGIN_ALTERNATE** tag. |
| **#NOFNR** | This tag tells the system to avoid using NetBIOS-directed name queries for LAN Manager Unix systems. |
| **#MH** | This tag tells the system that multiple entries exist due to one or more multihomed computers. |

The LMHOSTS file is parsed; in other words, it is read from top to bottom, left to right. Computers that are accessed more frequently should be placed toward the top of the list. The entries that precede the **#PRE** tag should appear toward the bottom of the file because the entries are always already in the cache. In Windows 2000, the LMHOSTS file is used by default. To disable the use of an LMHOSTS file, on the WINS tab in Advanced TCP/IP settings, clear the checkbox Enable LMHOSTS Lookup.

# WINS Overview

Windows Internet Name Service (WINS) gives Windows 2000 a way to provide services for clients to obtain name resolution while reducing network broadcast traffic. These services include name registration, name renewal, name release, and name resolution.

Each client registers its name in the WINS database when it starts up. The client then performs a name query to find other hosts that are also registered in the database. If the name-to-IP-address mapping exists in the database and is active, WINS returns the IP address to the client.

## Name Registration

When a client computer starts, it registers its name and IP address with the WINS server by sending a name-registration request directly to the WINS server. The WINS server then ensures that no other client has the same name. Once this has occurred, the WINS server returns a successful registration message to the client. In the message, the amount of time that the registration will be active is specified as the time to live (TTL) value.

In Windows 2000, the registration includes not only the name, but also the Workstation service, the Server service, the Messenger service, the workgroup or domain that the computer pertains to, and the user who was logged on to the client when it registered its name.

If the name is already registered to another client in the database, WINS sends a name query request to the original name in the database to verify that the name is indeed in use and active. If the client that first registered the name is a multihomed computer, WINS sends a query to each interface. If the registered owner answers the query, or the name is a static entry, the registration request receives a negative acknowledgement and displays an error message.

# Name Renewal

The process of name renewal (or *refresh* as it is sometimes called) resembles children in a car on their way to a destination: "Dad, are we there yet?" then a few minutes later, "Mom, are we there yet?" and again, "Dad, are we there yet?" This process continues until the destination is reached. When a client computer registers its name with the WINS server, the server returns a TTL value to the client.

At the midpoint of expiration, the client requests a renewal of its registration. If the primary WINS server does not respond to this request, the client retries in 10 minutes and every 10 minutes thereafter for one hour. If after an hour the primary WINS server does not respond, the client then requests name renewal from the secondary WINS server. It also does this every 10 minutes for one hour, and then guess what? It tries again with the primary WINS server every 10 minutes for one hour until its name is renewed. If the name is still not renewed, the client returns to the secondary WINS server and goes through this process again. It goes back and forth between the primary and secondary WINS servers until its TTL expires. If at any time during this process a WINS server responds, the name is renewed and a new TTL value is set.

# Name Release

There are two ways a name gets released: when a client shuts down and when a client fails to renew its name within the TTL value. When a client shuts down, it sends a release request to the WINS server. The WINS server "unmaps" the NetBIOS name/IP address pair in the database and marks it for extinction by giving it an extinction interval. The *extinction interval* is the interval between when an entry is marked as released and when it is marked as extinct. The interval between when an entry is marked as extinct and when it is removed (scavenged) from the database is called the *extinction timeout period.*

## Name Resolution

A client that is configured to use WINS sends name-resolution requests to the WINS server when the client performs any of a number of actions, such as mapping a drive. To determine whether the client is configured to use WINS, at the command prompt type **ipconfig /all**. If the Node Type is listed as Hybrid or Peer-to-Peer (or Peer), the client is configured to use WINS.

# WINS in Windows 2000

In a Windows 2000 network, the need for WINS depends on the types of clients that are present and the types of applications used in the enterprise. As stated earlier, WINS is Microsoft's implementation of the RFC for a NetBIOS name server, which resolves NetBIOS names to IP addresses. WINS is the most prevalent name-resolution solution for the local area network, even eclipsing DNS.

*Note: Microsoft says the preferred name resolution solution is DNS. It seems to forget that many applications in networks today require NetBIOS, and doing away with WINS is not a viable option. In a perfect world (a world consisting solely of Windows 2000 Servers and Windows 2000 Professional computers, and containing no applications that require NetBIOS), you can do away with WINS.*

## WINS Client Configuration

To configure WINS on a Windows 2000 client computer, follow these steps:

1. Select Start|Settings|Control Panel. Go to Network And Dial Up Connections, and double-click Local Area Connections.

2. Click the Properties button, and select the Internet Protocol (TCP/IP) entry in the list.

3. Click Properties, then click Advanced, and select the WINS tab.

4. Click Add and add the IP address of the WINS server(s) that will provide name resolution for the machine.

To create a static mapping for clients who cannot use WINS, follow these steps:

1. Select Start|Settings|Control Panel. Double-click Administrative Tools and then double-click WINS.

2. In the WINS management console, click Active Registrations in the console tree for the appropriate active WINS server.

3. From the Action menu, select New Static.

4. In the Create Static Mapping dialog box, type the static address in the IP Address box. Click OK.

# WINS Proxy

Some clients cannot use WINS but are configured as DNS clients. The only way for these clients to resolve NetBIOS names to IP addresses is through broadcast. In a routed environment, this process becomes difficult or even impossible to tolerate. For this reason, Microsoft introduced the *WINS proxy*. As the name suggests, the proxy acts on behalf of the client, receiving the broadcast on the local network and then sending a direct request to the WINS server if the WINS proxy does not have the information already in its cache.

To configure a Windows 2000 computer as a WINS proxy, you must edit the Registry of that computer. You'll need to add a value to the following Registry key:

```
HKEY_LOCAL_MACHINE\SYSTEM\CurrentControlSet\Services\NetBT\
    Parameters
```

The value you add, **EnableProxy**, must be set to 1.

# Installing WINS

Before you install a Windows 2000 computer as a WINS server, you must first have a static IP address. This is no different from the requirement in Windows NT.

To install WINS, do the following:

1. Select the Add Network Components link from the left side of the screen in Network And Dial-up Connections.

2. In the Windows Components Wizard, select Networking Services from the Components list (see Figure 5.1). Click Next.

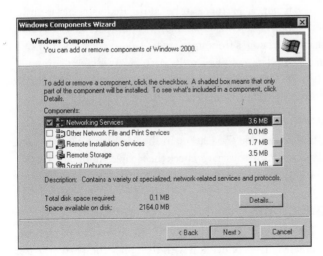

**Figure 5.1** The Windows Components dialog box.

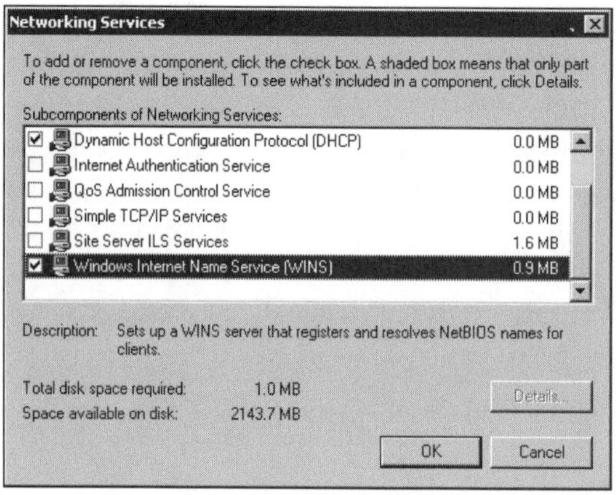

**Figure 5.2**   The Network Services dialog box.

3. In the Networking Services dialog box (shown in Figure 5.2), select the Windows Internet Name Service (WINS) checkbox. Click OK.

4. In the Files Needed dialog box, specify the location of the source files (wherever the i386 directory is located). When the configuration is complete, click Finish. You don't even have to reboot!

## WINS Replication

WINS replicates its database to other WINS servers in the network, thereby "sharing" what it knows with the other WINS servers. This replication is beneficial for all the clients in the network and can reduce network traffic. For replication to work, each WINS server must be configured with at least one other WINS server as its replication partner. A partner can be configured as either a push-partner, a pull-partner, or both (which is the default). A *pull-partner* is a WINS server that requests database changes from its partner. A *push-partner* is a WINS server that sends database update messages to its partner. As a client computer registers its name with a WINS server, that server propagates the registration to its partners, who in turn propagate the registration to their partners.

You can configure a WINS replication partner manually or automatically through the autodiscovery feature. To enable the feature, in the Microsoft Management Console Replication Partners Properties page, check the Enable Automatic Partner Configuration checkbox.

## Persistent Connections

When a Windows NT server configured as a WINS server needed to replicate its database, it had to create a new connection with its replication partner. After the replication took place, it broke its connection with its partner. In Windows 2000, WINS has a feature that keeps a persistent connection with its partner. Keeping a persistent connection uses less processor time, thus freeing up the WINS server to resolve names. Also, WINS databases are not as inconsistent as they were with Windows NT because changes are more current.

## Manual Tombstoning

In Windows NT, WINS records were not deleted on multiple servers simultaneously. It was possible that replication could occur between WINS servers that had conflicting information in the database. A server might receive the record of a client that had been previously deleted from another server.

Windows 2000 WINS has a new feature called *manual tombstoning*. This feature prevents WINS servers from sending deleted records back to other WINS servers. When a record is tombstoned, it is given a value (state) at which, once expired, the record is deleted. WINS servers replicate a tombstoned entry whose length is longer than the propagation delay in WINS replication. The length of the tombstoned state is greater than the propagation delay incurred with replication across the network.

Each WINS server updates the tombstone status and replicates this status to other WINS servers, and they store the replicated copies of these records. Once all WINS servers have replicated these records, the records are automatically removed from WINS.

To enable the tombstoning feature:

1. Open the WINS dialog box, select the owning server, and then view all the records of that server.

2. Highlight the record you want to delete, and delete it from the Action menu.

3. At this point, you can either delete or tombstone the record. Although manually tombstoning records requires Windows 2000 WINS servers, tombstoned records do replicate to Windows NT 3.51 and Windows NT 4 servers.

## Burst Handling

One of the new features of Windows 2000 WINS is *burst mode*. Several clients registering themselves can cause a heavy load on the WINS server. When the WINS server is in burst mode (which it is in by default), the WINS server responds positively to clients that submit registration requests before the WINS server has processed and physically entered these requests in the WINS server database, thus keeping network traffic down.

To configure a Windows 2000 computer burst mode default setting:

1. Open Control Panel and double-click Administrative Tools.

2. Choose Computer Management and open Services and Applications.

3. Right-click on WINS and choose Properties.

4. Click the Advanced tab.

5. In the Enable Burst Handling area, modify the settings as appropriate.

# Practice Questions

## Question 1

> Which of the following are some of the new features in Windows 2000 WINS? [Check all correct answers]
>
> ❑ a.  Persistent connections
>
> ❑ b.  Database replication
>
> ❑ c.  Manual tombstoning
>
> ❑ d.  Autodiscovery

The correct answers are a, c, and d. Persistent connections, manual tombstoning, and autodiscovery are among the new features of Windows 2000 WINS. Database replication existed in Windows NT, so answer b is incorrect.

## Question 2

> What must a Windows 2000 computer have before installing WINS?
>
> ○ a.  A connection to the Internet
>
> ○ b.  A default gateway
>
> ○ c.  A static IP address
>
> ○ d.  A dynamic IP address

The correct answer is c. WINS requires the computer to have a static IP address configured before you install the WINS service. A connection to the Internet and a default gateway are not necessary. Therefore, answers a and b are incorrect. WINS servers cannot have dynamic IP addresses or clients might not locate them. Therefore, answer d is incorrect.

## Question 3

> If you have client computers that use NetBIOS but are not configured to use WINS, how do you provide NetBIOS name resolution for those clients for servers that are registered with DNS?
>
> ○ a.  Install and configure a WINS proxy.
>
> ○ b.  Install and configure DHCP.
>
> ○ c.  Configure the client for B-node name resolution.
>
> ○ d.  Configure the client for I-node name resolution.

The correct answer is a. A WINS proxy acts on behalf of the client and obtains the IP-to-NetBIOS name mapping. Installing and configuring a DHCP server will not aid the client in name resolution, so answer b is incorrect. Configuring the client for B-node name resolution will not work past routers, so answer c is incorrect. Configuring the client for I-node name resolution is impossible because there is no such thing as I-node. Therefore, answer d is incorrect.

## Question 4

> Which of the following does a WINS client use to interact with a WINS server? [Check all correct answers]
>
> ❑ a.  Name registration
>
> ❑ b.  Name release
>
> ❑ c.  Name rejection
>
> ❑ d.  Name renewal

The correct answers are a, b, and d. A WINS client registers its name when it starts. The client releases its name when it shuts down gracefully. It tries to renew its name after 50 percent of its TTL has expired. Name rejection is a fictitious setting. Therefore, answer c is incorrect.

# Question 5

> Which of the following methods does not employ a WINS server? [Check all correct answers]
>
> ❑ a. B-node
>
> ❑ b. P-node
>
> ❑ c. M-node
>
> ❑ d. H-node

The correct answer is a. B-node does not employ a NetBIOS name server at all. B-node only implements a local broadcast. All other nodes employ a NetBIOS name server in some way, so answers b, c, and d are incorrect.

# Question 6

> WINS resolves fully qualified domain names (FQDNs) to IP addresses.
>
> ○ a. True
>
> ○ b. False

The correct answer is b. DNS resolves FQDNs to IP addresses. WINS resolves NetBIOS names to IP addresses.

# Question 7

> Bob has a network with three subnets. He uses LMHOSTS for name resolution. As his company grows, managing by LMHOSTS files will become too cumbersome. What service should Bob install to provide for name resolution?
>
> ○ a. DHCP
>
> ○ b. DNS
>
> ○ c. WINS
>
> ○ d. HOSTS

The correct answer is c. Because LMHOSTS resolves local names to IP addresses, Bob should install the WINS service. DHCP dynamically assigns IP addresses. Therefore, answer a is incorrect. DNS resolves fully qualified domain names (FQDNs) to IP addresses. Therefore, answer b is incorrect. A HOSTS file resolves DNS names to IP addresses. Therefore, answer d is incorrect.

## Question 8

---

Dave is designing a network with six subnets. For name resolution, he plans to install a WINS server on each subnet. What should Dave do to ensure that all Windows-based computers register their names with the local WINS server?

○ a.  Install DHCP relay agents on the routers.

○ b.  Place a WINS proxy on each subnet.

○ c.  Set up each computer with the WINS server's address.

○ d.  Install DNS.

---

The correct answer is c. By adding the WINS server's address to each computer, each computer will attempt to register itself. DHCP relay agents do not help a computer register its name. Therefore, answer a is incorrect. Because there is a WINS server on every subnet, a WINS proxy is not needed, so answer b is incorrect. Installing DNS does not register a computer's name with WINS. Therefore, answer d is incorrect.

## Question 9

---

Your Windows 2000 computer is enabled to use WINS for NetBIOS name resolution. In which order will your computer perform name resolution if WINS fails?

○ a.  local broadcast, LMHOSTS, HOSTS, DNS

○ b.  local broadcast, DNS, HOSTS, LMHOSTS

○ c.  LMHOSTS, HOSTS, DNS, local broadcast

○ d.  LMHOSTS, DNS, HOSTS, local broadcast

---

The correct answer is a. Because the computer is configured to use WINS for its NetBIOS name resolution, it is an H-node. All the other answers do not correspond to any node type. Therefore, answers b, c, and d are incorrect.

# Question 10

David has 500 Windows 2000 computers and 100 Unix computers. The Windows 2000 computers are all configured to use WINS. How should David configure his computers to resolve both NetBIOS names and FQDNs without using static name-resolution methods?

○ a. David should create a centralized LMHOSTS file on the server acting as forest root.

○ b. David should create an LMHOSTS file on each client computer.

○ c. David should set up DNS.

○ d. David should set up DNS to use WINS.

The correct answer is d. Although DNS is dynamic in Windows 2000, DNS can be set to use WINS for name resolution. LMHOSTS files are static. Therefore, answers a and b are incorrect. If DNS cannot resolve a name, name resolution may fail. Therefore, answer c is incorrect.

# Need to Know More?

 Lee, Thomas, and Joseph Davies. *Microsoft Windows 2000 TCP/IP Protocols and Services Technical Reference*. Redmond, Wash.: Microsoft Press, 2000. ISBN 0-7356-0556-4. This book is a comprehensive guide to TCP/IP and Windows 2000.

 Minasi, Mark, Christa Anderson, Brian M. Smith, and Doug Toombs. *Mastering Windows 2000 Server 2nd Edition*. San Francisco: Sybex Network Press, 2000. ISBN 0-7821-2774-6. Check out Chapter 18, "Building a Windows 2000 TCP/IP Infrastructure: DHCP, WINS, DNS, Sites, and More."

 See Chapter 7 of the *Microsoft Windows 2000 Server Resource Kit* for a complete discussion on WINS.

# Remote Access Services

**Terms you'll need to understand:**

✓ Dial up

✓ Virtual private network

✓ Point-to-Point Tunneling Protocol

✓ Layer 2 Tunneling Protocol

✓ Multilink

✓ Authentication

✓ Encryption

✓ Internet Authentication Server

**Techniques you'll need to master:**

✓ Configuring a virtual private network server

✓ Specifying the correct authentication protocol on the server and client

✓ Using the correct encryption for communicating data

✓ Creating a remote access policy

✓ Configuring a profile for a remote access policy

Remote access is one of the two functions provided by Windows 2000 Routing and Remote Access Server (RRAS). You can configure the Windows 2000 RRAS to allow inbound connections to the corporate network for authorized users. This remote access connection allows access to resources from remote locations as if it, the connection, was physically attached to the network.

The Windows 2000 remote access server provides two types of connections:

➤ *Dial-up access*—A remote client uses the public telephone line or Integrated Services Digital Network (ISDN) line to create a connection to a Windows 2000 remote access server.

➤ *Virtual private network (VPN) access*—A remote client uses an Internet Protocol (IP) internetwork to create a virtual connection to a Windows 2000 remote access server.

*Note: An internetwork is a network that links two disparate networks. The best-known and largest internetwork is the Internet.*

# Dial-Up Access

The reasons why most people choose dial-up access for remote clients are ease of administration and reduction in overall cost. Dial-up access provides a means for remote clients to access a network of computers. This network of computers is typically the company network. The client uses the telephone line to connect to the Windows 2000 server that is configured to accept dial-up access.

## Configuring the Dial-Up Access Server

You initiate the configuration of the dial-up access server by running the Routing and Remote Access Server Setup Wizard. Start the wizard by first accessing the Routing and Remote Access snap-in. Within the snap-in, right-click the server name and select Configure And Enable Routing And Remote Access, which is shown in Figure 6.1 as grayed out.

The wizard will want answers about the key configurations of the dial-up server, including the following:

➤ *Supported client protocols*—Supported protocols include NetBEUI, IPX, TCP/IP, and AppleTalk.

➤ *Network connection interface*—For dial-up access (typically a modem).

➤ IP address allocation for remote clients:

➤ *DHCP*—Uses the Dynamic Host Configuration Protocol (DHCP) server located on the remote access server network to allocate IP addresses to remote access clients.

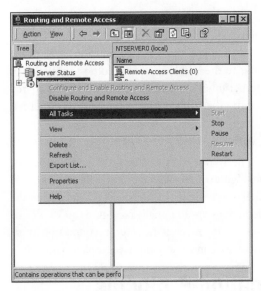

**Figure 6.1**    The Routing and Remote Access action menu.

➤ *Static pool*—Allows the remote access server to allocate IP addresses to remote access clients.

 The static pool of addresses cannot overlap the DHCP scope of IP addresses. If there is overlap, the network will have IP address conflicts.

➤ *Remote Authentication Dial-In User Service (RADIUS) client*—This feature uses a server to centrally authenticate and control remote access policies for all dial-in users.

➤ *DHCP relay agent configuration*—Although this topic is presented in a warning message, it is important to configure the relay agent with the IP address of the DHCP server after the wizard is completed.

 Do not forget this step. If the DHCP relay agent is not configured, clients do not receive the critical IP configurations to communicate effectively on the network. The DHCP relay agent is responsible for forwarding the requests of the remote access client to the DHCP server.

# Virtual Private Network Access

Virtual private networks are finally beginning to take hold in much of the corporate world. A VPN gives remote users the ability to connect to the company LAN through a common network, usually the Internet. This scenario actually has two connections. The first connection is to a local Internet service provider (ISP). Commonly, this connection type is dial-up, Digital Subscriber Line (DSL), cable, or satellite. The second connection is a "tunneled" connection through the first connection. This connection is to the VPN server located on the outside of the LAN, which also has an Internet interface. The key to a VPN is the shared network between the remote user and the LAN, which is typically the Internet.

## Configuring the VPN Server

The configuration for the VPN is nearly the same as that for the dial-up access, which happens through the wizard. Figure 6.1, shown earlier in the chapter, indicates the initial step to start the wizard. Refer to the list in the section "Configuring the Dial-Up Access Server" for the required steps to initially configure the VPN. The only difference in the configuration is that you select the Internet connection interface for the VPN instead of the network connection interface (usually a modem).

# RRAS Communication Protocols

The communication between client and server requires a protocol to encapsulate the data, which in turn is sent over the wire. The core of most communication protocols, both dial-up and VPN, is Transmission Control Protocol/Internet Protocol (TCP/IP). The LAN protocol the client uses is wrapped in a remote access protocol communication packet and then shipped on the wire.

## Dial-Up Protocols

There are two options for communicating over a dial-up connection with Windows 2000: One is both inbound and outbound; the other is only outbound:

➤ *Point-to-Point Protocol (PPP)*—This industry-standard protocol suite is used to transport multiprotocol packets over point-to-point links.

➤ *Serial Line Internet Protocol (SLIP)*—SLIP is an older TCP/IP remote access communication protocol used in Windows 2000 for outbound communication only.

## VPN Protocols

You can use two protocols when connecting to a Windows 2000 VPN server. When planning for which protocol to use, consider that not all clients support both protocols:

➤ *Point-to-Point Tunneling Protocol (PPTP)*—PPTP is a communication protocol that tunnels through another connection, encapsulating PPP packets. The encapsulated packets are IP datagrams capable of being transmitted over IP-based networks, such as the Internet.

➤ *Layer 2 Tunneling Protocol (L2TP)*—L2TP is a communication protocol that tunnels through another network, such as IP, X.25, Frame Relay, or Asynchronous Transfer Mode (ATM). L2TP is a combination of PPTP and Layer 2 forwarding technology, which encapsulates PPP packets and provides additional security functionality.

# Configuring the Communication Protocols

You need to configure at least one, but possibly two, communication protocols. PPP is required for both dial-up and VPN connections. The other configuration, either PPTP or L2TP, is only necessary for a VPN connection. Both of these VPN protocols rely on PPP for the initial packaging of the data.

## Configuring PPP

PPP is a vital part of any remote access server because most communication relies on it. PPP is configured at the server level, not the remote access port level. Figure 6.2 shows the different PPP configuration options. To access the PPP configuration, right-click on the RRAS server name in the routing and remote access snap-in and then move to the properties of the server.

PPP has four configuration options:

➤ *Multilink connections*—Multilink aggregates multiple physical links into a single logical link for data communication. Multilink is commonly used with dial-up connections and ISDN connections.

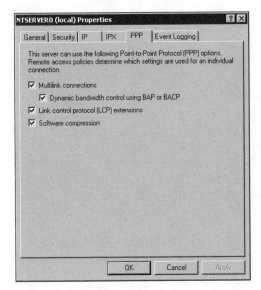

**Figure 6.2**  PPP configuration options.

You must configure multilink on both ends of the remote access communication for it to work.

➤ *Dynamic bandwidth control using (BAP) or (BACP)*—Bandwidth Allocation Protocol (BAP) is the PPP control protocol that allows for the dynamic addition and removal of links through multilink. You can control the dynamic links through remote access policies, which are based on the percentage of line utilization and the length of time the bandwidth is reduced. Bandwidth Allocation Control Protocol (BACP) uses Link Control Protocol to regulate which multilink request has precedence.

➤ *Link Control Protocol (LCP) extensions*—LCP is a PPP control protocol that dynamically configures the Data Link layer of the connection after negotiating link and PPP parameters.

You must enable the LCP extensions to support the call-back feature of remote access services.

➤ *Software compression*—This enables the Microsoft Point-to-Point Compression Protocol (MPPC), which compresses the data that is sent over a demand-dial or remote access connection.

## Configuring PPTP

The configuration of the PPTP protocol or port, as it is referred to in the routing and remote access interface, is not in an intuitive location. To configure the PPTP ports, right-click on the Ports option in the routing and remote access interface and then select Properties. Figure 6.3 shows the Ports Properties window, where PPTP configurations are completed. The list shows routing and remote access devices. Select PPTP, and click the Configure button. This opens the WAN Miniport (PPTP) configuration window, as shown in Figure 6.4.

PPTP ports can support either inbound-only connections or inbound and outbound connections. The inbound and outbound configuration is for the demand-dial routing connection. You also configure the number of ports in the PPTP Ports Properties window. You must complete this configuration within this interface.

It is important to configure more than enough PPTP ports in comparison to the number of remote access users who will connect over the VPN.

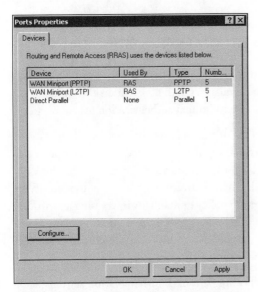

**Figure 6.3**    Ports Properties page showing the PPTP and L2TP ports.

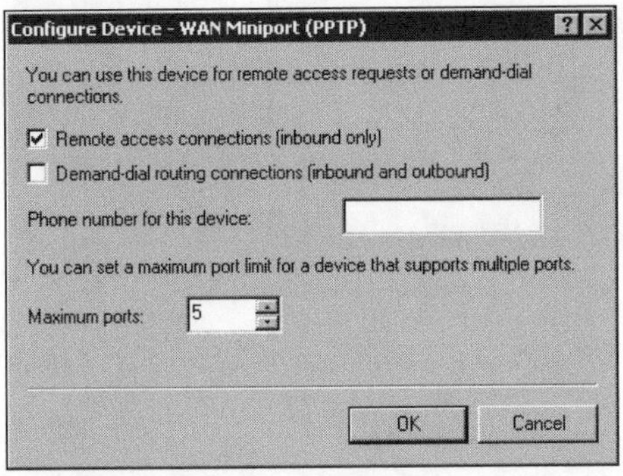

**Figure 6.4**    The PPTP configuration window.

When a PPTP-based connection is established through a VPN server, the authentication mechanisms are no different from those for a PPP connection. These authentication mechanisms include those described in the section "Authentication Protocols" later in this chapter. With these options, only Extensible Authentication Protocol (EAP)-Transport Level Security or Microsoft Challenge Handshake Authentication Protocol (MS-CHAP—v1 or v2) encrypts the payload using Microsoft Point-to-Point Encryption (MPPE). If you need more security than this link encryption mode provides, you must use Internet Protocol Security (IPSec). IPSec is an end-to-end encryption method that requires the use of L2TP.

### Configuring L2TP

You configure L2TP by accessing the Ports Properties page shown in Figure 6.3. This is the same location described for the PPTP configuration. L2TP has the same configurations as PPTP in this interface and supports the same authentication protocols, but this is where the similarities end. L2TP offers the option to use IPSec for end-to-end encryption and additional authentication for connections.

L2TP authentication of the VPN client occurs at two different levels: The computer is authenticated, and then the user is authenticated. IPSec computer authentication is established when both the remote access computer and the VPN server have a certificate installed. The certificate is obtained automatically by configuring an auto-enrollment group policy or manually by creating a certificate using the Certificate Authorization server with Windows 2000. The user is authenticated using the same PPP authentication protocols described in the section "Authentication Protocols" later in this chapter.

You can configure additional encryption and data authentication settings using an IPSec policy, located in the local machine policy, or a group policy object. These settings determine the levels of encryption and requirements for connectivity. The different encryptions for L2TP over IPSec connections are the strong and basic strength encryption settings detailed in the section "Data Encryption" later in this chapter. Data authentication for L2TP over IPSec connections includes the following:

➤ *Hash Message Authentication Code (HMAC) Message Digest 5 (MD5)*—A hash algorithm producing a 128-bit hash of the authenticated payload.

➤ *HMAC Secure Hash Algorithm (SHA)*—A hash algorithm using a 160-bit hash of the authenticated payload.

# Remote Access Policies

Like any other policy in Windows 2000, a *remote access policy* is a set of decisions for a user who connects via remote access. You can configure multiple policies for remote access, which lets you customize how different types of users access the network remotely. The complexity of these policies should not be taken lightly for two reasons. The first is that there are numerous options and the combinations of the options are almost countless. With the multitude of options, you face obvious learning curves. The second reason to not take policies lightly is that the exam requires that you know all of the different combinations!

 Remote access policies are one area in particular that applies the exam philosophy that you must have one year of hands-on experience. A clear understanding of the following remote access conditions and remote access policy profiles is essential for performing well on the exam.

Remote access policies configure many of the functions discussed in other sections of this chapter. Some of the configurations are duplicated, and others are unique for the policy configuration. A remote access policy has three primary elements:

➤ Remote access conditions

➤ Remote access permissions

➤ Remote access policy profile

# Remote Access Conditions

A remote access policy condition is a single attribute or multiple configured attributes that are compared to the variables when a remote user attempts to access the remote access server. If there are multiple configured attributes for the policy, all of the attributes must match correctly for the connection attempt to succeed. Figure 6.5 shows all of the different attributes you can configure for any policy.

Some of the more important attributes follow:

➤ *Windows-Groups*—This condition includes a Windows 2000 group intended for the users of the group. The conditions allow for the addition of multiple groups or a single group that has nested groups within it. Therefore, there is no need to configure a separate policy for each group.

To configure a group of users who require the same remote access policy, first configure them in the same security group in Active Directory Users and Computers. Then, configure a remote access policy that has the Windows-Groups condition as the group just configured.

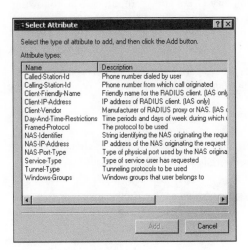

**Figure 6.5** Policy attribute selection window.

*Note: You cannot use the built-in local groups of a standalone remote access server running Windows 2000 for the Windows-Groups attribute.*

➤ *Day-And-Time-Restrictions*—Both the day of the week and the time of the day can be conditions of the policy. The policy is based on the day and time of the attempt relative to the server providing the authorization.

➤ *Tunnel-Type*—This condition determines the tunnel type of the requesting client. The two types are PPTP and L2TP. Both remote access clients and demand-dial routers can be affected by this policy condition. This policy then works directly with the policy profile for the authentication method and encryption strength.

 Both the client and the server must have matching attributes for the policy to apply and therefore allow access. With this in mind, it is important to remember that not all Windows operating systems support L2TP.

If you want to define different authentication, encryption, or other settings for PPTP or L2TP connections, create separate remote access policies using the Tunnel-Type remote access policy condition set to either Point-to-Point Tunneling Protocol or Layer 2 Tunneling Protocol.

## Remote Access Permissions

Whether or not a user has permission to log on to the remote access server is a complex issue due to the addition of remote access policies. A user can be configured to either Allow Access or Deny Access in one of two places. The first is in the remote access policy. The other location is on the Dial-In tab of the user property sheet through Active Directory Users and Computers. The following decision tree indicates the order in which all permissions are checked to determine whether a user can log on:

 The order of the remote access permission application is elaborate and is tested in depth on the exam.

1. The first remote access policy in the list of possible policies is checked against the attempted remote user's credentials and configurations:

 If no remote access policy is configured, the connection attempt is rejected.

➤ If the connection attempt does not match the policy, the next policy is checked.

➤ If the connection attempt matches the policy, the remote access permission settings for the user are checked.

| If no policies match the connection attempt, the user is rejected from the remote access server.

2. The remote access permission settings for the user can be one of three settings, as shown in Figure 6.6:

➤ If the Deny Access permission is selected, the connection attempt is rejected.

➤ If the Allow Access permission is selected, the user's account properties and remote access policy profile properties are applied. If the connection attempt does not match the user's account and remote access policy profile properties, the connection attempt is rejected. If the connection attempt does match the user's account and remote access policy profile properties, the connection attempt is accepted.

➤ If Control Access Through Remote Access Policy is selected, the permissions of the policy are then checked. Figure 6.7 shows the two different configurations for remote access permissions at this level:

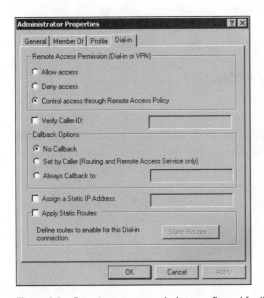

**Figure 6.6**   Remote access permissions configured for the user.

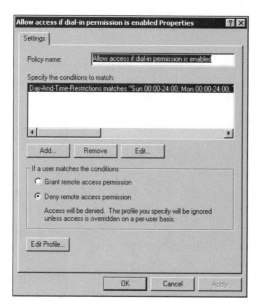

**Figure 6.7** Remote access policy permissions.

➤ If Deny Remote Access Permission is selected, the connection attempt is rejected.

➤ If Grant Remote Access Permission is selected, then the user's account and remote access policy profile properties are checked. If the connection attempt does not match the user's account and remote access policy profile properties, the connection attempt is rejected. If the connection attempt does match the user's account and remote access policy profile properties, the connection attempt is accepted.

# Remote Access Policy Profile

The remote access policy profile is new in Windows 2000, and there is a profile associated with each remote access policy. As indicated in the preceding permission process, the profile plays a key role in whether a user is accepted or rejected for remote access. Each profile has six different configuration categories. These six categories are separated into different tabs in the Edit Dial-In Profile window, as shown in Figure 6.8. The combination of each profile configuration, user dial-up configuration, and policy setting can create different access scenarios. Paying special attention to each configuration is important on the exam.

## Dial-In Constraints Settings for a Remote Access Policy

The dial-in constraints are important configurations that require special attention on the exam. The key parts of the dial-in constraints are Disconnect If Idle,

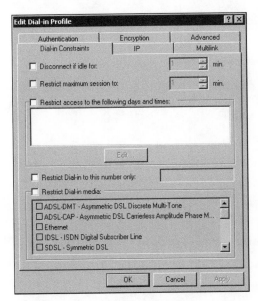

**Figure 6.8**   The Edit Dial-In Profile window displaying the default tab, Dial-In Constraints.

Restrict Maximum Session, and the day and time restrictions. Figure 6.8 shows the possible configurations for the dial-in constraints:

➤ *Disconnect If Idle For (X) Minutes*—Allows the remote access server to disconnect the connection if there is no communication between the two for a certain amount of time.

➤ *Restrict Maximum Session To (X) Minutes*—Allows the remote access server to dictate how long a remote user is connected for any one session.

➤ *Restrict Access To The Following Days And Times settings*—Controls the scheduled access times for the policy.

## IP Settings for a Remote Access Policy

The profile can configure the manner in which the client can obtain an IP address. The policy can also dictate IP filters based on inbound and outbound IP addresses. Figure 6.9 shows the IP tab configurations:

➤ *IP Address Assignment Policy*—Determines how the client interacts with the remote access server to obtain an IP address. The configuration allows the client to request an IP address from the server. The server must configure the client with the IP address, or the server configuration defines how the client receives the IP address.

➤ *IP Packet Filters*—Determines whether the ingress or egress traffic is routed based on the protocol being used. The source network or the destination

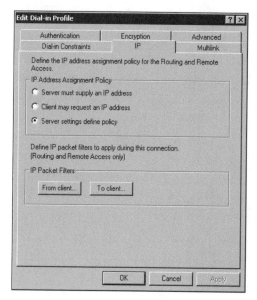

**Figure 6.9** Remote access profile IP configuration tab.

network must be configured and then set to permit or deny traffic. The common protocols that are filtered include Transmission Control Protocol (TCP), User Datagram Protocol (UDP), and Internet Control Message Protocol (ICMP).

## Multilink Settings for a Remote Access Policy

The multilink configuration in the remote access policy profile is not only the configuration for the multilink, but also the BAP settings. The settings in this location of the profile only take effect if the multilink and BAP configurations shown in Figure 6.2 are selected. Figure 6.10 shows the possible configurations for multilink and BAP in the remote access profile settings tab:

➤ *Multilink Settings*—Configure whether multilink is allowed and to what degree of support. The settings allow the client to be restricted to a single port or to use a multitude of ports for the multilink connection.

➤ *Bandwidth Allocation Protocol (BAP) Settings*—Profile configurations that can dynamically reduce the number of multilink connected lines to a single line if certain criteria are met. The criteria you can configure includes the percentage the line capacity must have for a set amount of minutes or seconds.

## Authentication Settings for a Remote Access Policy

The Authentication tab in the profile settings is a key tab to understand and know for the exam. Each of the different authentication methods indicates a unique type of connection from the server to the client. Refer to the section

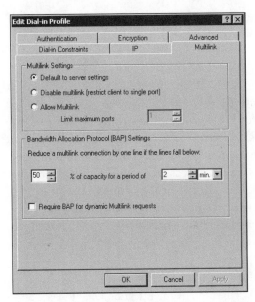

**Figure 6.10**    Multilink configuration tab in the remote access profile.

"Authentication Protocols" later in the chapter to get a definition of each type of authentication. Figure 6.11 indicates the different types of authentication you can configure through the Authentication tab. You must select each type of authentication to make that type available for the remote access client connection.

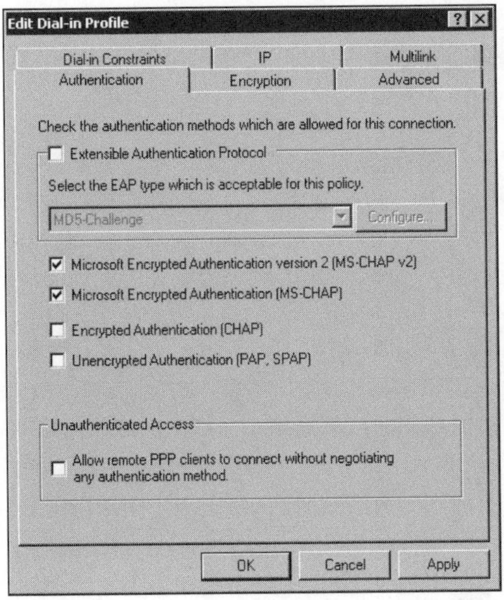

**Figure 6.11**    Authentication methods for a policy profile.

Keep in mind on the exam that this is a different configuration from that for Windows NT 4.

## Encryption Settings for a Remote Access Policy

The encryption settings configured in the remote access policy profiles are only applied to the Windows 2000 RRAS service. The settings for the encryption levels are described in detail in the section "Data Encryption" later in this chapter. When all three of the settings are selected, as shown in Figure 6.12, any one of the encryption strengths can be utilized. The final encryption depends on the client configurations. When a single encryption setting is configured in the remote access policy profile, the client must have a matching encryption setting to connect to the remote access server.

## Advanced Settings for a Remote Access Policy

The Advanced tab allows for specific Remote Authentication Dial-In User Service (RADIUS) and vendor attribute settings. These settings specify a series of RADIUS attributes that are sent back to a RADIUS client by the Internet Authentication Service (IAS) server. These attributes are specific to the RADIUS authentication and are ignored by the remote access server. (Refer to the "Internet Authentication Service and Remote Authentication Dial-In User Service" section later in this chapter for more details). Figure 6.13 shows a partial list of attributes for the advanced configuration of a remote access policy profile.

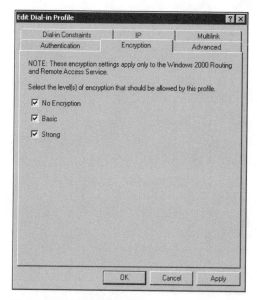

**Figure 6.12** Encryption settings for a remote access policy profile.

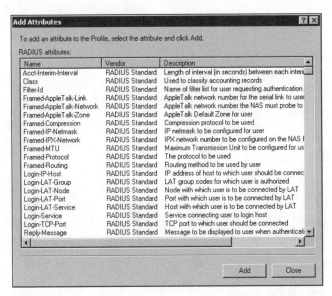

**Figure 6.13** Attributes that can be added to a remote access policy profile.

# Managing Remote Access

The core management of remote access for users starts in the Active Directory. A user must belong to the correct Windows group and have the correct remote access permission to get authenticated. This administration takes place in Active Directory Users and Computers if you are configuring users within Active Directory, or Local Users and Groups if you are configuring a standalone server. The Dial-In tab has the configurations required to let the user successfully use the remote access server. This configuration also lets you customize how the user interacts with the remote access server:

➤ *Remote Access Permission*—This configuration applies to both dial-up and VPN access. Depending on the configuration of the domain, either native mode or mixed mode, the default setting differs. Native-mode domains have users set to Control Access Through Remote Access Policy. Mixed-mode domains set the user remote access to Deny Access.

 Be certain to pay attention to the exam question stem about whether the remote access server is involved in a native-mode domain or a mixed-mode domain. This affects how the default configurations are set, such as the user Remote Access Permission.

➤ *Verify Caller ID*—This configuration allows the server to verify the originating caller's phone number. The phone number must match the caller's initiating phone number; otherwise, the call is rejected. Both the caller and the remote access server must support Caller ID. The caller must have the required phone system and related equipment. The server must have the correct call-answering equipment that supports Caller ID.

➤ *Callback Options*—This option is an excellent way to enable a secure connection. The setting has either the caller or the network administrator specify the callback number.

➤ *Assign A Static IP Address*—This configures the remote client with a predetermined static IP address.

➤ *Apply Static Routes*—This configuration is for one-way demand-dial routed connections. The static routes are applied to the routing table of the answering router. This allows the network, using the demand-dial connection, to communicate with the network on the other side of the answering remote access server.

*Note: Windows NT 4 RAS cannot use remote access policies. The Windows NT 4 RAS server needs to have RRAS (which includes routing) for Windows NT installed or be upgraded to a Windows 2000 server.*

# Security of Dial-Up Clients

The security of a dial-up client and the data transferred across the connection is extremely important. To keep this data and communication secure, you can configure a number of authentication and encryption protocols.

## Authentication Protocols

The security of the users' credentials as they authenticate with the remote access server is important for your network protection. The additional protocols that help in this defense include:

➤ *Password Authentication Protocol (PAP)*—Permits clear text authentication.

➤ *Shiva Password Authentication Protocol (SPAP)*—Typically used by third-party clients and servers. The encryption for the protocol is two-way, but it is not as good as CHAP.

➤ *Challenge Handshake Authentication Protocol (CHAP)*—A one-way challenge-response authentication protocol for PPP connections. When you use CHAP, you can use additional types of encryption, such as Message Digest 5 (MD5) and Data Encryption Standard (DES). Windows operating systems such as Windows NT, Windows 9x, and Windows for Workgroups always use CHAP when communicating with each other.

➤ *Microsoft Challenge Handshake Authentication Protocol (MS-CHAP v1)*—A special version of CHAP used by Microsoft. The encryption is still two-way and consists of a challenge from the server to the client that consists of a session ID. The client uses a Message Digest 4 (MD4) hash to return the username to the server.

➤ *Microsoft Challenge Handshake Authentication Protocol (MS-CHAP v2)*—Offers more secure encryption than CHAP or MS-CHAP v1 through mutual authentication and asymmetric encryption keys.

➤ *Extensible Authentication Protocol (EAP)*—A mutual authentication protocol that is an extension to PPP. The extensions allow for arbitrary authentication mechanisms such as Smart Cards and MD5 Challenge encryption.

## Data Encryption

Depending on what is sent over the wire, either by telephone or Ethernet, the data might require that you take additional measures to keep it secure. This security is required in some enterprises and companies. If you are not certain whether you need data encryption, most likely you do not. Data encryption causes overhead on the transmission and can cripple a network connection if the hardware and network are not configured for the overhead. Some of the possible data encryption types include:

➤ *Microsoft Point-to-Point Encryption (MPPE)*—Link encryption used with MS-CHAP v2 or EAP-Transport Layer Security (TLS) authentication. This encryption takes advantage of 40-bit, 56-bit, and 128-bit encryption keys.

➤ *Strong strength encryption*—Allows for MPPE 56-bit key encryption over PPTP VPN connections and dial-up connections. 56-bit DES encryption is used if L2TP over IPSec is the protocol for the VPN connection.

➤ *Basic strength encryption*—Allows for MPPE 40-bit key encryption over PPTP VPN connections and dial-up connections. 40-bit DES encryption is used if L2TP over IPSec is the protocol for the VPN connection. This encryption provides backward compatibility with non-Windows 2000 clients.

# IAS and RADIUS

For remote users to gain access to a dial-up or VPN connection, a remote access server must authenticate them. If the enterprise is large, this process could involve a number of remote access servers. To eliminate the mind-numbing process of managing remote access permissions for every remote user across a multitude of remote access servers, you can use the Internet Authentication Service (IAS). IAS provides central management capabilities to control the access that remote users have to the remote access server itself as well as to network resources.

IAS uses the RADIUS protocol to enable the communication of authentication, authorization, and accounting to the homogeneous and heterogeneous dial-up or VPN equipment in the enterprise. The IAS server then takes the data from the network access server (NAS) or remote access server and authenticates the user to the Windows NT 4 or Windows 2000 domain controller.

*Note: A network access server (NAS) is just a server that accepts PPP requests from remote users. Windows 2000 uses the term remote access server.*

Figure 6.14 illustrates a typical configuration using NAS, RRAS, IAS, and Windows 2000 Active Directory.

The IAS server performs the centralized management of more than just the user authentication. It also provides for the management features described in the following sections.

## Centralized User Authentication

When the user attempts a connection, the user credentials are passed along to the NAS or RAS. The NAS or RAS negotiates a session based on the most secure protocol possible, which depends on the remote access server configuration and

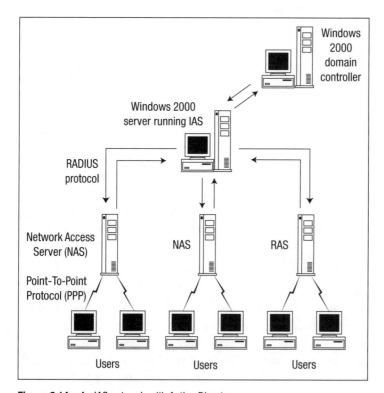

**Figure 6.14** An IAS network with Active Directory.

the client support and configuration. The IAS server can support the following possible negotiations:

➤ Authentication protocols, including PAP, CHAP, MS-CHAP, and EAP

➤ Authentication of the user based on the number called by the user

➤ Authentication of the user based on the number the user is calling from, also referred to as *Caller ID*

 To be able to authenticate users, the primary and backup IAS servers must be registered on the domain controllers in Active Directory in the built-in groups as members of the RAS and IAS Servers security group.

## Centralized User Authorization

Authorization defines what the remote user has been given the privilege to access on the network. This control is established through remote access policies on the IAS server. You can configure remote access policies for the IAS server for the following conditions:

➤ Windows group membership

➤ Connection attempt device, such as ISDN, modem, or VPN tunnel

➤ The protocol for the remote access user

➤ The destination phone number the remote access user dials

➤ The source phone number from which the remote access user calls

➤ Time and day restrictions of the connection attempt

➤ RADIUS attributes

## Centralized Auditing and Usage Accounting

Because the network has an exposure through the remote access server, it is important to monitor and audit the access to the server. IAS supports auditing information related to authentication success, rejections, account lockouts, and logon/logoff records. The information is stored in a log file in a format that can be analyzed by standard data-analysis packages.

You can configure dial-up access or VPN access to use either Windows or RADIUS as an accounting provider. If you select Windows as the accounting provider, the accounting information accumulates on the remote access server. If you select RADIUS, RADIUS accounting messages are sent to the RADIUS server for accumulation and later analysis.

## Integration with Windows 2000 RRAS

The configuration of IAS is consistent with that of Windows 2000 RRAS, which makes it an easy choice on the Windows 2000 network. IAS and RRAS share remote access policies and accounting capabilities. This integration makes your RRAS infrastructure scalable. If you have only a few remote access servers, then you might not need IAS. If the RRAS structure grows, the migration to an IAS solution is seamless due to the integration of the two.

 Consider the environment where you have Windows NT 4 Routing and Remote Access Service (RRAS) servers. You can only use the access-by-policy in a Windows 2000 mixed-mode domain administrative model if the NT 4 RRAS servers are configured as RADIUS clients to a Windows 2000 IAS server. You cannot use the access-by-policy in a Windows 2000 mixed-mode domain administrative model for Windows NT 4 RAS servers.

## Managing IAS Configurations in a Multiple IAS Server Environment

When multiple IAS servers are configured to handle the remote access authentication, authorization, and auditing functions, the flexibility to save and restore the IAS configurations is important. In some instances, it is also important to export configurations from one IAS server and import those configurations to another IAS server. For any of these functions, you can use the **netsh** (Netshell) command to manipulate the database and the configurations.

# Practice Questions

## Question 1

You are the administrator of an enterprise that has 200 remote access users. The users dial in to the network from different locations at different times of the day and week. Five of the Windows NT 4 RAS servers have been replaced with Windows 2000 RRAS servers. All of the remote access servers are configured to use DHCP to allocate the IP addresses to remote access users.

Users are having problems resolving computer names when connected to the Windows 2000 RRAS servers. The remote access users have no problem when connected through the Windows NT 4 servers. What needs to be done to fix the problem?

○ a. DCPROMO the Windows 2000 RRAS servers.

○ b. Install the DHCP relay agent on the Windows 2000 servers.

○ c. Enable the DHCP server to Always Update DNS for the client.

○ d. Create a BOOTP scope to allocate IP addresses for the remote access clients.

The correct answer is b. Windows 2000 RRAS servers need the DHCP relay agent configured to point to the DHCP server for additional options that are configured for the DHCP-enabled clients. Answer a does not affect the name resolution; it only promotes a Windows 2000 server to a domain controller or demotes a Windows 2000 server from a domain controller. Answers c and d are not related to name resolution, so they do not solve any of the problems that are present in the stem of the question.

## Question 2

---

You are responsible for ACME Enterprise's remote access servers and access to resources through remote access. ACME is a Windows 2000 Active Directory mixed-mode domain. All remote access users are able to successfully dial in and gain access to the resources appropriately.

ACME has just acquired the WIDGET company. The WIDGET company is very small, but it does have several Windows NT 4 RAS servers. The NT 4 RAS servers have joined the ACME domain to broaden the remote access server availability for the expanding ACME domain.

Users are now complaining that they cannot gain access to the network at all times. After investigating the problem, you discover that the Windows NT 4 attempted connections are not being validated properly from the Windows 2000 Active Directory.

What needs to be done?

○ a.  Manually add the Windows NT 4 servers to Active Directory integrated DNS.

○ b.  Manually add the remote access users to Active Directory integrated DNS.

○ c.  Add the Windows NT 4 servers to the Pre-Windows 2000 Compatible Access group.

○ d.  Add the Everyone group to the Pre-Windows 2000 Compatible Access group.

---

The correct answer is d. Because the Windows NT 4 servers cannot validate the remote access users correctly to the Active Directory, you must add the Everyone group to the Pre-Windows 2000 Compatible Access group in Active Directory Users and Computers. Answers a and b are incorrect because adding anything to DNS here does not solve any computer name resolution. If there were any domain name or FQDN resolution issues, then DNS might solve the problem. Answer c does not work because the addition of the computers to the Pre-Windows group does not fix the problem; it only adds users.

# Question 3

You are the network administrator of the largest financial company in the Midwest. The auditors in the company have been complaining that they would like to work at home and gain access to tax information, but they currently do not have access to the network remotely.

The only users that have access to the network remotely are the members of the IS group. The permissions for the IS members are currently configured through the User Property page in Active Directory Users and Computers.

You are instructed to give the auditors remote access permissions but limit their access to Monday through Saturday from 6 A.M. until 9 P.M.

Select the required steps and arrange them in the order in which they would be performed:

Delete the original remote access policy.

Move the new remote access policy to a higher priority than the default remote access policy.

Select Allow Access for each auditor in Active Directory Users and Computers.

Select Grant Remote Access Permission in the new remote access policy.

Select Control Access Through Remote Access Policy for each auditor in Active Directory Users and Computers.

Place all of the auditors in a group in Active Directory Users and Computers called REMAUDIT.

Modify the default remote access policy to include the Windows Groups condition with REMAUDIT.

Create a new remote access policy to include the Windows Groups condition with REMAUDIT and the day and time restrictions of Monday through Saturday, 6 A.M. to 9 P.M.

The correct answer is:

Select Control Access Through Remote Access Policy for each auditor in Active Directory Users and Computers.

Place all of the auditors in a group in Active Directory Users and Computers called REMAUDIT.

Create a new remote access policy to include the Windows Groups condition with REMAUDIT and the day and time restrictions of Monday through Saturday, 6 A.M. to 9 P.M.

Select Grant Remote Access Permission in the new remote access policy.

Move the new remote access policy to a higher priority than the default remote access policy.

The core of this problem is that you must configure a new group with special remote access permissions and constraints. You should configure the permission for allowing access in the policy because there is no information given about the existing policy structure. This way, the auditors are guaranteed access. The existing remote access policy cannot be affected because it applies to the current IS member group (even though it has Allow Access configured through the user properties). Therefore, the existing policy cannot be modified or deleted. The new policy must be first in the listing because it will be the first policy to match the conditions of the attempted connection from the auditors. The IS members do not match the policy, so they receive their original policy, even though it is second in the list.

## Question 4

You are configuring a new VPN connection for a client. The client will use the VPN connection to give its vendors access to a portion of its network to communicate bid information. Because the nature of the information from the vendor is sensitive, you want to configure the most secure authentication possible to reduce the possibility of interception and decryption. Which authentication setting will you use?

○ a.  MS-CHAP v2

○ b.  MS-CHAP v1

○ c.  MD5 and EAP

○ d.  SPAP

The correct answer is c. MD5 configured within EAP is the best authentication available through Windows 2000 remote access. The alternative to this is EAP configured with Smart Card use, which would also be the level of authentication required for the answer. Answers a, b, and d are all less secure but provide good levels of authentication.

# Question 5

> You are responsible for configuring the remote access servers for the ACME company. One group of users will access the corporate LAN to do routine word processing and send internal memos through email. The second group will run one of the corporate applications to perform weekly database updates. The second group will require additional bandwidth on an as-needed basis.
>
> You must optimize the bandwidth, so configurations must ensure that additional bandwidth is freed when the link utilization drops below 50 percent for more than 20 seconds.
>
> What needs to be done? [Check all correct answers]
>
> ❑ a. Configure multilink connections on the database users' computers.
>
> ❑ b. Configure multilink connections for the RRAS servers.
>
> ❑ c. Configure Bandwidth Allocation Protocol (BAP) for the RRAS servers.
>
> ❑ d. Configure a remote access policy to drop to a single line when the link utilization drops below 50 percent for more than 20 seconds.

The correct answers are a, b, c, and d. Every answer is needed to complete the task. First, you must configure both the client and server for multilink. The server must be configured to support BAP, and the multilink and BAP must be configured for the group of users. This configuration comes in the form of a remote access policy.

## Question 6

> You are the network administrator responsible for the central administration of all the remote access servers. The network is configured with 10 remote access servers. Five of the remote access servers are running Windows 2000 Server, and the other five are Windows NT 4 servers. An IAS server is configured to manage the authentication and remote policies of all 10 remote access servers.
>
> You now need another IAS server to help carry the load of remote access client authentication and remote access policies. The policies from the first IAS server need to be copied to the second IAS server to ensure that the same policies are applied to users, regardless which IAS server authenticates them.
>
> How will you accomplish this task?
>
> ○ a.  Force replication through Active Directory Sites and Services.
>
> ○ b.  Place the IAS policy file in the Netlogon share.
>
> ○ c.  Use the **netsh** command to copy the profile.
>
> ○ d.  Configure DFS as a master and replica to replicate the policy.

The correct answer is c. The **netsh** (Netshell) command permits the backup and restoration of the policy file to the correct IAS server. The replication through Active Directory Sites and Services is for Active Directory database replication between domain controllers. Therefore, answer a is incorrect. The Netlogon share is where the NT system policies and logon scripts are located to be replicated among all of the domain controllers. Therefore, answer b is incorrect. DFS is designed to create a logical listing of resource shares. The remote access policy used with IAS would not be an item shared as a resource to users. Therefore, answer d is incorrect.

## Question 7

You are testing the new phone lines and remote access servers for your company. A Windows 2000 server is configured as the remote access server. There are 10 users performing the remote access tests. The users can access the remote access server and the correct applications on the LAN.

To take the test one step further, you place each user in a group called REMTEST and remove all remote policies. You configure the Allow Access permission for each user in Active Directory Users and Computers. Now, none of the users can log on to the remote access server.

What can be done to fix the problem?

- ○ a. Change the remote access configuration for each user to Control Access Through Remote Access Policy.

- ○ b. Create a new remote access policy allowing access with the REMTEST group as the Windows Groups condition.

- ○ c. Add the Everyone group to the Pre-Windows 2000 Compatible Access group.

- ○ d. Add the REMTEST group to the RAS and IAS Servers security group.

The correct answer is b. There needs to be at least one remote access policy that meets the dial-in users' connection credentials. If this policy is not configured, no remote user can be authenticated to the remote access server. The remote access permission setting of Control Access Through Remote Access Policy configured in the user permissions still requires a remote access policy. Therefore, answer a is incorrect. The Pre-Windows 2000 Compatible Access and RAS and IAS Servers groups do not help any of the problems associated with the stem of the question. Therefore, answers c and d are incorrect.

## Question 8

> There are five remote locations at the security department where you work. Each of the five remote locations has highly secure data that needs physical security for the computers as well as some form of user validation beyond a username and password.
>
> It has been decided to use Smart Cards for the user authentication. You have installed the appropriate hardware at each remote location, but you now need to configure the remote access server for LAN access from each remote site. You have configured a remote access policy for these five remote locations but need to configure the correct encryption protocol.
>
> Which protocol will you select?
>
> ○ a.  MD5 CHAP
>
> ○ b.  EAP
>
> ○ c.  MS-CHAP v2
>
> ○ d.  SPAP

The correct answer is b. EAP is the protocol required to support Smart Card authentication. Both the client and the server must be configured for EAP. MD5 CHAP is a two-way authentication protocol, but it does not use Smart Card authentication. Therefore, answer a is incorrect. MS-CHAP v2 and SPAP are not at the high level of EAP authentication and do not support Smart Card authentication either. Therefore, answers c and d are incorrect.

# Need to Know More?

 Shinder, Debra LittleJohn, and Thomas W. Shinder. *Managing Windows 2000 Network Services*. Rockland, Mass.: Syngress Media, Inc., 2000. ISBN 1928994067. Good overall book for networking Windows 2000, with emphasis on remote access services.

 Search the RRAS help file within the Windows 2000 Server operating system. The help file provides details for configuring, implementing, and troubleshooting.

 Search the TechNet CD (or its online version through **www. microsoft.com**) and the *Windows 2000 Server Resource Kit* CD using the keywords "RRAS", "VPN", "PPTP", "L2TP", "RADIUS", and "IAS".

 The Web site **www.ietf.org/html.charters/radius-charter.html** is the absolute authority for RADIUS authentication.

# Routing in a Windows 2000 Network Infrastructure

**Terms you'll need to understand:**

✓ Static route

✓ Demand dial

✓ Routing Information Protocol (RIP)

✓ Open Shortest Path First (OSPF)

✓ Internet Group Membership Protocol (IGMP)

✓ Internet Connection Sharing (ICS)

✓ Network Address Translation (NAT)

**Techniques you'll need to master:**

✓ Configuring a two-way demand-dial connection

✓ Setting up the RIP v2 protocol

✓ Developing a border router topology

✓ Configuring IGMP routers and proxies

✓ Learning when to use the **netsh** command

✓ Understanding the differences between NAT and ICS

Windows NT 4 was equipped with some routing functionality, but it wasn't until Routing and Remote Access Service (RRAS) for Windows NT 4 was developed that routing for the Windows NT environment was optimized. RRAS for Windows NT 4 brought with it RIP v2, OSPF, demand-dial routing, the Remote Authentication Dial-In User Service (RADIUS) client (see Chapter 6 on remote access), and IP packet filtering. Windows 2000 RRAS includes these incredible features, but also brings new and improved routing support. These new routing features include support for multicast routing, small office/home office (SOHO) Internet routing, Layer 2 Tunneling Protocol (L2TP) over IP Security (IPSec) (see Chapter 8 on Internet Protocol Security), and some new administrative tools.

# Why Use Windows 2000 Routing?

There are many advantages to using the routing functionality that is included with Windows 2000. One overall reason for using Windows 2000 routing is the seamless integration with Windows 2000 Active Directory. Another reason for implementing Windows 2000 routing is the excellent solution it creates when combined with Windows 2000 remote access services.

All the reasons for using Windows 2000 routing can be broken down into three main categories: small office/home office support, corporate enterprise support, and reduced total cost of ownership. Some of the routing features are designed specifically for an individual category, whereas other features overlap categories. Internet Connection Sharing (ICS) is designed specifically for the SOHO environment. Network Address Translation (NAT) routing is a feature that can fall within both the SOHO environment and the corporate enterprise. The use of demand-dial routing can directly affect the SOHO or corporate enterprise, while reducing the cost of connectivity along the way. Routing Information Protocol (RIP) and Open Shortest Path First (OSPF) are designed for the corporate environment to expand the network in an efficient manner.

Regardless of the routing feature that is implemented, using Windows 2000 routing can reduce the total cost of ownership dramatically over a mid-range routing solution, either software or hardware. Core knowledge of each feature, including the implementation, configuration, and troubleshooting of the functionality of the product, is the key to making good decisions while using Windows 2000 routing.

# Static Routing

Static routing is designed for small enterprises, typically 2 to 10 networks in size. A static route is best suited for a single path, which means there is only one path for a packet to travel between any two endpoints on the network. As the name indicates, a static route is also ideal for static environments, where the network topology and routes do not change often. Typically, a static route is used in a home office IP network, small business, or branch office.

There are, of course, drawbacks to almost everything, and static routing is no different. One of the major problems with static routing is the lack of fault tolerance. When a router or link goes down, a static route cannot determine another route or inform other routers that the route is down. Another disadvantage to static routing is the overhead it creates from an administrative standpoint. When you add any new route or remove an old route, you must configure the change on every computer that requires the update.

Static routing has some inherent problems that can occur if some planning is not implemented during the configuration of the network. To reduce the overhead of the static route configurations, you can instantiate a peripheral router in the plan. A peripheral router is a router attached to multiple networks, with only one of those routes to a neighboring router.

# Demand-Dial Routing

Demand-dial routing is not a new feature in the Microsoft suite of routing solutions. However, it is a great solution for those environments that need to route between two different locations and optimize the amount of time the link between the two locations is active. As the name indicates, demand-dial routing is a solution for an environment with a dial-up connection to the remote segment for which it needs to route information. The connection established by the dial-up is active only when it needs to transport traffic between the two segments.

## On-Demand and Persistent Connections

You can establish two different types of connections for demand-dial routing. The first type is for an environment that pays for the time the link is active, so the link is established only when data needs to be transferred. This type is known as *on demand*. On-demand demand-dial routing is a great solution, but also has drawbacks. The first drawback is performance. If the link is not active when data needs to be transmitted to the other segment, the connection must first be activated. Another drawback is based on the application or traffic you are using or sending over the network. If the link is not established quickly enough, the application might time out or the data packets might extinguish the time to live (TTL).

For example, you start Internet Explorer to view a Web page. The request is sent to the demand-dial interface, which is not active because it has not been used recently. The demand-dial connection is established, which can take up to 20 seconds for analog phone lines. Depending on the configurations of Internet

Explorer, the application might time out, indicating that the Web site was not available. If the Web site is then refreshed after the connection is made, the Web site appears as if there was never a problem.

The other demand-dial type is a *persistent connection*. A persistent connection is designed for WAN connectivity when the cost of the link is fixed and the connection can be active 24 hours a day. This might include analog connections, but only when the phone call is a local one. Regardless of the connection, the persistent connection automatically reestablishes the connection if the connection is lost.

For persistent connections to work properly, both routers must be configured for persistent behavior. The calling router will have the Persistent Connection option selected, and the answering router must have the Disconnect If Idle For checkbox cleared.

# One-Way and Two-Way Demand-Dial Connections

There is more flexibility built into demand-dial routing than meets the eye. The ability to choose on-demand or persistent connections is one example of this flexibility. Another example of demand-dial's flexibility is the one-way and two-way connection option. Depending on the network structure and the requirements placed on the demand-dial route, the initiation of the route can come from one direction at all times or from either direction.

If the initiation of the demand-dial only comes from one direction, you need to create a one-way demand-dial connection. In this scenario, only one network can force the connection to the other network. The benefits of this configuration include the ability to limit the traffic from the receiving side to the calling side as well as reducing the connection time, which is important if the connection price is dependent on the time of use. The only time traffic can flow in this direction is when the connection is active.

One-way connections require close attention to detail when you configure the service. If you leave out or slightly alter any of the steps for a one-way connection, the connection might fail.

## One-Way Demand-Dial Computer Making the Call

The following list describes the steps for creating a one-way demand-dial connection:

*Note: Detailed steps are given here, but typically you will use the Demand-Dial Interface Wizard, shown in Figure 7.1.*

1. Create a demand-dial interface for the Windows 2000 Routing and Remote Access server. Following is a list of the critical settings for the interface:

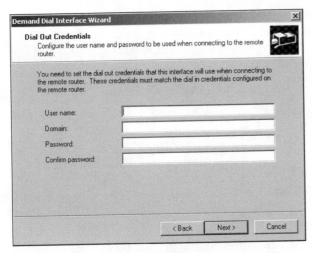

**Figure 7.1** Demand Dial Interface Wizard user account settings.

➤ Interface name. (Be certain to type the name correctly and document the name to be referenced in future steps.)

➤ Phone number of the computer on the receiving end.

➤ Device and COM port that will be used for the demand-dial connection.

➤ Protocols and security settings, as shown in Figure 7.2.

➤ Dial-out credentials.

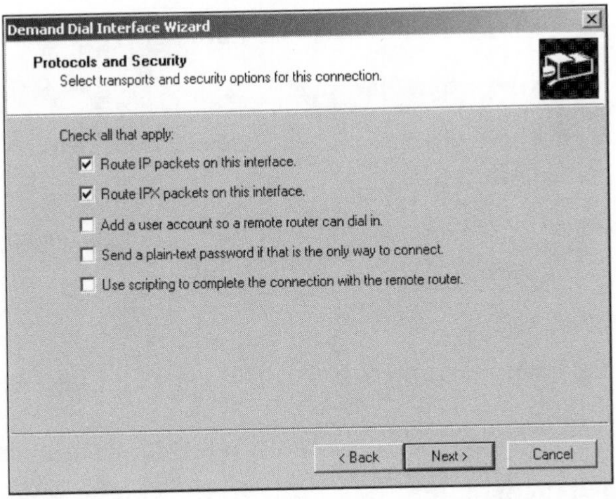

**Figure 7.2** Demand Dial Interface Wizard protocols and security settings.

The credentials must match the user account configured on the answering computer. If the answering computer is not a Windows computer, the domain name might not be required and could cause connection problems.

2. Create a static IP route with the following configuration:

> ➤ Interface name created in Step 1

> ➤ Destination network

> ➤ Network mask of the destination network

*Note: Remember that the demand-dial connection is a point-to-point connection. On a point-to-point connection, the gateway IP address is not required for the static route.*

### One-Way Demand-Dial Computer Receiving the Call

The initiating computer is not the only one that needs to be configured; the receiving computer has the following list of configurations:

1. Create a user account that will be used to authenticate the connection:

> ➤ The user account name must match the name of the calling demand-dial interface.

 The user account name on the answering computer must match the demand-dial interface name of the calling computer.

> ➤ Clear the User Must Change Password At Next Logon checkbox.

> ➤ Select the Password Never Expires checkbox.

> ➤ The user account must have dial-in permission and correct remote access policy permissions (see Chapter 6).

2. Configure a static route for the user account with the following required information:

> ➤ Destination network

> ➤ Network mask for destination network

> ➤ Number of hops to the destination network

### Two-Way Demand-Dial Computers

Two-way configurations are similar to one-way configurations, but have some distinct additions. These slight changes are extremely important to note when

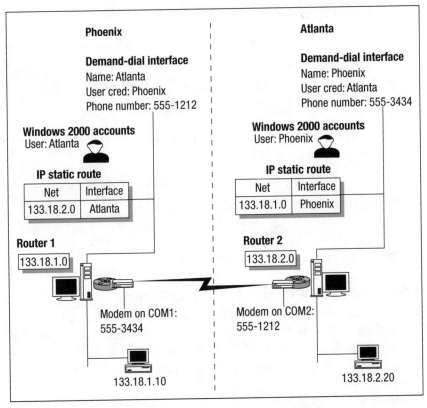

**Figure 7.3** A two-way demand-dial example detailing both configurations.

configuring the interface, and they are critical to delineate on the exam. Figure 7.3 shows a sample configuration for a two-way demand-dial connection.

The following list describes the steps for creating a two-way demand-dial connection:

1. Create a demand-dial interface for the Windows 2000 Routing and Remote Access server. Following is a list of the critical settings for the interface:

   ➤ Interface name. (Be certain to type the name correctly and document the name to be referenced in future steps.)

   ➤ Phone number of the computer on the receiving end.

   ➤ Device and COM port that will be used for the demand-dial connection.

   ➤ Protocols and security settings, as shown in Figure 7.2.

   ➤ Dial-out credentials.

2. Create a user account that will be used to authenticate the connection:

> ➤ The user account name must match the name of the calling demand-dial interface.

> ➤ Clear the User Must Change Password At Next Logon checkbox.

> ➤ Select the Password Never Expires checkbox.

> ➤ The user account must have dial-in permission and correct remote access policy permissions (see Chapter 6).

3. Create a static IP route with the following configuration:

> ➤ Interface name created in Step 1

> ➤ Destination network

> ➤ Network mask of the destination network

# Additional Demand-Dial Configurations

When planning the implementation of a demand-dial configuration, it is important to consider some additional settings to control the connection. These additional configurations are designed to enhance the security of the connection as well as keep the cost of running the demand-dial route to a minimum.

## Demand-Dial Filtering

You can establish a filter for the demand-dial connection that controls the connectivity based on the IP traffic. You can make configurations to either initiate the connection or deny the connection. You can configure the filter to connect based on the type of traffic that is being requested. For example, if you want to allow Web-based traffic to create a connection, then configure the filter to successfully connect port 80.

Demand-dial filters are completely different from IP packet filters. *Demand-dial filters* determine whether the demand-dial connection is established. *IP packet filters* determine the traffic that is allowed in and out of the demand-dial interface once the connection is established.

## Dial-Out Hours

An extremely important feature that you can configure for your demand-dial connection is the time of day the connection can be initialized. This setting affects the router that initiates the connection, not the receiving router. This configuration can help reduce the network traffic during busy times of the day as well as reduce the load on the demand-dial routers during peak times.

## Static Routes

The best solution for creating the route tables for demand-dial routers is with static routes. You create the initial static routes within the Routing and Remote Access interface for each router. You can configure static routes for demand-dial links in two different ways: default mode and auto-static mode.

 Auto-static mode does not mean that the process is automatic, only that the routes are added automatically instead of manually. You must initiate the process manually or by scheduling it with the Windows 2000 Scheduler.

The default mode offers an advantage because there is only a single route to configure. The disadvantage to the default route is that the demand-dial connection attempts a connection to all routes that are destined for another network, including unreachable networks. Auto-static routes are static routes that are automatically added to the routing table for a router after routes are requested across a demand-dial connection. You add these routes by using the RIP-for-IP routing protocol. The advantage of auto-static routes is that unreachable destinations do not cause the router to call connecting routers. Auto-static routing requires periodic updates to reflect the networks that are reachable at connecting locations.

 When an auto-static update is performed, the first thing the system does is delete the existing auto-static routes for the interface. This happens before the request is sent off to the router for updates. A serious problem arises if there is no response to the request. The router cannot replace the routes it has deleted, which in most cases leads to a loss of connectivity to remote networks.

## Dynamic Routes

You should use dynamic routing for persistent connections only. The dynamic nature of a persistent demand-dial connection mirrors that of a dedicated link. To create a dynamic route for demand-dial connections, simply add the demand-dial interface to the IP or Internetwork Packet Exchange (IPX) routing protocol.

## Monitoring Demand-Dial Connections

You can monitor demand-dial interfaces by using the snap-in for Routing and Remote Access. This option can only monitor the connection status, however. If you want more details, you can use the rasmon utility to determine line speed, device statistics, connection statistics, and device errors.

# Routing Information Protocol

Routing Information Protocol (RIP) is designed for small- to medium-sized enterprises, typically 10 to 50 networks wide. RIP is best suited to provide routing solutions in a multipath, dynamic environment. RIP communicates with other RIP routers to exchange route table information. RIP has a version 1 and a version 2. Both have benefits, but RIP v2 is usually the best solution in most cases. RIP also supports routing for both IP and IPX.

## RIP-for-IP Networks

RIP is a good solution for routing in an IP environment, but there are limitations to using RIP. One such limitation is the diameter of the RIP internetwork. The maximum diameter for a RIP-for-IP network is 16 hops.

*Note: The diameter of the internetwork is defined as the size of the internetwork in terms of hops or other metrics. A metric indicates the order of the gateways for a particular router.*

Another consideration for RIP is the cost of a particular route. RIP uses the hop count as a metric to determine the best route for the data. Because the metric for any route can be customized, it is best to set the desirable route to the lowest metric. With the metric altered, the best route is predetermined by the configuration of the metric.

### RIP v1

RIP v1 is designed for environments that implement classful routing because RIP v1 does not announce the subnet mask for each route. RIP v1 uses broadcasting to announce the route changes to other RIP routers. If you want classless interdomain routing (CIDR) or variable-length subnet masks (VLSM) for the network, you must implement RIP v2 instead of v1.

### RIP v2

RIP v2 supports all of the features that v1 offers, plus some new options that optimize the routing structure. Like v1, v2 supports broadcast announcements, but it also supports multicast announcements. Another key feature of v2 is that it supports simple password authentication between RIP routers. You must configure RIP v2 on each router that will use the password authentication. The password must be the same case-sensitive name on each router. The password is transmitted across the network in clear-text, so the security of the password is very weak.

Only RIP v2 routers can utilize password authentication.

If you use RIP v2 with a demand-dial link, you have additional options to select. As stated earlier in the demand-dial section, the link can be either on demand or persistent. Two settings for RIP v2 correlate to these different demand-dial types. If the demand-dial link is on demand, then the RIP operation mode should be auto-static. If the link is persistent, the operation mode should be periodic update.

## Mixing RIP v1 and v2 Environments

Providing additional features and benefits to performance, RIP v2 is by far the better choice over RIP v1 for any network. If circumstances prohibit the use of RIP v2 over v1, you should consider the design and implementation of both types in the same environment. First, remember that v1 does not support class-less routing. Therefore, the IP subnets must be simple. Another consideration is the configuration for the RIP v2 announcements. You must configure all v2 routers for broadcast announcements because v1 does not support multicast announcements. A final consideration is what the v2 router will accept for announcements. You should configure the v2 router to accept both v1 and v2 announcements, as shown in Figure 7.4.

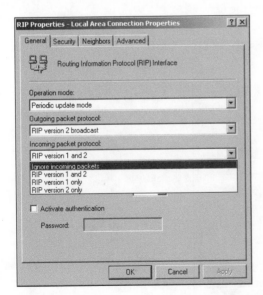

**Figure 7.4**    RIP v2 interface configuration for incoming packets.

## Silent RIP

Another type of RIP configuration, called *silent RIP*, supports the processing of RIP announcements, but does not broadcast any routing information. The processed RIP announcements are used to build the routing table for the host. This configuration is an excellent solution for a host that wants a dynamic routing table but does not want to contribute to updating other routing tables. Windows 2000 Professional supports a silent RIP component called the RIP Listener. Windows 2000 Server supports this feature under the Outgoing packet protocol configuration for the RIP v2 interface, which is shown in Figure 7.5.

## Additional RIP Configurations

You can make additional configurations for the RIP interface to include settings for security and structure. RIP-for-IP security includes features such as RIP v2 authentication (see the section "RIP v2" earlier in this chapter), peer security, route filters, and neighbors:

➤ Peer security is the ability to create a list of other RIP routers, by IP address, from which RIP announcements will be accepted.

➤ Route filters are created at each RIP interface to control the networks that are accepted or announced. The configuration allows for both inbound and outbound filtering. This configuration optimizes the route table to include only the routes that are required for the network.

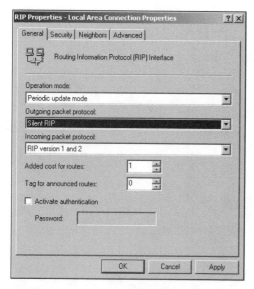

**Figure 7.5**   RIP Listener configuration for a Routing and Remote Access server.

➤ RIP neighbors are designed to ensure that the RIP announcements are sent to specific routers. The initial intent of the neighbor unicast announcement was for nonbroadcast multi-access network technologies such as Frame Relay, but you can still leverage the concept here. The configuration of the neighbors include broadcast and multicast announcements only; neighbors in addition to the broadcast and multicast announcements; and informing only neighbors.

 When you configure RIP routers to unicast to neighboring RIP routers, the ability of silent RIP hosts to receive RIP traffic is impaired. Therefore, you need to either add the silent RIP hosts as neighbors or configure the Windows 2000 router to broadcast or multicast as well as unicast to neighboring RIP routers.

## Testing the RIP-for-IP Internetwork

Because RIP is an automatic feature for updating routing tables throughout the routing environment, there must be some methodology for testing the configurations to ensure that the routes are properly configured:

➤ The Routing and Remote Access Service snap-in supports the viewing of RIP neighbors.

➤ You can view the IP routing table from the Routing and Remote Access Service snap-in or from the command prompt. If a particular route has changed within the routing environment but the RIP router has not received the update, there could be a problem with the configuration of the RIP routers. Another reason could be simply that the RIP routers have not had sufficient time to announce the changes to all of the RIP routers.

➤ Ping and tracert are excellent tools for determining the status of a route and the route that is taken to a particular location on the internetwork.

## RIP and SAP for IPX

RIP for IPX provides the same functionality for the IPX protocol as it did for the IP protocol list. Service Announcement Protocol (SAP) for IPX is the advertising protocol commonly used on IPX internetworks to advertise services and their locations. The Routing and Remote Access service also provides the ability to configure static SAP services and SAP service filters.

## RIP and SAP for IPX Considerations

Along the same lines as the RIP-for-IP routing, the IPX option also has some items you must consider for network design and implementation:

➤ The maximum diameter of a RIP and SAP for IPX is 16 routers.

➤ If you do not want NetBIOS for IPX traffic, you can disable the propagation of this traffic on specific interfaces. You can also configure static NetBIOS names to eliminate the need for NetBIOS for IPX traffic.

➤ You can configure SAP filters to control the propagation of the SAP service outside a group of IPX networks.

# Open Shortest Path First

Open Shortest Path First (OSPF) is designed to handle the exchange of routing information for large, to sometimes very large, internetworks. There are definite advantages to using OSPF in comparison to static routing or RIP. One advantage is that it does not have a limit of 16 hops for the routing environment. OSPF is extremely efficient not only for updating the routing tables, but also for choosing the route that is selected to transmit the data over the internetwork.

This efficiency is a result of the algorithm used to determine and compile the routing table. The algorithm, Shortest Path First (SPF), computes the least costly route between the router and all of the networks that are part of the internetwork.

 The OSPF algorithm always produces routes that are loop free.

The reason OSPF is more efficient when exchanging routing table information is that it creates a map of the internetwork. This map, called the link state database (LSDB), is updated after any change to the network topology. When a change has occurred on the network, the database is synchronized with other OSPF routers to keep the database accurate at all times. After the router receives the changes to the database, it recalculates the routing table.

The drawback to this method of routing is that the database can get quite large for some networks. This is where the planning and implementation of OSPF become critical.

## Topology of an OSPF Internetwork

An OSPF internetwork can become complex, which is its main disadvantage compared to other dynamic routing options. However, the power that the OSPF network provides for performance, efficiency, and redundancy is nearly unmatched. An OSPF network usually consists of the following characteristics: autonomous system (AS), areas, backbone area, border routers, and virtual links.

## Autonomous System

The core design structure behind the OSPF routing environment is the autonomous system (AS), which is illustrated in Figure 7.6. An AS includes all of the networks that share a common administrative authority.

The group of routers that exchange routing information within the AS is a critical component to the entire structure. A typical AS should adhere to the following recommendations:

➤ The AS should be divided into OSPF areas.

➤ The backbone area of the AS should be designated on a high-bandwidth network.

➤ The backbone area should be able to maintain a high capacity so that the inter-area traffic is not bottlenecked.

➤ All inter-area traffic should directly communicate through the backbone area.

## Areas

The OSPF routing environment should consist of subdivisions called *areas*. These areas are collections of contiguous subnets. An area is an administrative boundary used for separate sites or domains.

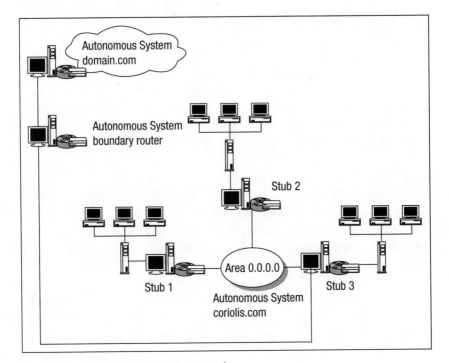

**Figure 7.6**   OSPF autonomous system example.

When planning the areas, follow the guidelines listed here:

➤ You should assign IP addresses in a contiguous manner. This allows for the summarization of the ranges of IP addresses in the route calculation.

➤ Use summary route advertisements when possible. When areas are developed with a summary route advertisement, the area border router advertises the internal network subnets in the form of [*Destination, Network Mask*] pairs to the other area border routers. This summary appears under the router ID number, represented by four numbers in dotted notation, such as 0.0.0.2. The route table generation and the replication overhead of the link state database are more efficient because of the summary.

*Note: The router ID is an arbitrary number specified when the area is created. This ID is typically used to denote the subnets that are contained in the area, but it is not required.*

➤ You should use stub areas whenever possible. Stub areas have a couple of outstanding benefits that can reduce the administrative overhead and make troubleshooting easier:

➤ When you use stub areas, a single static route can summarize all external routes as well as routes destined for outside of the AS.

➤ Stub areas also ensure that all external routes outside of the AS are not routed through another stub area. This reduces the traffic on the stub areas as well as the boundary routers.

➤ When designing the internal structure of the area, keep the inter-area communication to a minimum by locating appropriate servers in the areas. This includes DNS servers, DHCP servers, WINS servers, and Windows 2000 domain controllers. It is an excellent idea to synchronize the design of the OSPF areas with the Windows 2000 sites. You can limit the replication of Active Directory to within the area and site until the scheduled replication occurs.

## Backbone Areas

The backbone area of the OSPF AS is certainly the most critical part of the AS routing topology. The backbone area is connected to all of the other OSPF areas, which are typically stub areas. All traffic that enters or exits a stub area is routed through the backbone area. This area is always designated as Area 0.0.0.0, as indicated in Figure 7.6.

## OSPF Routers

An OSPF AS environment has many types of routers. Following is a description of each type of router. Keep in mind that there can be many routers of each type within each AS:

➤ *Internal router*—A router with all of the routing interfaces connected to the same area. An internal router contains only one LSDB.

➤ *Area border router (ABR)*—A router with interfaces connected to different areas. These routers have more than one LSDB, one for each of the areas it services.

➤ *Backbone router*—A router with at least one interface linked to the backbone area. Backbone routers include all of the ABRs as well as the internal routers of the backbone area.

➤ *AS boundary router (ASBR)*—A router responsible for exchanging routes with sources outside of the OSPF AS. These routers are also responsible for advertising external routes throughout the OSPF AS. Supported external route providers include local routes, auto-static routes, RIP v2, SNMP routes, non–demand-dial static routes, and static routes.

 You can also configure ASBRs to filter certain route sources and subnets.

## Virtual Links

A virtual link is a logical link between a backbone area border router and an area border router that do not have a backbone area between them. Figure 7.7 illustrates this concept with the new area linked to the backbone only by two ABRs.

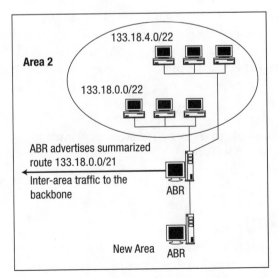

**Figure 7.7** OSPF topology, including a virtual link.

You create virtual links by setting both ABRs as virtual link neighbors. The other settings you need to establish for this virtual link include the same transit area, the router ID of the virtual link neighbor, matching hello and dead intervals, and a matching password.

 You should use virtual links only in rare instances. They can cause routing and other problems on top of being difficult to configure. You should plan the AS design to eliminate all virtual links and to make all areas directly connected to the backbone area.

## Additional OSPF Considerations

Planning and implementing an OSPF routing topology can be a tremendous amount of work. Even though the initial stages of establishing the AS can be complex, keep in mind the additional features of OSPF that Windows 2000 offers:

➤ Route filters can be established to control the interaction with other routing protocols.

➤ OSPF can coexist with RIP on the same network and exchange information successfully.

➤ It is best to configure only a single protocol per interface if you are using multiple IP routing protocols.

## Monitoring OSPF Internetworks

Keeping in mind the complexity of the OSPF design and implementation, think of how great it would be to have a utility that lets you control the OSPF AS and all the details involved. That utility is available! The tool is the **netsh** command-line and scripting utility. With **netsh**, you can control more than just the OSPF routing on the Routing and Remote Access server; you can also control other routing protocols on the server.

 The **netsh** utility is a replacement for the **routemon** utility that was available for Windows NT 4 RRAS.

# Multicast Routing

Multicasting technology is provided to deliver data in a point-to-multipoint method on an internetwork. Some examples of multicasting include Microsoft NetShow, RealAudio, and RealVideo. The information that is multicasted must be routed to the correct networks, where the computers and devices are listening for the data. Windows 2000 provides these routing options through the IGMP routing protocol that consists of the IGMP router mode and IGMP proxy mode. These technologies provide multicast forwarding in a single router environment or when you connect through a single router to the Internet.

## Internet Group Management Protocol

Internet Group Management Protocol (IGMP) is the protocol used to register IP clients within a multicast environment. There are two versions of IGMP, version 1 and version 2. IGMP version 2 is the supported version in Windows 2000. This version is also supported in Windows NT 4 SP 4 and later and Windows 98. The good news is that IGMP version 2 is backwards compatible with IGMP version 1.

*Note: IGMP is not the protocol used to initiate the IP multicast traffic; it is only used to maintain the host group membership on a local subnet. You can also use the protocol to forward the multicast traffic from one segment to another segment with the IGMP routing functionality.*

You install and configure IGMP by using the Routing and Remote Access plug-in on the Windows 2000 computer. IGMP lets an interface operate in one of two modes: IGMP proxy mode or IGMP router mode. Figure 7.8 illustrates a simple IGMP routed environment where a multicast client is on the IGMP router-mode interface and the Internet is on the IGMP proxy-mode interface.

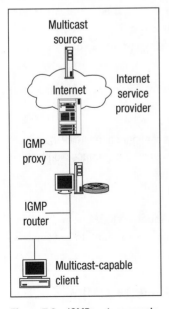

**Figure 7.8**   IGMP router example.

A Windows 2000 server that is performing IGMP routing needs both an IGMP router-mode interface and an IGMP proxy-mode interface.

# IGMP Router Mode

The key to using the IGMP router mode is keeping track of the multicast hosts on the network. There can be multiple IGMP router-mode interfaces on any one Windows 2000 IGMP router. The router-mode feature of IGMP has many functions, most of which are included in the following list:

➤ The router functions in promiscuous mode, which catches all traffic on the network wire.

*Note: The network card in the router that is functioning as an IGMP router must support multicast promiscuous mode, or the router manager will report errors.*

➤ The router listens for specific messages from the multicast hosts on the network. The Host Membership Report message and the Leave Group message are recorded on the IGMP router.

➤ The router is also responsible for sending IGMP Host Membership queries to keep track of the existing hosts.

➤ The router keeps a multicast forwarding table, which is the current group membership of hosts on the subnet.

➤ The IP multicast traffic can be forwarded to the required multicast group. That can be the router itself, for a process that is running on the router, or it can be a network segment that contains multicast group members or other multicast routers.

You can establish the configurations shown in Figure 7.9 for each interface that is running IGMP v2 in IGMP router mode.

The **netsh** command is also capable of configuring the IGMP v2 interface settings. The command to configure the interface would be:

```
netsh routing ip ipmg set interface
```

The configurations available for the IGMP router mode include controlling how the router queries the multicast hosts and setting the susceptibility to lost packets.

# IGMP Proxy Mode

IGMP proxy-mode interfaces are designed to work with the IGMP router-mode interfaces. The purpose of the IGMP proxy mode is to connect the Windows

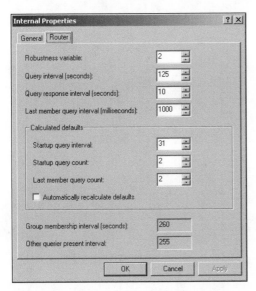

**Figure 7.9**   IGMP v2 Router mode configuration tab.

2000 multicast router to a multicast IP internetwork. The internetwork can be either a private intranet or the Internet.

 Private intranets typically run a multicast routing protocol such as Distance Vector Multicast Routing Protocol (DVMRP) or Protocol Independent Multicast (PIM). The special multicast-capable portion of the Internet is known as the Internet multicast backbone, or the MBone.

An IGMP router configuration is illustrated in Figure 7.10. Note that the IGMP router-mode interfaces are directed to the internal networks, and the IGMP proxy-mode interface is on the Internet MBone side.

The IGMP proxy-mode interface acts like a host and joins host groups on behalf of hosts on its IGMP router-mode interfaces. When traffic that is destined for host members located on the IGMP router-mode interface (the local network in this case), the IGMP proxy-mode interface receives and forwards the packets using the IP multicast forwarding process. When multicast traffic is sent by hosts on the IGMP router-mode interface side, the packets are received by the IGMP router-mode interfaces and routed out the IGMP proxy-mode interface, where a downstream IP multicast-enabled router can either forward the traffic or ignore it.

## The MBone

The MBone is the portion of the Internet that supports multicast routing and forwarding of Internet-based IP multicast traffic. The MBone is a series of

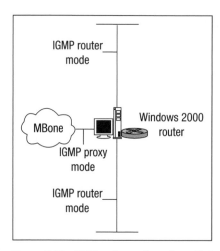

**Figure 7.10** IGMP router configuration with two router-mode interfaces and a connection to the Internet MBone.

multicast-enabled islands—contiguous network structures—all connected together by tunnels. The tunnel is responsible for passing the multicast traffic from one island to another island, encapsulating the IP multicast packets along the way. The tunnel is required to allow the multicast traffic to traverse portions of the Internet that do not support multicast forwarding.

# Multicast Boundaries

The administrator uses a boundary to control the forwarding of the IP multicast traffic to portions of the internetwork. The two primary types of multicast boundaries are multicast scope boundaries and time to live (TTL) boundaries.

## Multicast Scope-Based Boundaries

Scope-based boundaries prevent the multicast traffic from being forwarded to a specific range of multicast IP addresses. The range of possible multicast IP addresses that can be configured in a scope are 239.0.0.0 to 239.255.255.255.

 To create a scope-based boundary, you must first create the scope. You create the scopes using the Multicast Scopes tab of the Properties of the General node under IP Routing in the Routing and Remote Access Service snap-in.

You configure the scope-based boundaries using the scope name that was created for the multicast IP address range. Each interface can have a unique scope-based boundary configuration. A scope-based boundary prevents both the sending and receiving of multicast packets beyond the interface of the IGMP router.

## Multicast TTL-Based Boundaries

TTL-based boundaries also prevent multicast traffic from being forwarded to specific portions of the internetwork. However, the prevention is based on the TTL on the packet that is being forwarded.

 TTL-based boundaries are not as effective as scope-based boundaries. TTL-based boundaries can also cause undesired multicast traffic on portions of the network. Use scope-based boundaries when you must prevent or control multicast traffic.

TTL-based boundaries are independent of the multicast group membership; that is, the boundaries apply to all multicast packets. The TTL-based boundary prevents the traffic based on a threshold that the multicast traffic has specified. Table 7.1 lists the typical thresholds for different scopes.

# Multicast Heartbeat

The heartbeat of multicast routing is the ability of the Windows 2000 router to listen for the regular multicast notification for a specific group address. This notification verifies whether the multicast connectivity is available on the network. Multicast heartbeats are typically used with Simple Network Management Protocol (SNMP) and Simple Network Time Protocol (SNTP).

# IP-in-IP Tunnels

Similar in function to the MBone tunnels, the IP-in-IP tunnels on your network are responsible for forwarding multicast traffic from one network to another network, traversing a network that does not support multicast forwarding or routing. The multicast traffic is encapsulated with an IP header addressed to and from the endpoints of the IP-in-IP tunnel.

| Table 7.1 | TTL-based thresholds. |
|---|---|
| **TTL Threshold** | **Scope** |
| 0 | Restricted to the same host |
| 1 | Restricted to the same subnet |
| 15 | Restricted to the same site |
| 63 | Restricted to the same region |
| 127 | Worldwide |
| 191 | Worldwide; limited bandwidth |
| 255 | Unrestricted in scope |

## Monitoring and Troubleshooting Multicast Routing

Certain tools built into Windows 2000 Routing and Remote Access service help you monitor and troubleshoot multicast routing:

➤ The **mrinfo** command displays the configuration of a multicast router.

➤ The **netsh** command allows for command-line configuration of the IGMP router interfaces.

➤ IGMP event logging is built into the IGMP routing protocol.

# Routing to the Internet

RRAS that came with Windows NT 4 was limited in the ability to connect users on a network with the Internet quickly and painlessly. Knowing that limitation, Microsoft added some features to Windows 2000 that allow users on smaller to medium-sized networks to easily connect to the Internet. You even have a choice about how painless and how easy you want to make this connection.

The two options for connecting a SOHO to the Internet are Internet Connection Sharing (ICS) and Network Address Translation (NAT). Each option has advantages and disadvantages. The decision about which option to use for your environment is an easy choice, if you just look at the structure and robustness of each solution. A discussion of each option follows.

## Internet Connection Sharing

Internet Connection Sharing (ICS) is an additional feature that Windows 2000 offers over Windows NT 4. ICS is also available on Windows 98, but not on Windows 95. ICS gives small networks, typically small offices or home offices, access to the Internet without the overhead of additional Windows 2000 server components. ICS can be configured on both Windows 2000 Server and Professional.

ICS is a translated connection for users who want to gain access to the Internet. The Windows 2000 computer that runs ICS acts as a network address translator for routing the data. A translated connection is not as complex to configure or manage because the underlying technology does not have the advanced features of a routed solution. Translated connections require less knowledge about IP and routing, which results in easier configurations for the host computers and the Windows 2000 computer running the service.

The design of ICS is such that it only takes a single step, selecting a single checkbox, to configure the service, which is shown in Figure 7.11.

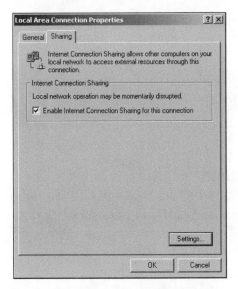

**Figure 7.11**   Single-step configuration for ICS.

If the entire network is configured correctly around ICS, it takes only a single step to configure ICS. ICS provides services that replace network-centric servers and services. Following is a list of what ICS provides:

➤ The ICS computer is automatically assigned the IP address of 192.168.0.1 with a subnet mask of 255.255.255.0.

➤ The DHCP allocator uses the 192.168.0.0 range of IP addresses and a subnet mask of 255.255.255.0.

➤ An autodial feature is built in and enabled by default.

➤ A static IP route is created automatically when the dial-up connection is established.

➤ The ICS service is started automatically.

➤ A DNS proxy is enabled for the ICS clients to achieve proper name resolution.

## ICS Precautions

ICS is a great solution but should be used in situations that do not require extensive access to the Internet, where only a few users need the connection. Here are some other warnings about using ICS:

➤ All client computers must be DHCP enabled.

➤ There cannot be a DHCP server on the network, or the ICS service will not function properly.

➤ Any clients configured on the network with any IP address other than the 192.168.0.0/24 subnet will not be able to communicate with the ICS clients or server.

➤ ICS does require two network access cards in the ICS computer. They can both be NICs, or they can be a NIC and a modem.

➤ ICS only allows certain services and applications to be controlled over the connection.

# Network Address Translation

Network Address Translation (NAT) is a technology that has appeared in other networking devices and software for some time. It is a new solution for the Windows 2000 revolution, however. NAT solves many problems that SOHOs and some medium-sized companies had connecting to the Internet.

NAT is a routed connection that can only be installed on Windows 2000 Server. The service routes IP packets between the LAN and the Internet. The routed connection requires knowledge about the IP addressing scheme and the routing configuration to successfully transmit the data. NAT is a better solution than ICS for most SOHO-to-Internet environments because of the ability to control the IP network and traffic through the NAT router. However, with the flexibility and control come additional configurations.

## NAT Network Addressing

NAT lets you choose between using the built-in DHCP allocator or using a network-based DHCP server. The NAT service does not auto-detect the DHCP server on the network, so you must make the configuration properly in the NAT interface, as shown in Figure 7.12.

Configuring NAT network addressing is somewhat confusing and should be noted for exam preparation. If the box is selected to Automatically Assign IP Addresses By Using DHCP, then the NAT router assigns IP addresses to the DHCP-enabled clients on the network. If the network-based DHCP server is supposed to allocate the IP addresses to the client computers, you should clear the checkbox, as shown in Figure 7.12.

The IP address scheme for the network should be one of the private address classes to eliminate any IP conflicts with IP addresses that were allocated by InterNIC. The default IP address range is 192.168.0.0/24.

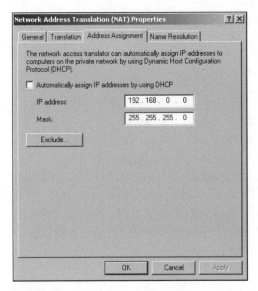

**Figure 7.12**    NAT Address Assignment tab.

## Inbound NAT

If you must configure multiple public IP addresses for the public to gain access to the internal computer, you make these settings for the public interface of the NAT protocol in the Routing and Remote Access Service snap-in. You configure the range of IP addresses in the NAT Properties, as shown in Figure 7.13.

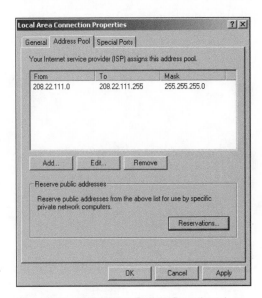

**Figure 7.13**    NAT Address Pool configuration tab.

After you configure the address pool, you must establish a reservation for the public address to be linked to the private address. The final step is to configure a special port for the public interface. The special port indicates which private address and port the inbound packet should be routed to, based on the public address and port to which it was sent.

## VPN Connections through NAT

The NAT route can support a VPN connection with Windows 2000. This is only available due to an additional component included with Windows 2000, a NAT editor. The NAT editor lets you route Point-to-Point Tunneling Protocol (PPTP) packets across the NAT router. Without the NAT editor, the PPTP packet is not supported for forwarding across the NAT router. L2TP is also supported with the NAT editor, but not if Internet Protocol Security is also implemented with the L2TP configuration.

# Practice Questions

## Question 1

You are the network administrator for the marketing.acme.local domain. The company has just purchased another company that will need access to the main office. The main office will also require access to the new company network. Because the remote office was just acquired, there will not be too much traffic over the WAN link. The decision is made to use a standard analog connection for the link. A demand-dial connection is the final choice for the WAN link. The following requirements are also placed on the link:

- The demand-dial should be able to be initiated from either direction.

- MS-CHAP is the authentication protocol.

- The demand-dial connection should be on demand.

- The most efficient routing protocol should be used.

The following configurations are made for the Windows 2000 routers on each end:

- A remote access policy is configured for the demand-dial connections, with MS-CHAP as the authentication protocol.

- OSPF is configured as the routing protocol.

- The appropriate interfaces are configured for the demand-dial routers.

- The appropriate user accounts are created on each demand-dial router.

- The appropriate static routes are created for each demand-dial router.

- Both demand-dial interfaces have the Persistent Connection option selected and the Disconnect If Idle checkbox cleared.

Which of the requirements are obtained? [Check all correct answers]

- ❏ a. The demand-dial should be able to be initiated from either direction.

- ❏ b. MS-CHAP is the authentication protocol.

- ❏ c. The demand-dial connection should be on demand.

- ❏ d. The most efficient routing protocol should be used.

The correct answers are a, b, and c. With the configurations of the appropriate remote access policies and the demand-dial interface established, the demand-dial connection will work appropriately and be on demand. Because the demand-dial connection is on demand, the OSPF routing protocol will not function properly. Therefore, answer d is incorrect. In this case, a static route with the auto-static setting would be a better solution.

## Question 2

You are configuring the WAN connectivity for a remote location to the main office. The remote office has an ISDN connection to the main office already established and in working order. The cost for the ISDN connection is established based on the amount of time that the connection is live. Therefore, the connection must be optimized for time.

It is decided to create an on-demand demand-dial connection. The connection should only support the link being initiated by the remote office. The demand-dial interface is correctly established, but the static route needs to be finalized. Where will the static routes need to be configured? [Check all correct answers]

❏ a. Within the Routing and Remote Access Service on the receiving computer

❏ b. Within the Routing and Remote Access Service on the initiating computer

❏ c. For the user account on the receiving computer

❏ d. For the user account on the initiating computer

The correct answers are b and c. For a one-way demand-dial connection, the initiating computer needs a static route configured for the demand-dial interface. The receiving computer needs a static route configured for the user account because the user account is used to create the connection. The receiving computer does not have a static route configured for the interface on a one-way demand-dial connection. Therefore, answer a is incorrect. The user account on the receiving computer is where the static route is configured for a one-way demand-dial connection. Therefore, answer d is incorrect.

# Question 3

You are upgrading some of the Windows 2000 routers in the enterprise to take advantage of the new features included in RIP v2. The existing Windows 2000 routers are all using RIP v1. After two of the computers are upgraded, a test is performed to make sure that the new environment is working properly. After the test and further investigation, it is determined that the two RIP v2 routers are communicating with each other and receiving updates from the RIP v1 routers, but the remaining RIP v1 routers are communicating only with each other. What is the problem?

○ a.  The RIP v1 routers are configured for broadcast announcements.

○ b.  RIP v1 and RIP v2 are not mutually supported on the same network.

○ c.  The RIP v2 routers are configured for broadcast announcements.

○ d.  The RIP v2 routers are configured for multicast announcements.

The correct answer is d. Because the RIP v2 routers are announcing the route updates via multicasting, the RIP v1 computers cannot communicate with the RIP v2 routers. RIP v1 only uses broadcast announcements. Therefore, answer a is incorrect. RIP v1 and RIP v2 are compatible on the same network, with the proper configuration. Therefore, answer b is incorrect. If the RIP v2 routers were configured with a broadcast announcement, the problem would be solved. Therefore, answer c is incorrect.

## Question 4

You are developing a solution for one of the remote offices in your company. The remote office wants everyone on the network to gain access to the Internet through a single access point. The problem is that the budget is slim and there is no money for the purchase of multiple IP addresses or a dedicated link to an ISP. The current internal network subnet is the 10.1.1.0/24 network. The IP address that was allocated to you by the ISP is 24.1.24.24/28:

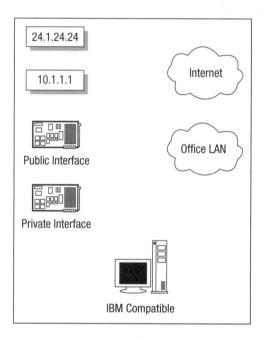

It is decided to use NAT coupled with a demand-dial connection. This will give every user access to the Internet over the 56Kbps ISP connection. Arrange the objects in the exhibit in the correct order to create the required configuration and link the correct devices together as appropriate.

The correct answer is shown here:

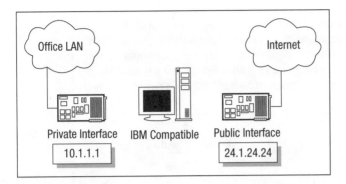

## Question 5

You are creating an Internet connectivity solution for one of the branch offices using Internet Connection Sharing (ICS). You place two network cards in the Windows 2000 server that will perform the connection and change the current static IP configurations on the client computers to have the private side of the ICS computer as the default gateway. The clients cannot gain access to the Internet even though the ICS computer can. What could be the problem?

○ a. The client computers need to be configured as DHCP enabled.

○ b. The ICS computer needs to have NAT running first.

○ c. There needs to be a DHCP server installed on the network.

○ d. There is no DNS server on the network.

The correct answers is a. The clients need the IP address configured for DHCP. This will force the client computers to obtain an IP address from the ICS computer. NAT is a solution you use instead of ICS, so answer b is incorrect. It is a better solution than ICS, but it is not needed to have ICS run correctly. ICS will not function properly if there is a DHCP server on the network. Therefore, answer c is incorrect. DNS does not have to be on the network. Therefore, answer d is incorrect. The ICS computer will allocate the DNS server it has to the client computers that are using the ICS service.

# Question 6

You are the network administrator responsible for the implementation of the new OSPF topology for the new branch. You have determined that there needs to be three areas in addition to the backbone area. Unfortunately, one of the areas must be connected via a virtual link. There is a question about what the traffic pattern will be because the virtual link is required.

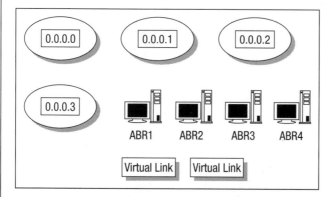

Arrange the objects in the exhibit in the correct order for the topology described here. Then, connect the areas together representing the traffic pattern from the area that has the virtual link to the area on the other side of the backbone area.

The correct answer is shown here:

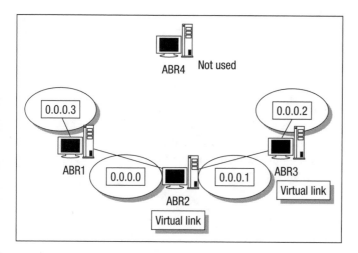

## Question 7

You are the network administrator of the sales.acme.local domain. You are trying to get the new training group application to work properly on the network. The new application is using multicasting to provide the training to users within the enterprise. There are too many multicast operations occurring at any one time, which is causing too much traffic on portions of your network.

You need to control the traffic by only forwarding some multicast traffic to certain parts of the network. What options do you have to accomplish this? [Check all correct answers]

❏ a. Configure the multicast heartbeat.

❏ b. Configure multicast TTL-based boundaries.

❏ c. Configure multicast scope-based boundaries.

❏ d. Configure the multicast scopes.

The correct answers are b and c. Both boundaries will provide the capability to control the forwarding of multicast broadcasts. The heartbeat listens for a regular multicast notification to a specified group address to verify that IP multicast connectivity. Therefore, answer a is incorrect. A multicast scope cannot control the forwarding of the traffic. Therefore, answer d is incorrect.

# Question 8

You are the network administrator for the sales.acme.local domain. You need to set up a two-way demand-dial connection from the Windows 2000 Routing and Remote Access server located in the main office to the Windows 2000 Routing and Remote Access server in the remote office. The main office is located in Boston, and the remote office is located in Phoenix. You are going to use the naming standards that your company has instituted, which result in the following names for the different two-way demand-dial link:

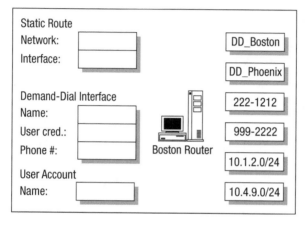

Demand-dial interface names:

- DD_Boston

- DD_Phoenix

User accounts for the demand-dial connections:

- DD_Boston

- DD_Phoenix

IP addresses:

- Boston users have addresses in the 10.1.2.0/24 subnet.

- Phoenix users have addresses in the 10.4.9.0/24 subnet.

Phone numbers:

- The Boston modem phone number is 222-1212.

- The Phoenix modem phone number is 999-2222.

Place the items in the exhibit to fill in the missing items for only the Boston router. (Note: Some items may be used more than once, whereas others may not be used at all.)

The correct answer is shown here:

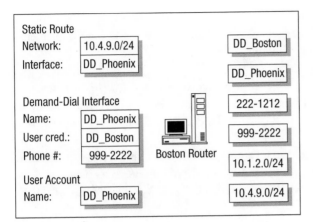

# Need to Know More?

 Search the RRAS Help file within the Windows 2000 Server operating system. The Help file provides details for configuring, implementing, and troubleshooting.

 Refer to the *Windows 2000 Server Resource Kit TCP/IP Core Networking Guide*. Detailed information is available about IP multicasting in the sections "Introduction to TCP/IP" and "Windows 2000 TCP/IP."

 Search the TechNet CD (or its online version through **www.microsoft. com**) and the *Windows 2000 Server Resource Kit* CD using the keywords "RIP", "OSPF", "NAT", "ICS", "IGMP", and "Demand-Dial".

 Refer to **www.ietf.org/ids.by.wg/nat.html**. This Web site includes a tremendous amount of information related to Network Address Translation.

# Protocol Security and IPSec

### Terms you'll need to know:

✓ IPSec

✓ Internet Key Exchange (IKE)

✓ Phase I and Phase II security associations (SA)

✓ Authentication Header (AH) protocol

✓ Encapsulated Security Payload (ESP) protocol

✓ Hash functions

✓ Diffie-Hellman (DH) encryption

### Techniques you'll need to master:

✓ Setting IPSec filters and policies

✓ Monitoring IPSec communications

✓ Troubleshooting IPSec errors

Like it or not, computer networks are not always safe places for the transfer of data. Your servers or data can be maliciously attacked in multitudes of ways, and these attacks can come from many different places both inside and outside of your private network.

Although establishing the physical security of buildings and servers is an important step, usually data must be transmitted from one computer to another. Once the data leaves the sending computer, and until the receiving computer correctly receives the data, attacks can happen to hamper the effective conveyance of the data.

Windows 2000 implements cryptography-based protection services, dynamic key management, and IP Protocol Security (IPSec) to protect data packets.

The functions of IPSec include:

➤ Protecting the integrity of the packet while en route

➤ Ensuring the confidentiality of the packet

➤ Authenticating credentials for established entities in the secured conversation

➤ Protecting computers against network protocol attacks

IPSec's end-to-end model involves the sending computer securing the data prior to transmission and the receiving computer unsecuring the data only after it has been received. For this reason, IPSec should be one of the components in a layered enterprise security plan.

# Common Types of Network Attacks

Your networks and data are vulnerable to many types of attacks. They vary in complexity and propensity for damage, but all should be anticipated. Each of these types of attacks has some sort of defense involving one or more of the components of IPSec.

## Eavesdropping

In general, the majority of network communication occurs in an unsecured or "clear-text" format, which allows an attacker who has gained access to data paths in your network to "listen in" or interpret (read) the traffic. Eavesdropping on your communications is referred to as *sniffing* or *snooping*. Without strong encryption services, your data can be read by others as it traverses the network.

## Data Modification

After an attacker has read your data, the next logical step is to alter it. An attacker can modify the data in the packet without the knowledge of the sender or receiver.

Even if you do not require confidentiality for all communications, you do not want any of your messages to be modified in transit.

## Identity Spoofing (IP Address Spoofing)

Most networks and operating systems use the IP address of a computer to identify a valid entity. In certain cases, it is possible for an IP address to be falsely assumed—a technique called *identity spoofing*. An attacker might also use special programs to construct IP packets that appear to originate from valid addresses inside the corporate intranet. After gaining access to the network with a valid IP address, the attacker can modify, reroute, or delete your data. The attacker can also conduct other types of attacks.

## Denial-of-Service Attack

Unlike a password-based attack, the denial-of-service attack prevents normal use of your computer or network by valid users.

After gaining access to your network, the attacker can do any of the following:

➤ Send invalid data to applications or network services, which causes abnormal termination or behavior of the applications or services

➤ Flood a computer or the entire network with traffic until a shutdown occurs because of the overload

➤ Block traffic, which results in a loss of access to network resources by authorized users

## Man-in-the-Middle Attack

As the name indicates, a man-in-the-middle attack occurs when someone between you and the person with whom you are communicating is actively monitoring, capturing, and controlling your communication transparently. When computers are communicating at low levels of the Network layer, the computers might not be able to determine with whom they are exchanging data.

## Compromised-Key Attack

A key is a secret code or number necessary to interpret secured information. Although obtaining a key is a difficult and resource-intensive process for an attacker, it is possible. After an attacker obtains a key, that key is referred to as a *compromised key*.

An attacker uses the compromised key to gain access to a secured communication without the sender or receiver being aware of the attack. With the compromised key, the attacker can decrypt or modify data and try to use the compromised

key to compute additional keys, which might allow the attacker access to other
secured communications.

# Attack Protection

IPSec has a number of features that significantly reduce or prevent the attacks
discussed previously:

➤ *Encapsulating Security Payload (ESP) protocol*—Provides data privacy by encrypting the IP packets.

➤ *Cryptography-based keys*—Creates a digital checksum for each IP packet. Any
modifications to the packet data alter the checksum, which indicates to the
receiving computer that the packet was modified in transit.

➤ *Mutual verification (authentication headers, or AH)*—Establishes trust between
the communicating systems; only trusted systems can communicate with each
other. IPSec combines mutual authentication with shared, cryptography-based
keys.

➤ *Packet filtering*—Determines whether communication is allowed, secured, or
blocked according to the IP address ranges, protocols, or specific protocol ports.

# How IPSec Works

The security of protocol traffic through IPSec follows steps dependent on the
configuration of various security settings. Packets not set to be secured pass through
without modification, but packets set for one or more security modifications are
changed by various components of the IPSec process. The processes are as follows:

1. An application on Computer A generates outbound packets to send to Computer B across the network.

2. Inside TCP/IP, the IPSec driver compares the outbound packets against
   IPSec filters, checking to see whether the packets need to be secured. The
   filters are associated with a filter action in IPSec security rules. You can configure IPSec rules in many combinations on a single computer. Figure 8.1
   illustrates an IPSec filter.

3. If a matched filter has to negotiate a security action, Computer A begins
   security negotiations with Computer B, using a protocol called the *Internet
   Key Exchange (IKE)*. The two computers exchange identity credentials according to the authentication method specified in the security rule. Authentication methods could be Kerberos authentication, public-key certificates,
   or a pre-shared key value (much like a password). The IKE negotiation

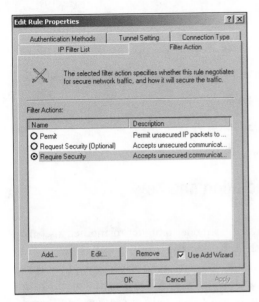

**Figure 8.1**    An IPSec filter.

establishes two types of agreements, called *security associations,* between the two computers:

➤ *Phase I IKE SA*—Specifies how the two computers trust each other and protects their negotiation.

➤ *Phase II IPSec SAs*—Consists of an agreement on how to protect a particular type of application communication.

*Note: The two SAs specify security methods and keys for each direction of communication. IKE automatically creates and refreshes a shared, secret key for each SA. The secret key is created independently at both ends without being transmitted across the network.*

4. The IPSec driver on Computer A signs the outgoing packets for integrity and optionally encrypts them for confidentially using the methods agreed upon during the negotiation. It transmits the secured packets to Computer B.

*Note: Firewalls, routers, and servers along the network path from Computer A to Computer B do not require IPSec. They simply pass along the packets in the usual manner.*

5. The IPSec driver on Computer B checks the packets for integrity and decrypts their content if necessary. It then transfers the packets to the receiving application.

# IPSec Protocols

IPSec provides four protocols for use in securing protocol packets:

➤ Internet Security Association and Key Management Protocol (ISAKMP)

➤ Oakley key determination protocol

➤ Authentication Header (AH) protocol

➤ Encapsulating Security Payload (ESP) protocol

## Internet Security Association and Key Management Protocol

Before IP packets can be transmitted from one computer to another, a security association (SA) must be established. An *SA* is a set of parameters that defines the services and mechanisms, such as keys, necessary to protect communications for a security protocol. An SA must exist between the two communicating parties using IP Security. Internet Security Association and Key Management Protocol (ISAKMP) defines a common framework to support the establishment of security associations. ISAKMP is not linked to one specific algorithm, key-generation method, or security protocol.

An SA is a combination of a mutually agreed-upon key, security protocol, and security parameters index (SPI) that together define the security used to protect the communication from sender to receiver. The SPI is a unique, identifying value in the SA used to distinguish among multiple security associations existing at the receiving computer. For example, multiple associations might exist if a computer is securely communicating with multiple computers simultaneously. This situation occurs mostly when the computer is a file server or a remote access server that serves multiple clients. In these situations, the receiving computer uses the SPI to determine which SA is used to process the incoming packets.

### Phase I SA

To ensure successful, secure communication, IKE performs a two-phase operation. Confidentiality and authentication during each phase is ensured by the use of encryption and authentication algorithms agreed on by the two computers during security negotiations. With the duties split between two phases, keying can be accomplished with great speed.

During the first phase, the two computers establish a secure, authenticated channel—the Phase I SA. It is so named to differentiate between the SAs established in each of the two phases. IKE automatically provides the necessary identity protection during this exchange. This ensures that no identity information is sent without encryption between the communicating computers, thus enabling total privacy.

Following are the steps in a Phase I negotiation:

1. *Policy negotiation*—The following four mandatory parameters are negotiated as part of the Phase I SA:

   ➤ The encryption algorithm (DES or 3DES)

   ➤ The hash algorithm (MD5 or SHA)

   ➤ The authentication method (certificate, pre-shared key, or Kerberos v5 authentication)

   ➤ The Diffie-Hellman (DH) group to be used for the base keying material

2. *DH exchange (of public values)*—Information specific to this session and its encryption is exchanged.

*Note: At no time are actual keys exchanged; only the base information needed by DH to generate the shared, secret key is exchanged. After this exchange, the IKE service on each computer generates the master key used to protect authentication.*

3. *Authentication*—The computers attempt to authenticate the DH exchange. Without successful authentication, communication cannot proceed. The master key is used, in conjunction with the negotiation algorithms and methods, to authenticate identities. The entire identity payload—including the identity type, port, and protocol—is hashed and encrypted using the keys generated from the DH exchange in the second step. The identity payload, regardless of which authentication method is used, is protected from both modification and interpretation.

The sender presents an offer for a potential security association to the receiver. The responder cannot modify the offer. Should the offer be modified, the initiator rejects the responder's message. The responder sends either a reply accepting the offer or a reply with alternatives.

Once an offer reaches agreement, Phase II SA begins.

## Phase II SA

The following are the steps in Phase II negotiation:

1. *Policy negotiation*—The IPSec computers exchange their requirements for securing the data transfer:

   ➤ The IPSec protocol (AH or ESP)

   ➤ The hash algorithm for integrity and authentication (MD5 or SHA)

   ➤ The algorithm for encryption, if requested (3DES or DES)

A common agreement is reached, and two SAs are established: one for inbound and one for outbound communication.

2. *Session-key material refresh or exchange*—IKE refreshes the keying material and new, shared, or secret keys are generated for authentication and encryption (if negotiated) of the packets. If a re-key is required, a second DH exchange (as described in the section "Phase I SA") takes place prior to this, or a refresh of the original DH is used for the re-key.

3. *Passing the SAs and keys*—The SAs and keys are passed to the IPSec driver, along with the SPI.

During this second negotiation of shared policy and keying material—this time to protect the data transfer—the Phase I SA protects the information.

As the first phase provides identity protection, the second phase provides protection by refreshing the keying material to prevent bogus SAs. IKE can accommodate a key exchange payload for an additional DH exchange if a re-key is configured (the master key Perfect Forward Secrecy [PFS] is enabled). Otherwise, IKE refreshes the keying material from the DH exchange in the first phase.

Phase II results in a pair of security associations: one SA for inbound communication and one SA for outbound, each with its own SPI and key.

The retry algorithm for a message here is almost identical to the process in Phase I, with one major difference: If this process reaches a timeout for any reason during the second or greater negotiation off the same Phase I SA, a re-negotiation of the Phase I SA is attempted. A message for Phase II received with no Phase I SA established is rejected.

Using a single Phase I SA for multiple Phase II SA negotiations makes the process extremely fast. As long as the Phase I SA does not expire, re-negotiation and re-authentication are not necessary. The number of Phase II SA negotiations that can be performed is determined by IPSec policy attributes.

## SA Lifetimes

The Phase I SA is cached to allow multiple Phase II SA negotiations (unless PFS is enabled for the master key or the session key policy lifetimes have been reached). When a key lifetime is reached for the master or session key, the SA is renegotiated and the key is refreshed or regenerated.

When the default timeout period is reached for the Phase I SA, or the master or session key lifetime is reached, the responder receives a delete message. The IKE delete message tells the responder to expire the Phase I SA. This prevents bogus Phase II SAs from being formed because Phase II SAs are valid until their lifetime is expired by the IPSec driver, independently of the Phase I SA lifetime.

IKE does not expire the Phase II SA because only the IPSec driver knows the number of seconds or bytes that have passed to reach the key lifetime.

 Use caution when setting very disparate key lifetimes, which also determine the lifetime of the SA. For example, setting a master key lifetime of eight hours and a session key lifetime of two hours can mean that you have a Phase II SA in place for almost four hours after the Phase I SA expired. This can occur if the Phase II SA is generated immediately before the Phase I SA expires.

## Oakley

Oakley is a key determination protocol that uses the Diffie-Hellman key exchange algorithm. Oakley supports Perfect Forward Secrecy (PFS), which ensures that if a single key is compromised, it permits access only to data protected by a single key. It never reuses the key that protects communications to compute additional keys and never uses the original key-generation material to compute another key.

IPSec protocols provide data and identity protection services for each IP packet by adding their own security protocol header to each IP packet.

## Authentication Header

Authentication Header (AH) provides authentication, integrity, and anti-replay for the entire packet (both the IP header and the data payload carried in the packet). It does not provide confidentiality, which means it does not encrypt the data. The data is readable but protected from modification. Integrity and authentication are provided by the placement of the AH between the IP header and the Transport layer (Layer 4) protocol header, which is shown as TCP/UDP in Figure 8.2. AH uses an IP protocol ID of 51 to identify itself in the IP header.

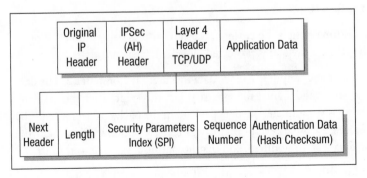

**Figure 8.2** AH fields.

AH can be used alone or in combination with the Encapsulating Security Payload (ESP) protocol.

The AH contains the following fields:

➤ *Next Header*—Identifies the next header that uses the IP protocol ID. For example, the value might be 6 to indicate TCP.

➤ *Length*—Indicates the length of the AH.

➤ *Security Parameters Index (SPI)*—Used in combination with the destination address and the security protocol (AH or ESP) to identify the correct security association for the communication. (For more information, see the section "Key Management" later in this chapter.) The receiver uses this value to determine with which security association this packet is identified.

➤ *Sequence Number*—Provides anti-replay protection for the SA. It is a 32-bit, incrementally increasing number (starting from 1) that is never allowed to cycle and that indicates the packet number sent over the security association for the communication. The receiver checks this field to verify that a packet for a security association with this number has not been received already. If one has been received, the packet is rejected.

➤ *Authentication Data*—Contains the Integrity Check Value (ICV) that is used to verify the integrity of the message. The receiver calculates the hash value and checks it against this value (calculated by the sender) to verify integrity.

AH signs the entire packet for integrity, except certain fields in the IP header that can change, such as the Time To Live and Type of Service fields.

## Encapsulating Security Payload

Encapsulating Security Payload (ESP) provides confidentiality, authentication, integrity, and anti-replay protection for data packets. You can use ESP alone or in combination with AH.

ESP does not normally sign the entire packet unless it is being tunneled; ordinarily, just the IP data payload is protected, not the IP header.

For example, a user at Computer 1 sends data to a user on Computer 2. The data payload is encrypted and signed for integrity. Upon receipt, after the integrity verification process is complete, the data payload in the packet is decrypted. The user on Computer 2 can be certain that it was really Computer 1 who sent the data, that the data was unmodified, and that no one else was able to read it.

ESP indicates itself in the IP header using the IP protocol ID of 50. The ESP header is placed prior to the Transport layer header (TCP or UDP) or the IP payload data for other IP protocol types. Figure 8.3 illustrates the ESP header fields.

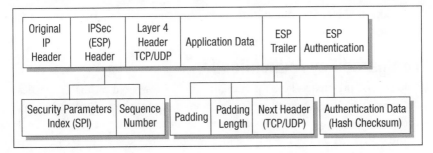

**Figure 8.3**   ESP header fields.

The ESP header contains the following fields:

➤ *Security Parameters Index*—When used in combination with the destination address and the security protocol (AH or ESP), identifies the correct security association for the communication. The receiver uses this value to determine the security association with which this packet should be identified.

➤ *Sequence Number*—Provides anti-replay protection for the SA. It is a 32-bit, incrementally increasing number (starting from 1) that indicates the packet number sent over the security association for the communication. The sequence number is never allowed to cycle. The receiver checks this field to verify that a packet for a security association with this number has not been received already. If one has been received, the packet is rejected.

The ESP trailer contains the following fields:

➤ *Padding*—Uses 0 to 255 bytes for 32-bit alignment with the block size of the block cipher.

➤ *Padding Length*—Indicates the length of the Padding field in bytes. This field is used by the receiver to discard the Padding field.

➤ *Next Header*—Identifies the nature of the payload, such as TCP or UDP.

The ESP authentication trailer contains the following field:

➤ *Authentication Data*—Contains the Integrity Check Value (ICV), and a message authentication code used to verify the sender's identity and message integrity. The ICV is calculated for the ESP header, the payload data, and the ESP trailer.

# Certificate Handling

Specific methods are needed to use the Certificate Services capabilities in Windows 2000. All service levels of IPSec handling must achieve an agreement about the services used before communication can begin or continue between the computers involved in data conveyance.

## Pre-Shared Key Authentication

IPSec can use pre-shared keys for authentication. Pre-shared means the parties must agree on a shared, secret key that becomes part of the IPSec policy. During security negotiation, information is encrypted before transmission using the shared key and decrypted on the receiving end using the same key. If the receiver can decrypt the information, identities are considered authenticated.

Pre-shared key methodology is provided only for interoperability purposes and to adhere to the IPSec standards set forth by the Internet Engineering Task Force (IETF). To safely use this authentication method, the policy must be restricted to administrator-only read and write access, encrypted for privacy when communicated between the domain controller and domain member computers, and restricted to system-only read access on each computer.

 Microsoft does not recommend frequent use of pre-shared key authentication because the authentication key is stored unprotected in the IPSec policy.

## Public-Key Cryptography

IPSec implements public-key cryptography methods for authentication (certificate signing) and key exchange (the Diffie-Hellman algorithm). Public-key cryptography has all the capabilities of secret-key cryptography but is generally more secure because it requires two keys—one for signing and encrypting the data and one for verifying the signature and decrypting the data. Public-key cryptography is often referred to as *asymmetric cryptography,* which simply means that two keys are required for the process. Each user has a private key known only to that person and a public key that is widely distributed.

# Hash Functions

Hash Message Authentication Codes (HMAC) "sign" packets to verify that the information received is exactly the same as the information sent (integrity). This is critical when data is exchanged over unsecured media.

HMACs provide integrity by means of a hash function (algorithm) combined with a shared, secret key. A hash is more commonly described as a signature on the packet, but in a technical sense, a hash differs from a digital signature: A hash uses a secret, shared key, but a digital signature uses public-key technology and the sending computer's key.

*Note: Hash functions are also sometimes referred to as message digests or one-way transforms. One-way transforms or functions are so named for two reasons: Each party must perform the computation on their respective end, and it is easy to go from message to digest but mathematically infeasible to go from digest to message. Conversely, two-way encryption functions can go either way.*

The hash signature itself is actually a cryptographic checksum or Message Integrity Code (MIC) that each party must compute to verify the message. For example, the sending computer uses an HMAC algorithm and shared key to compute the checksum for the message and includes it with the packet. The receiving computer must perform an HMAC computation on the received message and compare it to the original (included in the packet from the sender). If the message has changed in transit, the hash values are different and the packet is rejected.

You can choose between two hash functions when setting IPSec policy:

➤ *HMAC-MD5*—Message Digest 5 (MD5) is based on RFC 1321. MD5 makes four passes over the data blocks using a different number constant for each message word on every pass. This equates to 64 32-bit constants used during the MD5 computation and a 128-bit key.

➤ *HMAC-SHA*—Secure Hash Algorithm (SHA) was developed by the National Institute of Standards and Technology as described in Federal Information Standard PUB 180-1. The SHA process is closely modeled after MD5. SHA uses 79 32-bit constants during the computation, which results in a 160-bit key that is used for integrity check. Longer key lengths provide greater security, so SHA is considered the stronger of the two.

# DES

Data Encryption Standard (DES) uses a 56-bit key and maps a 64-bit input block into a 64-bit output block. The key appears to be a 64-bit key, but one bit in each of the 8 bytes is used for odd parity, resulting in 56 bits of usable key.

The input block is initially put through rounds to produce a 64-bit output block. A round is like shuffling a deck of cards—it is a randomization process to ensure that different values are produced each time. This key is used to generate 16 48-bit, per-round keys. Each round takes as its input the outcome (key) of the previous round plus the 48-bit key, and produces the next 56-bit key. After the 16th round, the key is permuted with the inverse of the initial permutation.

Cipher Block Chaining (CBC) hides patterns of identical blocks of data within a packet. An initialization vector (an initial random number) is the first random block to encrypt and decrypt a block of data. Different random blocks are used in conjunction with the secret key to encrypt each block. This ensures that identical clear-text data (unsecured data) results in unique, encrypted data blocks. Repeats can compromise the security of the key by providing a pattern with which an attacker can crack your encryption. A lack of repeats also prevents data expansion during encryption.

Windows 2000 IPSec supports the use of the following:

➤ *3DES*—This is highly secure and therefore slower in performance. 3DES processes each block three times, using a unique key each time:

  ➤ Encryption on the block with key 1

  ➤ Decryption on the block with key 2

  ➤ Encryption on the block with key 3

*Note: 3DES is the default in Windows 2000.*

➤ *DES*—This is provided when the high security and overhead of 3DES is not necessary.

# Key Management

A key is a secret code or number required to read, modify, or verify secured data. Keys are used in conjunction with algorithms (a mathematical process) to secure data. Windows 2000 automatically handles key generation and implements the following keying properties that maximize protection:

➤ *Dynamic re-keying*—IPSec policy controls how often a new key is generated during the communication, using a method called *dynamic re-keying.* The communication is sent in blocks, and each block of data is secured with a different key. This prevents an attacker who has obtained part of a communication, and the corresponding session keys, from obtaining the rest of the communication. IPSec policy lets you control how often a new key is generated. If no values are configured, keys are regenerated automatically at default intervals.

➤ *Key lengths*—Every time the length of a key is increased by one bit, the number of possible keys doubles, making it exponentially more difficult to break the key. IPSec policy provides multiple algorithms to allow for short or long key lengths.

➤ *Key material generation: the Diffie-Hellman algorithm*—To enable secure communication, two computers must be able to gain the same shared key (session key) without sending the key across a network because that would severely compromise the secret.

The Diffie-Hellman algorithm (DH) predates Rivest-Shamir-Adleman (RSA) encryption and offers better performance. It is one of the oldest and most secure algorithms used for key exchange.

The two parties publicly exchange some keying information, which Windows 2000 additionally protects with a hash function signature. Neither party ever exchanges the actual key; however, after the exchange of keying material, each is able to generate the identical shared key. At no time is the actual key ever exchanged.

DH keying material exchanged by the two parties can be based on 96 or 128 bytes of keying material, known as *DH groups.* The strength of the DH group is directly related to the strength of the key. Strong DH groups combined with longer key lengths increase the degree of computational difficulty in breaking the key.

IPSec uses the DH algorithm to provide the keying material for all other encryption keys. DH on its own provides no authentication; in the Windows 2000 IPSec implementation, identities are authenticated after the DH exchange takes place.

# IPSec Modes

You can implement the IPSec protocols, AH and ESP, in either tunnel or transport mode. There are four possible combinations of modes and protocols:

➤ AH in transport mode

➤ AH in tunnel mode

➤ ESP in transport mode

➤ ESP in tunnel mode

In practice, AH in tunnel mode is not used because it protects the same data that AH in transport mode protects.

The AH and ESP headers do not change between tunnel or transport mode. The difference is what they are protecting, the IP packet or an IP payload.

## Transport Mode

In transport mode, AH and ESP protect the transport header. In this mode, AH and ESP intercept the packets flowing from the Transport layer into the Network layer and provide the configured security.

When security is not enabled, Transport layer packets such as TCP and UDP flow into the Network layer, IP, which adds the IP header and calls to the Data Link layer. When security in the Transport layer is enabled, the Transport layer packets flow into the IPSec component. The IPSec component is implemented as part of the Network layer (when integrated with the operating system). The IPSec component adds the AH, ESP, or both headers and invokes the part of the Network layer that adds the Network layer header.

You use the transport mode of IPSec only when you want security from end to end. As stated earlier, the routers look mostly at the Network layer in making routing decisions, and the routers do not and should not change anything beyond the Network layer header. Inserting transport mode IPSec headers for packets flowing through a router is a violation of this rule.

When both AH and ESP are used in transport mode, ESP should be applied first. The reason is obvious. If the transport packet is first protected using AH and then using ESP, the data integrity is applicable only for the transport payload because the ESP header is added later. This is not desirable because the data integrity should be calculated over as much data as possible.

If the packet is protected using AH after it is protected using ESP, then the data integrity applies to the ESP payload that contains the transport payload.

# Tunnel Mode

You use the tunnel mode in cases when a device that did not originate the packets provides security—as is the case with virtual private networks (VPNs)—or when the packet needs to be secured to an intermediate destination that is different from the actual destination. It is also used when a router provides security services for packets it is forwarding. In tunnel mode, IPSec encapsulates an IP packet with IPSec headers and adds an outer IP header.

An IPSec tunnel-mode packet has two IP headers, inner and outer. The host constructs the inner header, and the device providing the security services adds the outer header. This can be either the host or a router. Nothing precludes a host from providing tunnel-mode security services end to end. However, in this case there is no advantage to using tunnel mode instead of transport mode. In fact, if the security services are provided end to end, transport mode is better because it does not add an extra IP header.

Authentication of the VPN client occurs at two different levels: The computer is authenticated, and then the user is authenticated.

## IPSec Computer Authentication

Mutual computer authentication of the VPN client and the VPN server is performed when you establish an IPSec ESP security association (SA) through the exchange of computer certificates. IPSec Phase I and Phase II negotiation occurs, and an IPSec SA is established with an agreed encryption algorithm, hash algorithm, and encryption keys.

To use Layer 2 Tunneling Protocol (L2TP) over IPSec, you must install a computer certificate on both the VPN client and the VPN server. You can obtain computer certificates automatically by configuring an auto-enrollment Windows 2000 Group Policy or manually by using the Certificates snap-in.

### IPSec User-Level Authentication

The user attempting the Point-to-Point Tunneling Protocol (PPTP) connection is authenticated using PPP-based user authentication protocols such as EAP, MS-CHAP, CHAP, SPAP, and PAP. Because IPSec encrypts the PPP connection establishment process, you can use any PPP authentication method. Mutual user-level authentication occurs if you use MS-CHAP v2 or EAP-TLS.

# IP Packet Filtering

An IP address identifies a computer system's location on the network. Each IP address is separated internally into two parts, a network ID and a computer ID:

➤ The network ID identifies a single network within a larger TCP/IP network (that is, a network of networks). This ID is also used to identify each network uniquely within the larger network. Figure 8.4 illustrates a filter for a particular network.

➤ The computer ID for each device (such as a workstation or router) identifies a system within its own network.

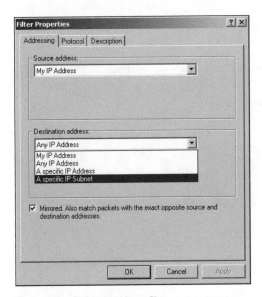

**Figure 8.4**   Network address filter.

# Filters and Rules

A rule provides the ability to trigger security negotiations for a communication based on the source, destination, and type of IP traffic, a process called *IP packet filtering*. This provides a way for the network administrator to define precisely what IP traffic triggers are secured, blocked, or passed through (unsecured).

Each filter within an IP filter list describes a particular subset of network traffic to be secured, both for inbound and outbound traffic:

➤ *Inbound filters*—Apply to traffic received, allowing the receiving computer to match the traffic with the IP filter list. Inbound filters respond to requests for secure communication or match the traffic with an existing SA and process the secured packets.

➤ *Outbound filters*—Apply to traffic leaving a computer toward a destination, triggering a security negotiation that must take place before traffic is sent.

*Note: You must have a filter to cover any traffic for which the associated rule applies.*

A filter contains the following parameters:

➤ *The source and destination address of the IP packet*—These can be configured from a very granular level, such as a single IP address, to a global level that encompasses an entire subnet or network.

➤ *The protocol over which the packet is being transferred*—This defaults to cover all protocols in the TCP/IP protocol suite. However, it can be configured to an individual protocol level to meet special requirements, including custom protocol numbers.

➤ *The source and destination port of the protocol for TCP and UDP*—This also defaults to cover all ports but can be configured to apply to only packets sent or received on a specific protocol port.

## Filter Actions

The filter action sets the security requirements for the communication. These requirements are specified in a list of security methods contained in the filter action, including which algorithms, security protocols, and key properties are to be used. Figure 8.5 illustrates a rule with specific filter actions set.

A filter action can also be configured as:

➤ *A pass-through policy*—Does not allow secure communication. IPSec simply ignores traffic in this case. This is appropriate for traffic that cannot be secured because the remote computer is not IPSec-enabled, traffic that is not sensitive enough to require protection, or traffic that provides its own security (such as Kerberos, SSL, and PPTP protocols).

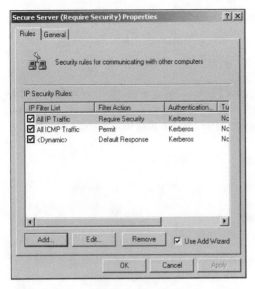

**Figure 8.5**   Rule with filter action settings.

➤ *A blocking policy*—Stops communication from a rogue computer.

➤ *A policy that negotiates for security but still enables communication with non-IPSec-enabled computers*—You can configure a filter action to use "fallback to clear." This allows secure communications if the client is able, but also allows clear-text communication with clients that cannot use secure communications. If the initiator of an IKE negotiation receives a reply from the responder, then the negotiation does not allow fallback to clear.

# Troubleshooting IPSec

When things go wrong, where should you look to find the answers? Most of the time, the problem is an inability for the client and server to agree on one or more components of the process. Examining the conditions of desired communications and the aspects of the failure lets you make a complete diagnosis of the problem.

## Normally Successful Communications Fail

If two computers have been communicating successfully and secured communication between them suddenly fails, do the following:

1. Ping the other computer to verify the computer is still on the network. You should receive a message indicating IPSec is being negotiated. If you do not, check whether the list of acceptable security methods in your filter action

has changed since the last communication with that computer. The old security associations based on previous security methods might still be in effect. If so, try the next step.

 If you are using unmodified default policies, ping will not be blocked by IPSec. However, if you have created custom policies and have not exempted the ICMP protocol used by the ping tool, it might erroneously fail.

2. Restart the policy agent. This clears any old security associations.

## Other Causes of Failure

Failure of IPSec is usually a result of misconfiguration of some sort. Whether the problem is that several administrators have made conflicting changes or that some dependent piece of configuration has been removed, there are several key items to check:

➤ Try a policy integrity check to verify that changes made to any policy settings have been updated in Active Directory or the Registry.

➤ If you have removed an existing computer from a domain or have changed to using local policy instead of Active Directory policy, you might have to restart the policy agent. Otherwise, the policy agent continues to attempt to reach Active Directory and does not use Registry policy.

➤ Multihomed computers have multiple default routes, which might cause problems.

## IPSec Policy Mismatch Error

Negotiations can fail due to incompatible IPSec policy settings. Follow these steps to correct the problem:

1. Run Event Viewer and examine the security log. Recent events include attempts at IKE negotiation with a description of their success or failure.

2. Check the security log on the computer specified by the IP address in the log message.

3. Determine the cause of the policy mismatch and fix it:

➤ Verify that authentication methods are compatible.

➤ Verify that there is at least one compatible security method.

## "Bad SPI" Messages in Event Viewer

The bad SPI error might occur if a key lifetime value is set too low or the SA has expired but the sender continues to transmit data to the receiver. It is a benign error, so you should take notice only if a large amount of these messages are being logged. To determine and correct the problem, follow these steps:

1. Run IPSec Monitor.

2. Examine the number of re-keys.

3. If the number of re-keys is very large compared to the amount of time the connections have been active, set the key lifetimes in the policy to be longer. Good values for high-traffic Ethernet connections are larger than 50MB and longer than 5 minutes.

## Tools and Settings

The following sections describe tools and procedures you can use to determine whether IPSec is active and to make sure IPSec-secured communication is successful.

### Using Ping to Verify a Valid Network Connection

The following ping procedure determines whether standard, unsecured communication can take place. This allows you to separate network problems from IPSec issues:

1. Open a command prompt window.

2. Type "ping *<IP address>*".

### IPSec Monitor

The IPSec Monitor allows for the enumeration of associations created between computers using IPSec. Run the tool from the computer you wish to test:

1. Click Start|Run.

2. Type "ipsecmon *<computername>*".

When IPSec Monitor opens, you see a message in the lower-right corner indicating whether IPSec is enabled on the computer. For IPSec to be enabled, a policy must be assigned. However, no policies are listed in the IPSec Monitor Security Association list unless an SA with another computer is currently active. Figure 8.6 illustrates the monitor program.

The IPSec Monitor can confirm whether your secured communications are successful by displaying the active security associations on local or remote computers.

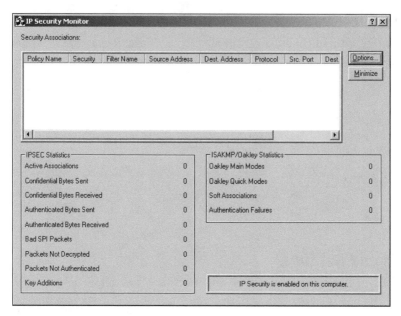

**Figure 8.6** The IP Security Monitor.

You also can use IPSec Monitor to determine whether there is a pattern of authentication or security association failures, possibly indicating incompatible security policy settings. You can run the IPSec Monitor on the local computer or remotely if you have a network connection to the remote computer.

The IPSec Monitor displays an entry for each active security association. Each entry includes the name of the active IPSec policy, the active filter action and IP filter list (including details of the active filter), and the tunnel endpoint (if one was specified). It can also provide statistics to aid in performance tuning and troubleshooting, including the following statistics:

➤ The number and type of active security associations.

➤ The total number of master and session keys. Successful IPSec security associations initially cause one master key and one session key. Subsequent key regenerations are shown as additional session keys.

➤ The total number of confidential (ESP) or authenticated (ESP or AH) bytes sent or received.

*Note: Because ESP provides authenticity and confidentiality, both counters are incremented.*

The refresh rate is the only configurable option. By default, the statistics update every 15 seconds. The statistics are accumulated with each communication that uses IPSec.

## IPSec Entries in Event Viewer

The IPSec policy agent makes entries to the system log to indicate the source of its policy. It also indicates the polling interval specified by the active policy for checking for policy changes in the Active Directory. If you edit the active IPSec policy on the local computer, the changes take effect immediately.

You can also see whether the computer is using local policy or policy from the Active Directory by viewing the event log. Specifically, examine the system log informational entry by the IPSec policy agent.

## TCP/IP Properties

By displaying the properties for Internet Protocol (TCP/IP), you can see the active IPSec policy. If the computer is running local IPSec policy, the name is displayed in an editable form. If the computer is running policy assigned through the Active Directory Group Policy, the name and dialog are grayed out, and they are not editable. Consult the Windows 2000 Help for instructions on displaying TCP/IP properties.

## Broken Links in Policy Components

Because Active Directory treats the last information saved as current, if multiple administrators are editing a policy it is possible to break the links between policy components. For example:

➤ Policy A uses Filter A.

➤ Policy B uses Filter B. (This means that Filter A has a link to Policy A, and Filter B links to Policy B.)

➤ Admin 1 edits Policy A and adds a rule that uses Filter C.

➤ At the same time, Admin 2 edits Policy B from a different location and adds a rule that also uses Filter C.

If both administrators save the changes simultaneously, it is possible for Filter C to link to both Policy A and Policy B. Because that is unlikely, if Policy A is saved last, it overwrites the link from Filter C to Policy B. Filter C only links to Policy A. This causes problems when Filter C is modified. Only Policy A picks up the new changes; Policy B does not.

The policy integrity check eliminates this problem by verifying the links in all IPSec policies. It is a good idea to run the integrity check after making modifications to a policy.

To check policy integrity, follow these steps:

1. Start the IP Security Management snap-in.

2. Click Action.

3. Point to All Tasks, and click Check Policy Integrity. (See Figure 8.7.)

All the IPSec policies listed in the console are checked. If any filters or settings are invalid, you see an error message.

## Restarting the Policy Agent

Restarting the policy agent might be necessary to clear up old SAs or to force a policy download from the Active Directory to domain clients. You must restart the computer to properly restart the policy agent. Restarting the policy agent also forces the restart of the IPSec driver.

Use Event Viewer to determine possible causes of failure if the policy agent does not start.

## Reinstalling IPSec Components

If the files necessary for IPSec components, such as IKE, the IPSec policy agent, or the IPSec Driver, have been removed or deleted, you can reinstall the IPSec components by removing and reinstalling TCP/IP. The IPSec components are reinstalled as part of the Internet Protocol installation.

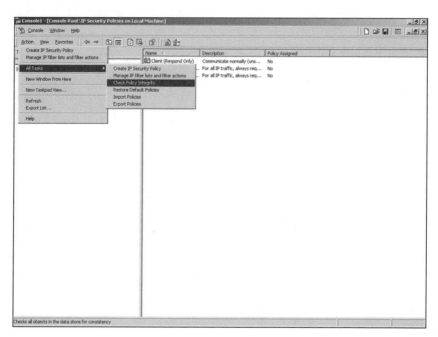

**Figure 8.7** IP security policy integrity check.

# Practice Questions

## Question 1

You are the network administrator for the acme.local domain. The network consists of a Windows 2000 domain in mixed mode. Windows NT 4 and Windows 2000 file servers are used for the departmental file storage and print servers.

During the past month, there have been some security breaches on one of the file servers that house the sales information. The file server that was breached is a Windows NT 4 server. You move the files to one of the Windows 2000 servers. After you move the files to the Windows 2000 server, you configure the IPSec properties to the secure server configuration.

Now, all sales users except those using Windows 2000 Professional are complaining that they can't access the files. What is the problem?

○ a.  The non-Windows 2000 Professional clients need the Active Directory client installed.

○ b.  The domain needs to be in native mode for IPSec to function properly.

○ c.  The **xcopy** command was not used to copy the files.

○ d.  The file server has a configuration that the down-level clients do not support.

The correct answer is d. Only Windows 2000 Professional computers support the IPSec feature. The other Windows clients will fail to access the files with the secure server option configured. The Active Directory client will not provide support for IPSec, even though it does provide excellent support for many other Active Directory features and accessibility. Therefore, answer a is incorrect. The domain does not have to be in native mode to support IPSec, so answer b is incorrect. IPSec is independent of Windows 2000 Active Directory. Because some users can access the files, the file permissions are not the issue. Therefore, the **xcopy** command is not the problem, and answer c is incorrect.

## Question 2

> You are structuring the organizational units (OUs) for the acme.local do-
> main. The marketing OU is working on some extremely important and se-
> cure documents that must be locked down. You have established NTFS
> permissions for the file server but would like to implement more security.
> You decide to enforce IPSec for communication to the server.
>
> You need to configure all of the different options available with the IPSec
> policy. You want to configure the MD5 or SHA option. Which portion of the
> IPSec feature set do you need to configure?
>
> ○ a.   Integrity algorithm
>
> ○ b.   Encryption algorithm
>
> ○ c.   Authentication type
>
> ○ d.   Session key settings

The correct answer is a. MD5 and SHA are both options for the Hash Message
Authentication Codes (HMAC) integrity algorithm. This algorithm is responsible for ensuring that the information received is the same as the information
sent. The encryption algorithms are based on the 3DES and DES standards.
Therefore, answer b is incorrect. The authentication typically used is Kerberos,
but certificates are also an option. Therefore, answer c is incorrect. The session
key settings are configurations for regeneration of the key. Therefore, answer d is
incorrect.

# Question 3

As the network administrator for the sales.acme.local domain, you are tasked with the responsibility of securing all data communications from the sales staff to the file server that holds the sales data. You have configured a group policy for the sales organizational unit (OU), of which all of the users are members. You also have configured a special group policy for the OU that has the sales file server as a member.

You now want to make sure that the IPSec configuration is complete. You need to configure the portion of IPSec that ensures the key generation is unique for additional keys and the original key generation is never used more than once. What configuration will you use?

○ a. AH security method

○ b. Perfect Forward Secrecy

○ c. ESP security method

○ d. Diffie-Hellman Group

The correct answer is b. The Perfect Forward Secrecy configuration ensures that the key generation is unique for all additional keys that are generated, and the original key is not used to generate any addition information. The AH and ESP security methods are configurations that either address data integrity or provide data integrity and encryption, respectively. Therefore, answers a and c are incorrect. The Diffie-Hellman group determines the key strength, so answer d is incorrect.

## Question 4

You need to configure security for the IP traffic from one particular file server in the environment. The information being transmitted is highly sensitive and needs the best security possible. The following describes the security requirements:

- The data should be protected with anti-replay security.
- The data should be encrypted when sent over the network.
- The reuse of keys to produce other keys should not be allowed.
- The algorithm to produce the data integrity should be the best available.

You implement the following configurations for the file server IPSec group policy:

- AH is set to use SHA.
- ESP is implemented to use SHA.
- Perfect Forward Secrecy is configured.
- Kerberos is used for authentication.
- DES encryption is used.

Which requirements are met with these settings? [Check all correct answers]

❑ a. The data should be protected with anti-replay security.

❑ b. The data should be encrypted when sent over the network.

❑ c. The reuse of keys to produce other keys should not be allowed.

❑ d. The algorithm to produce the data integrity should be the best available.

The correct answers are a, b, c, and d. All of the requirements are met with the configurations that were made. Authentication Header will ensure that the data cannot be replayed, and ESP will encrypt the data for transport. Perfect Forward Secrecy will ensure that the keys are not reused to produce other keys. SHA will enforce the best data integrity possible for the transportation of the information.

# Question 5

You need to configure security for the IP traffic from one particular file server in the environment. The information being transmitted is highly sensitive and needs the best security possible. The following describes the security requirements:

- The data should be protected with anti-replay security.

- The data should be encrypted when sent over the network.

- The reuse of keys to produce other keys should not be allowed.

- The algorithm to produce the data integrity should be the best available.

You implement the following configurations for the file server IPSec group policy:

- AH is implemented to use MD5.

- Perfect Forward Secrecy is configured.

- Kerberos is used for authentication.

Which requirements are met with these settings? [Check all correct answers]

- ❏ a.  The data should be protected with anti-replay security.

- ❏ b.  The data should be encrypted when sent over the network.

- ❏ c.  The reuse of keys to produce other keys should not be allowed.

- ❏ d.  The algorithm to produce the data integrity should be the best available.

The correct answers are a and c. The use of AH will ensure that the data cannot be replayed. Perfect Forward Secrecy will ensure that the keys will not be reused to produce other keys. Encryption was not configured for this file server because the ESP configuration was not made. Therefore, answer b is incorrect. SHA is a better algorithm for data integrity, so the use of MD5 will not suffice here. Therefore, answer d is incorrect.

## Question 6

You want to configure the Windows 2000 file server that contains the Human Resources information in such a way that all users who communicate with the server use IPSec. The following is a list of the requirements for communication with this HR file server:

- A user from HR cannot access the files if he or she is using a Windows NT client.

- All data that is sent is encrypted.

- The data encryption should use the best security.

- Certificates should be used for authentication.

The file server is configured with the following:

- A group policy object (GPO) is configured for the OU that houses the HR file server and HR computers.

- The IPSec policy within the GPO is configured for a secure server configuration.

- The ESP setting is set to use SHA encryption in the GPO.

- The authentication is set up to use Kerberos.

Which requirements are met with these configurations? [Check all correct answers]

- ❏ a. A user from HR cannot access the files if he or she is using a Windows NT client.

- ❏ b. All data that is sent is encrypted.

- ❏ c. The data encryption should use the best security.

- ❏ d. Certificates should be used for authentication.

The correct answers are a, b, and c. The configurations that were made will configure the file server to fulfill all of the requirements except the certificate authentication. Windows NT clients do not support the use of certificates, so by requiring certificates, answer a is correct. The configuration of ESP ensures that data is encrypted, making answer b correct. SHA is the best encryption that can be configured, which is better than the alternative MD5 encryption, making answer c correct. Separate settings are needed for authentication by certificates (such as Smart Cards). Therefore, answer d incorrect.

# Question 7

You want to configure the Windows 2000 file server that contains the Human Resources information in such a way that all users who communicate with the server use IPSec. The following is a list of the requirements for communication with this HR file server:

- A user from HR cannot access the files if he or she is using a Windows NT client.

- All data that is sent is encrypted.

- The data encryption should use the best security.

- Certificates should be used for authentication.

The file server is configured with the following:

- A group policy object (GPO) is configured for the OU that houses the HR client computers.

- The IPSec policy within the GPO is configured for a secure server configuration.

- The ESP setting is set to use SHA encryption in the GPO.

- The authentication is set up to use Kerberos.

Which requirements are met with the configurations? [Check all correct answers]

❏ a. A user from HR cannot access the files if he or she is using a Windows NT client.

❏ b. All data that is sent is encrypted.

❏ c. The data encryption should use the best security.

❏ d. Certificates should be used for authentication.

There are no correct answers to this question. Because the only group policy set for the computers is on the client computers, the file server does not have the correct configuration. The file server must be placed in the HR OU or have another group policy configured for the OU for which it is a member.

# Question 8

> You have just implemented a group policy to configure IPSec on all of the Windows 2000 Professional computers and Windows 2000 Servers that are members of the HR, IT, and Sales organizational units (OUs). There seems to be no difference in the communication or overhead with the transfer of information due to the IPSec configurations. You would like to check whether IPSec is running on the machines that are currently communicating with one another. What should you do?
>
> ○ a. View the IPSec properties under the IP configuration for the NIC.
>
> ○ b. Run Performance Monitor and log the IP object.
>
> ○ c. From a command prompt, run ipsecmon.
>
> ○ d. From a command prompt, run ping.

The correct answer is c. The ipsecmon tool will allow you to check whether IPSec is running on computers that are currently communicating. Using the **net view** command will only display the computers and shares available on the network. Therefore, answer a is incorrect. Performance Monitor will not log any information about the status of IPSec on the computer. Therefore, answer b is incorrect. Ping is a tool used to determine IP stack configurations. Therefore, answer d is incorrect.

# Need to Know More?

Doraswamy, Naganand, and Dan Harkins. *IPSec—The New Security Standard for the Internet, Intranets and Virtual Private Networks.* Prentice Hall: Lower Saddle River, N.J., 1999. ISBN 0130118982. The book details the IPSec components and the underlying configurations within the group policies.

Search the TechNet CD (or its online version through **www.microsoft. com**) and the *Windows 2000 Server Resource Kit* CD using the keywords "IPSec", "Tunnel Mode", "ESP near AH", "Diffie-Hellman", and "IKE".

For the latest IETF IPSec drafts, go to **www.ietf.org/html.charters/ ipsec-charter.html**.

For the latest IETF L2TP drafts, go to **www.ietf.org/html.charters/ pppext-charter.html**.

# Certificate Services

**Terms you'll need to understand:**

✓ Encryption
✓ Digital signatures
✓ Certificates
✓ Public-key infrastructure
✓ Authentication Header
✓ Encapsulated Security Payload
✓ Enterprise certificate authority
✓ Standalone certificate authority
✓ Subordinate certificate authorities

**Techniques you'll need to master:**

✓ Understanding how security services use certificates
✓ Using Group Policy to control the use of certificates
✓ Choosing the appropriate certificate authority

As the amount of data stored on and transferred between computers increases, so does the need for security. Many companies now leverage public networks (the Internet, for example) as part of their private networks by configuring virtual private networks (VPN), exposing their data to the world; mobile users have lightweight computers that are easy to carry, thus easy to steal; and impersonators may attempt to present bogus data in the hopes of gaining information based on the work done by others. Protection of data is a significant priority. With Windows 2000, the Certificate Services have been expanded beyond the Secure Sockets Layer (SSL) implementations available in Windows NT 4 to include the entire operating system, all of the computers and users on the network, and, potentially, all of the data transferred.

# Concepts of Cryptography

Cryptography is the science of protecting data by encrypting it from cleartext into ciphertext. Without the "secret decoder ring," you cannot read the file. This encryption is done by passing the raw data through some type of encryption key, making it unreadable to any except those who possess the decryption key. This ciphertext is nearly useless on its own, because a decryption key is required to put the data back into a readable state. In the broadest of terms, the two primary types of encryption are *secret* and *public*.

In secret (or symmetric) key cryptography, the encryption and decryption keys are identical. The two participants who communicate using this technology must securely exchange encryption/decryption keys before they can legitimately exchange encrypted data.

In contrast, the fundamental property of public-key (PK) cryptography is that the encryption and decryption keys are different. Encryption with a public key is a "one-way" function: A different decryption key (related but not identical to the encryption key) turns the ciphertext back into plain text. For PK cryptography, every user has a pair of keys consisting of a public key and a private key. By making the public key available, you can enable others to send you encrypted data that can only be decrypted using your private key.

Similarly, you can transform data using your private key such that others can verify it originated with you. This verification is called a *digital signature*.

The separation between public and private keys in PK cryptography has fostered a number of new technologies: The most important of these are:

➤ Digital signatures

➤ Entity authentication

➤ Secret key agreement via public key

➤ Bulk data encryption without prior shared secrets

There are a number of well-known PK cryptographic algorithms. Some, such as RSA (Rivest-Shamir-Adleman) and ECC (Elliptic Curve Cryptography), are general purpose in the sense that they can support all of the operations in the preceding list. Others support only a subset of these capabilities. Some examples include the Digital Signature Algorithm (DSA, which is part of the U.S. government's Digital Signature Standard, FIPS 186), which is useful only for digital signatures, and Diffie-Hellman (D-H), which is used for secret-key agreement.

## Digital Signatures

Perhaps the most important aspect of public-key cryptography is that of creating and validating *digital signatures*. This process is based on a mathematical algorithm that combines the private key with the data to be "signed" such that:

➤ Only someone possessing the private key could have created the digital signature.

➤ Anyone with access to the corresponding public key can verify the digital signature.

➤ Any modification of the signed data (even changing only a single bit in a large file) invalidates the digital signature.

Digital signatures are themselves just data, so they can be transported along with the signed data they "protect." For example, Joe can create an email message for Stephanie and send the signature along with the message text, providing Stephanie the information required to verify the message origin. In addition, digital signatures provide a way to verify that data has not been tampered with (either accidentally or intentionally) while in transit from the source to the destination.

## Entity Authentication

Entity authentication guarantees that the sender of data is the entity that the receiver thinks it is. One possible method involves the data receiver, Stephanie, sending a challenge to the data sender, Joe, encrypted with Joe's public key. Joe then decodes this challenge and sends it back to Stephanie, proving that he has access to the private key associated with the public key Stephanie used to issue the challenge.

An alternative is for Stephanie to send a plain-text challenge to Joe. Joe then combines the challenge with other information, which is digitally signed. Stephanie uses Joe's public key to verify the signature and prove Joe has the associated private key. The challenge makes this message unique.

## Secret Key Agreement via Public Key

Another feature of PK cryptography is that it permits two parties to agree on a shared secret using public, and nonsecure, communication networks. Basically, Joe and Stephanie each generate a random number that will form half of the shared secret key. Joe then sends his half of the secret to Stephanie encrypted using her public key, and Stephanie sends her half to Joe encrypted with his public key. Each side can then decrypt the message received from the other party, extract the half of the shared secret they did not generate, and combine the two halves to create the shared secret. Once the protocol is completed, the shared secret can be used for securing other communications.

## Bulk Data Encryption without Prior Shared Secrets

The fourth major technology enabled by PK cryptography is the ability to encrypt bulk data without the establishment of prior shared secrets. To get the advantages of PK cryptography along with efficient bulk encryption, you combine PK and secret-key technologies.

First, the user selects a secret-key encryption algorithm and generates a *random session key* to use for data encryption. If Joe is sending the message, he first encrypts this session key using Stephanie's public key. The resulting ciphertext key is then sent to Stephanie along with the encrypted data. Stephanie can recover the session key using her private key and then use the session key to decrypt the data.

In secret-key cryptography, Stephanie and Joe trust their shared secret key because they mutually agreed on it or exchanged it in a secure manner. This type of exchange, however, is usually impractical because the delivery of these keys would have to be done face to face, unless James Bond was available and could still be trusted. In contrast, using PK cryptography, Stephanie need only protect her private key and Joe his private key. The only information they need to share is each other's public key. They need to be able to identify each other's public key with high assurance, but they need not keep it secret. This ability to trust the association of a public key with a known entity is critical to the use of PK cryptography.

Stephanie might trust Joe's public key because Joe handed it to Stephanie directly in a secure manner, but this presupposes that Stephanie and Joe have had some form of prior secure communication. More likely, Stephanie has obtained Joe's public key through a nonsecure mechanism (for example, from a public directory, through email, or the like), so some other mechanism must give Stephanie confidence that the public key she holds claiming to be from "Joe" really is Joe's public key. One such mechanism is based on *certificates* issued by a *certificate authority (CA)*.

# Certificates

Certificates provide a mechanism for gaining confidence in the relationship between a public key and the entity owning the corresponding private key. A certificate is a particular type of digitally signed statement. The most common form of certificate in use today is based on the International Telecommunication Union-Telecommunication Standardization Sector (ITU-T) X.509 standard. (See the "Need to Know More?" section at the end of this chapter to learn more about standard certificates.) This fundamental technology is used in the Windows 2000 public-key infrastructure (PKI). However, it is not the only form of certificate. A certificate authority (CA) is simply an entity or service that issues and verifies certificates. A CA acts as a guarantor of the binding between the subject public key and the subject identity information contained within the certificates it issues. You can install Microsoft's Certificate Services, for example, to be a certificate authority for one or more domains.

## Trust and Validation

The fundamental question facing Stephanie when she receives a signed message is whether she should *trust* that the signature is valid and was made by whoever claimed to make it. Stephanie can confirm that the signature is mathematically valid; that is, she can verify the integrity of the signature using a known public key. However, Stephanie must still determine whether the public key used to verify the signature does in fact belong to the entity claiming to have made the signature in the first place. If Stephanie does not implicitly trust the public key to be Joe's, she needs to acquire strong evidence that the key used for the signing belongs to Joe.

If Stephanie can locate a certificate for Joe's public key, issued by a CA Stephanie implicitly trusts, then Stephanie can trust that Joe's public key really belongs to Joe.

Ultimately, Stephanie will end up constructing a *chain of certificates* leading from Joe and Joe's public key through a series of CAs and terminating in a certificate issued to someone whom Stephanie implicitly trusts. Such a certificate is called a *trusted-root certificate* because it forms the "root" (top node) of a hierarchy of public keys, or identity bindings, that Stephanie will accept as authentic.

 When choosing to explicitly trust a particular trusted-root certificate, trust is implied for the certificates issued by that trusted root, as well as all certificates issued by any subordinate CA certified by the trusted root.

The set of trusted-root certificates that Stephanie explicitly trusts is the only information that Stephanie must acquire in a secure manner. That set of certificates defines Stephanie's trust system and her belief in the public-key infrastructure.

## Windows 2000 PKI Components

Figure 9.1 presents a top-level view of the components that make up the Windows 2000 PKI. This logical view does not imply physical requirements for separate servers; in fact, you can combine many functions on a single-server system. A key element in the PKI is Microsoft Certificate Services, which allows you to deploy one or more enterprise CAs supporting certificate issuance and revocation. They are integrated with Active Directory, which provides CA location information and CA policy, and allows certificates and revocation information to be published. Layered on the cryptographic services is a set of certificate-management services. These support X.509 v3 standard certificates providing persistent storage, enumeration services, and decoding support. Finally, there are services for dealing with industry-standard message formats.

Other services take advantage of CryptoAPI to provide additional functionality for application developers. Secure Channel (schannel) supports network authentication and encryption using the industry-standard Transport Layer Security (TLS) and Secure Sockets Layer (SSL) protocols. Additionally, general-purpose Smart Card interfaces are supported. These interfaces have been used to integrate cryptographic Smart Cards in an application-independent manner and are the basis for Smart Card logon support integrated with Windows 2000.

*Note: The PKI does not replace the existing Windows 2000 domain trust and authorization mechanisms based on the domain controller (DC) and Kerberos Key Distribution Center (KDC).*

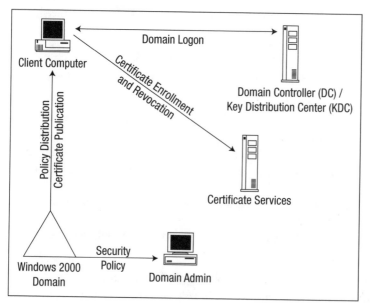

**Figure 9.1**   Public-key infrastructure components.

# Certificate Authorities

Microsoft Certificate Services, included with Windows 2000 and installed as a network service from Add/Remove Programs in the Control Panel, provides a means for an enterprise to easily establish CAs. Certificate Services includes a default Group Policy module for issuing certificates to enterprise entities (users, machines, or services). Within the PKI, you can easily support both enterprise CAs and external CAs, such as those associated with other organizations or commercial service providers.

*Note: The Microsoft PKI assumes a hierarchical CA model, but there is no requirement that all CAs share a common top-level CA parent (or root).*

In this hierarchical model, child CA-issued certificates are certified by parent CA-issued certificates, which bind a CA's public key to its identity and other policy-driven attributes. The CA at the top of a hierarchy is generally referred to as a *root CA*. The subordinate CAs are often referred to as *intermediate* or *issuing* CAs.

## Certificate Service Considerations

You install and configure certificate services after the Active Directory structure is completed. Key elements in this process include:

➤ *Selecting the host server*—The root CA can run on any Windows 2000 Server platform, including a DC.

➤ *Naming*—CA names are bound into their certificates and hence cannot change. You should consider factors such as organizational naming conventions and future requirements to distinguish between issuing CAs.

➤ *Generating a key*—The CA's public-key pair is generated during the installation process and is unique to this CA.

➤ *Generating CA certificates*—For a root CA, the installation process automatically generates a self-signed CA certificate using the CA's public-private key pair. For a child CA, you can submit a certificate request to either an intermediate or root CA.

➤ *Integrating Active Directory*—Information concerning the CA is written into a CA object in the Active Directory during installation. This provides information to domain clients about available CAs and the types of certificates they issue.

➤ *Issuing policy*—The enterprise CA setup automatically installs and configures the Microsoft-supplied Enterprise Policy Module for the CA.

By now, you can see that the keys and certificates generated for the various processes involved in a PKI are quite important. Their management and security involve several key elements:

➤ *Physical protection*—Because CAs represent highly trusted entities within an enterprise, it is often desirable to protect them from tampering. Physical isolation of the CA server, for example, can dramatically reduce the possibility of attacks.

➤ *Key management*—The CA's keys are its most valuable asset because the private key provides the basis for trust in the certification process. Cryptographic hardware modules (accessible to Certificate Services through a CryptoAPI certificate services provider) can provide tamper-resistant key storage and isolate the cryptographic operations from other software running on the server.

➤ *Restoration*—The loss of a CA can create a number of administrative and operational problems due to missing certificates, as well as prevent revocation of existing certificates. Certificate Services supports backing up a CA instance so it can be restored at a later time.

## Trust and Domain Clients

The use of PK technology is dependent upon the ability to generate and manage keys for one or more PK algorithms. Microsoft's CryptoAPI supports installable certificate service providers (CSPs) supporting key generation and management for a variety of cryptographic algorithms. The CryptoAPI defines standard interfaces for generating and managing keys that are the same for all CSPs. Mechanisms for storing key material depend on the selected CSP. The Microsoft-provided software CSPs (or *base* CSPs) store key material in an encrypted form on a per-user or per-machine basis. In addition, they support control over public-key pair exportability (**CRYPT_EXPORTABLE** flag) and usage control (**CRYPT_USER_PROTECT** flag). The former controls private key export from the CSP, and the latter determines user notification behavior when an application attempts to use the private key. Other CSPs might implement different mechanisms. For example, Smart Card CSPs store the public-key pair in the Smart Card tamper-resistant hardware and generally require entry of a PIN code to access operations involving the private key.

The principal client trust concern is that associated with certificate verification. This is generally based on the trust associated with the CA that issued the certificate. If a given end-entity certificate can be shown to "chain" to a known trusted-root CA, and if the intended certificate usage is consistent with the application context, then it is considered valid. If either of these conditions is not true, then it is considered invalid.

With Microsoft-based CSPs, the roaming of keys and certificates is supported by the roaming profile mechanism. Hardware token devices, such as Smart Cards, support roaming provided they incorporate a physical certificate store. The Smart Card CSPs that ship with the Windows 2000 platform support this functionality. Roaming support involves moving the hardware token with the user.

## Certificate Revocation

PK-based functionality assumes distributed verification in which there is no need for direct communication with a central trusted entity that vouches for these credentials. This creates a need for revocation information that can be distributed to individuals attempting to verify certificates.

Revocation information, and its timeliness, depends upon the application. To support a variety of operational scenarios, the Windows 2000 PKI incorporates support for industry-standard Certificate Revocation Lists (CRLs). Enterprise CAs support certificate revocation and CRL publication to the Active Directory under administrative control. Domain clients can retrieve this information, caching it locally, to use when verifying certificates. This same mechanism supports CRLs published by commercial CAs.

# PK Security Policy in Windows 2000

You can apply security policies to sites, domains, or organizational units (OUs) and affect the associated security groups of users and computers. PK security policy is simply one aspect of the overall Windows NT security policy, and it is integrated into this structure. It provides a mechanism to centrally define and manage policy while enforcing it globally. Trust in root CAs can be set via policy to establish trust relationships used by domain clients in verifying PK certificates. You configure the set of trusted CAs using the Group Policy Editor. You can configure the set on a per-machine basis, and it will apply globally to all users of that machine, as illustrated in Figure 9.2.

In addition to establishing a root CA as trusted, you can set usage properties associated with the CA. If specified, these properties restrict the purposes for which the CA-issued certificates are valid. Currently, they provide a means of restricting usage to any combination of the following:

➤ Server authentication

➤ Client authentication

➤ Code signing

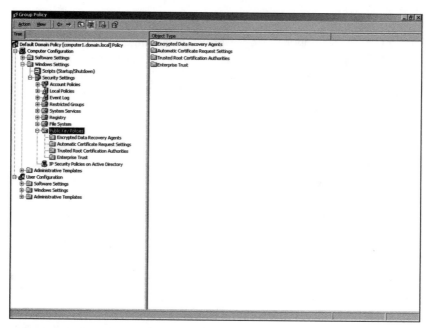

**Figure 9.2** Group Policy settings for certificate services.

➤ Email

➤ Internet Protocol Security (IPSec) end system

➤ IPSec tunnel

➤ IPSec user

➤ Timestamping

➤ Microsoft Encrypted File System

Certificate types provide a template for a certificate and associate it with a common name for ease of administration. The template defines elements such as naming requirements, validity period, allowable CSPs for private-key generation, algorithms, and extensions that should be incorporated into the certificate.

This mechanism is not a replacement for the enterprise CA issuing policy, but is integrated with it. The CA service receives a set of certificate types as part of its policy object. These are used by the Enterprise Policy Module to define the types of certificates the CA is allowed to issue. The CA rejects requests for certificates that fail to match these criteria.

The *auto-enrollment object* defines policy for certificates that an entity in the domain should have. This object can be applied on a machine and user basis. The types of certificates are incorporated by reference to the certificate type objects and can be any defined type. The auto-enrollment object provides sufficient information to determine whether an entity has the required certificates and to enroll for those certificates with an enterprise CA if they are missing. The auto-enrollment objects also define policy on certificate renewal.

Smart Card logon is controlled through policy associated with the user object in a manner analogous to password policy. You can set policy either to enable Smart Card logon, in which case you can still use password-based logon, or to enforce Smart Card logon. In the latter case, protection against unauthorized access to the account is significantly stronger. It does mean, however, that users will be unable to log on if they forget their Smart Card or attempt to use a machine lacking a Smart Card reader.

# Using PKI

The Web has rapidly become a key element in creating and deploying solutions for the effective exchange of information on a worldwide basis. For many uses, security is a key consideration. Of particular note for PKI are:

➤ *Server authentication*—Enabling clients to verify the server with which they are communicating

➤ *Client authentication*—Allowing servers to verify the client's identity

➤ *Confidentiality*—Encrypting data between clients and servers to prevent its exposure

The SSL protocol and the emerging Internet Engineering Task Force (IETF) standard TLS protocol play an important role in addressing these needs. SSL and TLS are flexible security protocols that can be layered on top of other transport protocols. They rely on PK-based authentication technology and use PK-based key negotiation to generate a unique encryption key for each client/server session. They are most commonly associated with Web-based applications and the HTTP protocol (referred to as HTTPS).

SSL and TLS are supported on the Windows platform by the secure channel (schannel) Security Support Provider Interface (SSPI) provider. Microsoft Internet Explorer and Internet Information Server both use schannel. Because schannel is integrated with Microsoft's SSPI architecture, it is available for use with multiple protocols to support authenticated and encrypted communications.

Taking full advantage of the SSL and TLS protocols requires both clients and servers to have identification certificates issued by mutually trusted CAs, allowing the parties to authenticate each other. In this mode, certificates are exchanged along with data that proves possession of the corresponding private key. Each side can then validate the certificate and verify possession of the private key using the certificate's public key. The identifying information included in the certificate can be used to make supplemental access control decisions. For example, the client can decide whether the server is someone it wants to conduct business with, and the server can decide what data the client will be allowed to access.

## Related Services

Many services related to PKI are either new or significantly revised in Windows 2000. No implementation of a solid PKI is complete without their proper consideration.

### Routing and Remote Access Services

As part of the Point-to-Point Protocol (PPP) connection establishment process, the calling router's credentials must be authenticated. (All externally connecting components are referred to as routers by RRAS.) User-level authentication occurs through one of the following PPP authentication methods:

➤ Password Authentication Protocol (PAP)

➤ Shiva Password Authentication Protocol (SPAP)

➤ Challenge Handshake Authentication Protocol (CHAP)

➤ Microsoft Challenge Handshake Authentication Protocol version 1 (MS-CHAP v1)

➤ Microsoft Challenge Handshake Authentication Protocol version 2 (MS-CHAP v2)

➤ Extensible Authentication Protocol-Message Digest 5 CHAP (EAP-MD5)

➤ Extensible Authentication Protocol-Transport Layer Security (EAP-TLS)

With EAP-TLS, the calling router's credentials consist of a user certificate that is validated by the answering router. EAP-TLS requires a public-key infrastructure (PKI) to issue and validate certificates.

Windows NT 4 with the Routing and Remote Access Service (RRAS) supports a feature called *two-way authentication.* Two-way authentication uses one-way authentication methods to perform mutual authentication. When two-way authentication is enabled on a demand-dial interface, the calling router forces the answering router to authenticate itself after the calling router authenticates itself. A Windows 2000 calling router never requests to authenticate a Windows NT 4 RRAS answering router. However, a Windows 2000 answering router authenticates itself when requested by a Windows NT 4 RRAS calling router.

## EFS

The Windows 2000 Encrypting File System (EFS) supports transparent encryption and decryption of files stored on a disk in the Windows NT file system (NTFS). The user can designate individual files to encrypt or folders whose contents are to be maintained in encrypted form. Applications have access to a user's encrypted files in the same manner as unencrypted files. However, they are unable to decrypt any other user's encrypted files.

 You cannot encrypt and compress data on a volume simultaneously. If compression is enabled, even for one file in a folder, that folder cannot be encrypted.

EFS makes extensive use of PK-based technology to provide mechanisms for encrypting files to multiple users and supporting file recovery. To do this, it leverages the ability of PK to support bulk encryption without prior shared secrets. In operation, each EFS user generates a public-key pair and obtains an EFS certificate. The certificate is issued by an enterprise CA in the Windows 2000 domain, although EFS generates a self-signed certificate for standalone operation where data sharing is not an issue. In addition, Windows 2000 supports an EFS recovery policy in which trusted recovery agents can be designated. These agents generate an EFS recovery public-key pair and are issued an EFS recovery certificate by the enterprise CA. The encrypted files can then be recovered to cleartext by using the cipher.exe or efsrecover.exe commands. The certificates of the EFS recovery agents are published to domain clients with the Group Policy Object, as illustrated in Figure 9.3.

## Smart Cards

Windows 2000 introduces PK-based Smart Card logon as an alternative to passwords for domain authentication. The authentication process uses the PKINIT protocol, proposed by the IETF Kerberos working group, to integrate PK-based authentication with the Windows 2000 Kerberos access control system.

In operation, the system recognizes a Smart Card insertion event as an alternative to the standard Ctrl+Alt+Del secure attention sequence to initiate a logon. The user is then prompted for the Smart Card PIN code, which controls access to operations with the private key stored on the Smart Card. In this system, the Smart Card also contains a copy of the user's certificate (issued by an enterprise CA). This allows the user to roam within the domain.

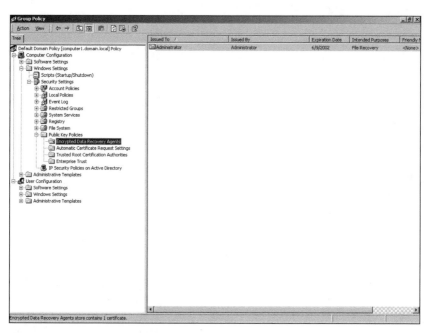

**Figure 9.3**   EFS certificate settings in Group Policy.

## IPSec

IPSec defines protocols for network encryption at the IP Protocol layer. IPSec does not require PK-based technology and can use shared secret keys, communicated securely through an out-of-band mechanism, at the network end points for encryption.

IP Security, as defined by the IETF, uses an Authentication Header (AH) and an Encapsulated Security Payload (ESP). The Authentication Header provides data communication with source authentication and integrity by digitally signing each transferred IP packet. The ESP provides confidentiality in addition to authentication and integrity. With IPSec, only the sender and recipient know the security key. If the authentication data is valid, the recipient knows that the communication came from the sender and that it was not changed in transit.

Windows IP Security builds upon the IETF model by mixing public-key and secret-key cryptography and by providing automatic key management for maximized security and high-speed throughput. This gives a combination of authentication, integrity, anti-replay, and (optionally) confidentiality to ensure secure communications. Because Windows IP Security is below the Network layer, it is transparent to users and existing applications.

Certificates provide the strongest security for authenticating non-Kerberos clients for IPSec communication. The use of shared secrets (passwords) for authentication provides relatively weak security.

# Types of Certificate Authorities

With the possibility of defining either an enterprise or standalone CA, both as an independent or subordinate issuer of certificates, four types of certificate authorities exist:

➤ Enterprise root CA

➤ Enterprise subordinate CA

➤ Standalone CA

➤ Standalone subordinate CA

## Enterprise Root CA

An enterprise CA is the root of a Windows 2000-based corporate CA hierarchy. You should set up an enterprise CA if the CA will be issuing certificates to users and computers within your corporation. For security reasons, the enterprise CA is typically configured to issue certificates only to subordinate CAs. The root CA is registered in the directory, and all computers in your enterprise using that directory automatically trust the root CA.

The enterprise CA requires the following:

➤ Windows 2000 DNS Service (required by Active Directory). See Chapter 4 for more details on DNS.

➤ Windows 2000 Active Directory. Enterprise policy places information into the Active Directory.

➤ Enterprise administrator privileges on the DNS, Active Directory, and CA servers. This is especially important because setup modifies information in numerous places, some of which require enterprise administrator privileges.

## Enterprise Subordinate CA

An enterprise subordinate is a CA that issues certificates within a corporation, but is not the most trusted CA in that corporation. (It is subordinate to another CA in the hierarchy.) You cannot designate an enterprise subordinate CA unless you have already installed an enterprise root CA. Typically, you will have multiple enterprise subordinate CAs. Each of these CAs either serves different communities of users or provides different types of certificates. With more than one subordinate, it is possible to revoke the subordinate's certificate in case of disaster and not have to reissue all the certificates in the organization.

The enterprise subordinate CA requires the following:

➤ A parent CA, which can be an external commercial CA or a standalone CA.

➤ Windows 2000 DNS service (required by Active Directory). See chapter 4 for more details about DNS.

➤ Windows 2000 Active Directory. Enterprise policy places information into Active Directory.

➤ Enterprise administrator privileges on the DNS, Active Directory, and CA servers.

## Standalone Root CA

If you will be issuing certificates to entities outside your enterprise and you do not want to use Active Directory or other Windows 2000 PKI features, then you want a standalone CA. A standalone CA is the root of a CA trust hierarchy, typically issuing certificates to subordinate CAs only. One example of when you would use a standalone root CA is if you want to issue certificates to your customers so they can access your Web site, and it is not feasible to give each one an account in your directory. Another example is if you intend to lock your root CA in a vault with no network access for security reasons, and you want to allow only a few trusted people to access this server.

The standalone root CA requires administrator privileges on the local server.

## Standalone Subordinate CA

A standalone subordinate CA operates as a solitary certificate server or exists in a CA trust hierarchy. You should set up a standalone subordinate CA when you will be issuing certificates to entities outside a corporation.

The standalone subordinate CA requires the following:

➤ An association with a CA that will process the subordinate CA's certificate requests. This can be an external, commercial CA.

➤ Administrative privileges on the local server.

## Installation Notes

If the Certificate Services Installation Wizard has options that are different from what you expect or need, several items may be influencing which options are available:

➤ You need to log on as an enterprise administrator when setting up the enterprise intermediary and enterprise-issuing certificate computers.

➤ If no Active Directory is detected, the two enterprise options are disabled.

➤ If an Active Directory is detected, the enterprise root CA option is selected if there are no CAs already registered in the Active Directory.

➤ If there are CAs registered in the Active Directory, the enterprise subordinate CA option is selected.

# Practice Questions

## Question 1

> You want to implement a PKI for your Windows 2000 network. Active Directory is present and functioning on three domain controllers in your domain. You want to implement an independent certificate system that is integrated with Active Directory. What type of certificate server will you install first?
>
> ○ a. Enterprise certificate authority
>
> ○ b. Enterprise subordinate certificate authority
>
> ○ c. Standalone certificate authority
>
> ○ d. Standalone subordinate certificate authority

The correct answer is a. To integrate with Active Directory, thus providing certificate services for the entire domain structure, you must install an enterprise certificate authority. Because no certificate service has yet been installed, a subordinate authority is not appropriate, making answer b incorrect. Standalone CAs do not have the ability to integrate with Active Directory, making answers c and d incorrect.

## Question 2

> You have an application that you want to allow use of digital signatures in your network. Users running this application log on to several different machines during the course of a workday. Roaming profiles are in place to minimize desktop setting changes and provide consistent settings between machines. You installed Microsoft Certificate Services as an enterprise root in the domain. EFS is used to encrypt sensitive data on the client computers. You want to supply certificates for use with the application. These certificates should only be available to the users running the application. What type of authority will you install to administer these certificates?
>
> ○ a. Enterprise certificate authority
>
> ○ b. Enterprise subordinate certificate authority
>
> ○ c. Standalone certificate authority
>
> ○ d. Standalone subordinate certificate authority

The correct answer is b. A subordinate certificate authority for the enterprise would allow for the independent management of the application-specific certificates and provide full integration with Active Directory for the management of all domain certificates through the roaming user profiles. An enterprise certificate authority is already installed, and installing another would make the application-specific certificates available to all users in the domain. Therefore, answer a is incorrect. Standalone authorities would not integrate with Active Directory, so accommodating roaming user profiles would not be possible, making answers c and d incorrect.

## Question 3

You want to verify all session communication between client computers and server computers in your network. No certificate services are currently installed. You do not want to add overhead to local network communication but want to configure secure data transfer for remote and Internet Web site users. Which of the following settings are appropriate for your security policy? [Check all correct answers]

- ❏ a.  AH for the local network
- ❏ b.  ESP for the local network
- ❏ c.  AH for remote users
- ❏ d.  ESP for remote users
- ❏ e.  AH for the anonymous Web user account
- ❏ f.  ESP for the anonymous Web user account
- ❏ g.  Enterprise certificate authority
- ❏ h.  Standalone certificate authority

The correct answers are a, c, d, e, g, and h. Authentication Headers (AH) verifies that the communication sessions are secure. You need this security for all accounts, including the anonymous Internet services account. Encapsulation security payload adds overhead as it brings security to data transfer for the remote users. Therefore, AH is required for all users, making answers a, c, and e correct. ESP encrypts the TCP data packets for remote users, making answer d correct. You need to install an enterprise certificate authority for the local accounts integration with Active Directory, making answer g correct. A standalone CA is best for providing secure data to the Internet users, who do not have user accounts in the Active Directory, making answer h correct.

Because ESP on the local network will add unnecessary overhead to the local network communication, answer b is incorrect. If data is encrypted in this fashion for Web users, however, this encapsulated encryption will likely cause failed decryption on the part of the Web site client, making answer f incorrect.

## Question 4

> You want to provide certificate services to external users connecting to your Internet Web site. You currently have one certificate hierarchy installed as an enterprise CA. You want to expand your current hierarchy to accomplish the goal. Which certificate authority is best suited to your needs?
>
> ○ a.  Enterprise certificate authority
>
> ○ b.  Enterprise subordinate certificate authority
>
> ○ c.  Standalone certificate authority
>
> ○ d.  Standalone subordinate certificate authority

The correct answer is d. A standalone subordinate certificate authority is the best choice, given the need for integration with a current authority. Standalone authorities can integrate with an enterprise authority, but external users of your Web site will not have accounts on the local domain, making answers a and b incorrect. A new hierarchy is not desired, making answer c incorrect.

## Question 5

> You want to use the Encrypting File System (EFS) on your network to secure data. Certificate Services is not installed. Which of the following will allow configuration of EFS?
>
> ○ a.  Install Certificate Services as an enterprise CA. Configure EFS through Group Policy.
>
> ○ b.  Install Certificate Services as an enterprise subordinate CA. Configure EFS through Group Policy.
>
> ○ c.  Install Certificate Services as a standalone CA. Configure EFS through Group Policy.
>
> ○ d.  Install Certificate Services as a standalone subordinate CA. Configure EFS through Group Policy.
>
> ○ e.  No installation of Certificate Services is necessary. Configure EFS through Group Policy.

The correct answer is e. Limited certificate services already exist in Windows 2000. You do not need to install Certificate Services unless new certificates are required. Therefore, answers a, b, c, and d are incorrect. Even without the installation of Certificate Services, configuring EFS certificate behavior is possible through Group Policy.

## Question 6

> You need to implement a secure method of authentication for remote users. Specifically, you are concerned that a remote user could have a laptop computer stolen. You want to ensure that no security breaches are possible either through the data local to the laptop being available or through that laptop's connection to the network. Which of the following services will you implement on the laptops to prohibit these situations? [Check all correct answers]
>
> ❑  a.  AH on the RRAS server
>
> ❑  b.  ESP on the RRAS server
>
> ❑  c.  EFS on the laptop
>
> ❑  d.  EFS on the RRAS server
>
> ❑  e.  Smart Card system for the network

The correct answers are c and e. EFS will encrypt the files on the laptop so that the files are unreadable if you cannot log on to the OS installed on the computer. A Smart Card system can provide certificate-level authentication both for the remote network and for the laptop (optional). TCP-level verification of communication between computers does not aid in this scenario because authentication will have taken place by then. The concern is not for data transmitted across the wire. Therefore, answers a and b are incorrect. Encrypting the files on the server will not help either because the concern is with the files on the laptop. Encrypting the files on the server would also prohibit anyone on the network from using the files. This makes answer d incorrect.

## Question 7

> You have removed the Encrypted Recovery Agent certificate from the Default Domain Policy. You attempt to re-create the certificate, but the process fails. What should you do?
>
> ○ a.  Install Certificate Services as an enterprise CA.
>
> ○ b.  Install Certificate Services as a standalone CA.
>
> ○ c.  Use efsrecover.exe to recover the certificate.
>
> ○ d.  Use cipher.exe to both encrypt and recover files as needed.

The correct answer is a. Installing Certificate Services as an enterprise CA allows for creation of certificates integrated with Active Directory, which is necessary for the implementation of EFS after certificates have been deleted. A standalone CA will not integrate with Active Directory. Therefore, answer b is incorrect. Efsrecover is used to gain access to previously encrypted files, assuming that a valid recovery certificate is available. Therefore, answer c is incorrect. Cipher.exe also works only with valid certificates, which must be created with an existing authority. Therefore, answer d is incorrect.

## Question 8

> You need to create digital certificates for your network. Microsoft Certificate Services is to be installed for this purpose. Which of the following tools will allow you to achieve this goal?
>
> ○ a.  Control Panel
>
> ○ b.  Group Policy
>
> ○ c.  Active Directory Installation Wizard (DCPromo)
>
> ○ d.  Internet Information Server

The correct answer is a. Add/Remove Programs, found in the Control Panel, is where you install Certificate Services. Group Policy lets you configure, not create, certificate publishing. Therefore, answer b is incorrect. DCPromo will install Active Directory, not Certificate Services, making answer c incorrect. Internet Information Server has Certificate Services available, but earlier versions of Certificate Services will not run on Windows 2000. Certificates can be imported but not created for use in Active Directory. Therefore, answer d is incorrect.

# Question 9

Which of the following allows for the verification of session information between client and server?

- ○ a. AH
- ○ b. Digital signatures
- ○ c. EFS
- ○ d. Group Policy

The correct answer is a. Authentication Headers allow for the verification of session communication between two computers. That is, there is assurance that the computer that initiated the conversation is the one with which it continues. Digital signatures verify user-level identity, not computer session connections. Therefore, answer b is incorrect. EFS encrypts data on a hard drive, making answer c incorrect. Group Policy provides configuration information to a computer, not imminent connection validity. Therefore, answer d is incorrect.

# Question 10

Another company has just purchased your company. You must install Certificate Services to allow integration with its Active Directory. All user accounts have been re-created in the parent-company domain. How should you install Certificate Services?

- ○ a. Enterprise certificate authority
- ○ b. Enterprise subordinate certificate authority
- ○ c. Standalone certificate authority
- ○ d. Standalone subordinate certificate authority

The correct answer is b. Because your user accounts are in the other domain, but you are installing Certificate Services in your domain, you must install an authority subordinate to the other company's while still integrating with its Active Directory. An enterprise root CA would need to use your accounts and generate certificates on its own, making answer a incorrect. Any standalone CA would not integrate properly with the accounts in the parent Active Directory. Therefore, answers c and d are incorrect.

# Need to Know More?

Kaufman, Charlie, Radia Perlman, and Mike Speciner. *Network Security: Private Communication in a Public World.* Upper Saddle River, N.J.: Prentice Hall, 1995. ISBN 0130614661. This is a comprehensive guide to scenario-based best practices and guidelines in setting up certificate services within a complete Public Key Infrastructure.

Stallings, William. *Cryptography and Network Security: Principles and Practice, Second Edition.* Upper Saddle River, N.J.: Prentice Hall, 1998. ISBN 0138690170. A little bit of history and detailed information on the algorithms used in cryptography.

*Windows 2000 Server Resource Kit* and *Microsoft TechNet: Step-by-Step Guides to Cryptography Services.* When it comes time to set up the various servers, these guides are quite handy.

Microsoft TechNet: Search for text containing "PKI", "Cryptography", and "Encryption".

These Windows 2000 Server Help files contain many references to specific setup procedures for services.

# Sample Test

## Question 1

Which layer of the TCP/IP model is responsible for putting raw data onto network media?

○ a. The Internet layer

○ b. The Transport layer

○ c. The Network Interface layer

○ d. The Session layer

## Question 2

Which of the following are layers of the TCP/IP model? [Check all correct answers]

❑ a. Network Interface

❑ b. Session

❑ c. Presentation

❑ d. Transport

## Question 3

If there is no response from the WINS server after the first attempt in the renewal process, how often will the WINS client attempt to renew its name?

○ a. Every 10 minutes until the time to live (TTL) has expired

○ b. Every two hours until one-half of the time to live (TTL) has expired

○ c. When one-eighth the time of the time to live (TTL) has expired

○ d. Every two minutes until half of the time to live (TTL) has expired

## Question 4

NWLink is Microsoft's implementation of which protocol?

○ a. TCP/IP

○ b. IPX/SPX

○ c. NetBEUI

○ d. DLC

## Question 5

How would a computer be configured as a WINS proxy?

○ a. Set the **EnableProxy** entry in the Registry to 1.

○ b. Set the **EnableWINS** entry in the Registry to 1.

○ c. Install a network interface card for each network ID in the computer acting as WINS proxy.

○ d. Remove all protocols except NetBEUI.

## Question 6

The IP address 191.107.2.200 is what class of IP address?

○ a. Class A

○ b. Class B

○ c. Class C

○ d. Class D

# Question 7

> You can use AppleTalk as a protocol in a pure Windows 2000 network.
>
> ○ a. True
>
> ○ b. False

# Question 8

> You are the network administrator for the marketing.corp.local domain. The domain is currently configured as a mixed-mode domain, with only a couple of Windows NT 4 domain controllers. Each remote location has at least one domain controller. You are configuring a two-way demand-dial connection between your office and the remote office. You have configured the following information for the connections:
>
> | Office | Interface | User Account | Phone Number |
> |--------|-----------|--------------|--------------|
> | Main | Remote_DD | Main_User | 14442121212 |
> | Remote | Main_DD | Remote_User | 15552121212 |
>
> When the connection is tested in either direction, the connection fails. What could be causing the connection problems?
>
> ○ a. The interfaces at each location need the same name.
>
> ○ b. With a two-way demand-dial connection, the user must be the same user account at each end.
>
> ○ c. The user account needs the same name as the interface for each location.
>
> ○ d. The domain needs to be in native mode for a two-way demand dial to function.

## Question 9

You are the network administrator for the corp.local domain. You have approximately 50 employees at one of your remote locations. The remote employees need to gain access to the Internet, but you do not want them to use the WAN connection through the main office because of the bandwidth issues.

You decide to install a Windows 2000 RRAS in the remote office to provide Internet access. The client computers and the Internet access need to meet the following requirements:

- All client computers will be able to access the Internet through the Windows 2000 RRAS server.

- The client computers should still use DHCP for obtaining their IP addresses.

- The client computers should continue to use the current IP address range of 10.1.10.0/24.

- The Windows 2000 RRAS server should resolve all DNS queries for the client computers.

You configure the new Windows 2000 RRAS server with the following settings:

- Network address translation is configured on the Windows 2000 RRAS server.

- The Windows 2000 RRAS server is configured to use DHCP.

- The existing DHCP scope options are configured with the IP address of the private interface as the default gateway.

- The Clients Using Domain Name System (DNS) checkbox is selected on the Windows 2000 RRAS server.

Which of the requirements are met? [Check all correct answers]

❏ a. All client computers will be able to access the Internet through the Windows 2000 RRAS server.

❏ b. The client computers should still use DHCP for obtaining their IP addresses.

❏ c. The client computers should continue to use the current IP address range of 10.1.10.0/24.

❏ d. The Windows 2000 RRAS server should resolve all DNS queries for the client computers.

# Question 10

You are the network administrator for the corp.local domain. You have approximately 50 employees at one of your remote locations. The remote employees need to gain access to the Internet, but you do not want them to use the WAN connection through the main office because of the bandwidth issues.

You decide to install a Windows 2000 RRAS in the remote office to provide Internet access. The client computers and the Internet access will need to meet the following requirements:

- All client computers will be able to access the Internet through the Windows 2000 RRAS server.

- The client computers should still use DHCP for obtaining their IP addresses.

- The client computers should continue to use the current IP address range of 10.1.10.0/24.

- The Windows 2000 RRAS server should resolve all DNS queries for the client computers.

You configure the new Windows 2000 RRAS server with the following settings:

- Internet Connection Sharing is configured on the Windows 2000 RRAS server.

- The Windows 2000 RRAS server is configured to use DHCP.

- The existing DHCP scope options are configured with the IP address of the private interface as the default gateway and the DNS server.

Which of the requirements are met? [Check all correct answers]

- ❑ a. All client computers will be able to access the Internet through the Windows 2000 RRAS server.

- ❑ b. The client computers should still use DHCP for obtaining their IP addresses.

- ❑ c. The client computers should continue to use the current IP address range of 10.1.10.0/24.

- ❑ d. The Windows 2000 RRAS server should resolve all DNS queries for the client computers.

# Question 11

You are creating a multicast environment for the corp.local network. Several servers are initiating the multicast traffic. Some of the traffic needs to get to the entire network, and some of the multicast traffic only needs to service specific subnets. What will you implement on the network to control the multicast traffic?

○ a.  DNS entry to control the TTL

○ b.  Auto-static route

○ c.  RIP v2

○ d.  Scope-based boundary

# Question 12

You are troubleshooting a routing problem that is occurring on your network. You have some IP multicast traffic that needs to be routed between two networks that are successfully using the IGMP routing protocol. However, the network that sits between the two networks does not support IP multicasting and therefore does not have any IGMP routing configured. What will you configure to allow the IP multicast traffic to traverse the middle network?

○ a.  RIP v2

○ b.  RIP v1

○ c.  IP-in-IP tunnel

○ d.  OSPF

# Question 13

You are configuring the new routed environment from the main office to primary and secondary remote offices. Some of the remote offices are directly connected to the main office, and others are routed through the primary remote offices. During the planning of the configurations, you decide on some criteria that must be met for the routing traffic. The criteria consist of the following:

- All dynamic route table changes need to be secure.

- Routed links should be dynamic to reduce the WAN link cost.

- Routing loops need to be eliminated.

- The routes need the flexibility to be organized into logical groupings.

You make the following configurations:

- RIP v1 is implemented.

- A two-way demand-dial configuration is made between all routes.

Which criteria are met with the configurations that were made? [Check all correct answers]

❑ a. All dynamic route table changes need to be secure.

❑ b. Routed links should be dynamic to reduce the WAN link cost.

❑ c. Routing loops need to be eliminated.

❑ d. The routes need the flexibility to be organized into logical groupings.

# Question 14

You are structuring your Windows 2000 DHCP servers (refer to the graphic).

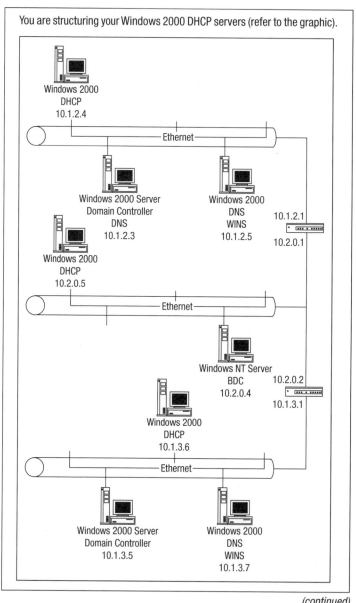

*(continued)*

## Question 14 *(continued)*

You have created three DHCP scopes to allocate addresses to your different segment. You need to configure the different DHCP options in the most efficient manner. The configuration should:

- Reduce network traffic
- Reduce DHCP scope option admin overhead
- Create fault tolerance for all name resolution for the clients

The following is a list of the DHCP scopes that you have configured:

Scope 1:

*IP Range* —10.1.2.10 to 10.1.2.200

*Subnet Mask*—255.255.255.0

Scope 2:

*IP Range* —10.1.3.10 to 10.1.3.200

*Subnet Mask*—255.255.255.0

Scope 3:

*IP Range*—10.2.0.10 to 10.2.0.50

*Subnet Mask*—255.255.255.192

Following is a list of the different option components that need to placed in the different DHCP option locations. Place the option component in the correct option location.

Server options:

Router

DNS

WINS

Scope 1 options

Router

DNS

WINS

Scope 2 options

Router

DNS

WINS

*(continued)*

## Question 14 *(continued)*

Scope 3 options

    Router

    DNS

    WINS

Possible IP addresses for the options:

| | |
|---|---|
| 10.1.2.1 | 10.1.3.6 |
| 10.1.2.3 | 10.1.3.7 |
| 10.1.2.4 | 10.2.0.1 |
| 10.1.2.5 | 10.2.0.2 |
| 10.1.3.1 | 10.2.0.4 |
| 10.1.3.5 | 10.2.0.5 |

# Question 15

You are configuring the new routed environment from the main office to primary and secondary remote offices. Some of the remote offices are directly connected to the main office, and others are routed through the primary remote offices. During the planning of the configurations, you decide on some criteria that must be met for the routing traffic. The criteria consist of the following:

- All dynamic route table changes need to be secure.

- Routed links should be dynamic to reduce the WAN link cost.

- Routing loops need to be eliminated.

- The routes need the flexibility to be organized into logical groupings.

You make the following configurations:

- RIP v2 is implemented.

- A one-way demand-dial configuration is made from all primary remote sites and the main office.

- A two-way demand-dial configuration is made from all secondary remote offices that link to the main office through a primary remote office.

Which criteria are met with the configurations that were made? [Check all correct answers]

❑ a. All dynamic route table changes need to be secure.

❑ b. Routed links should be dynamic to reduce the WAN link cost.

❑ c. Routing loops need to be eliminated.

❑ d. The routes need the flexibility to be organized into logical groupings.

# Question 16

You want to configure your DHCP server to update all DNS entries for both Windows 2000 and down-level clients. You have configured your DNS server to support only secure dynamic updates. You intend to use the DNSUpdateProxy group for all of the DHCP servers. You want to keep the records that are placed in DNS as secure as possible, with the configurations specified. Where will you place the DHCP server?

○ a. Windows NT 4 domain member server

○ b. Windows 2000 domain controller

○ c. Windows 2000 standalone server in a workgroup

○ d. Windows 2000 domain member server

# Question 17

You are having trouble with some of your clients that are configured as DHCP enabled. They are not obtaining an IP address from the DHCP server. The problem seems to be intermittent, so you use Network Monitor to determine the DHCP traffic on the network. Upon observation of the network capture, you observe the following DHCP-related packets:

DHCPINFORM

DHCPREQUEST

DHCPOFFER

DHCPDISCOVER

DHCPACK

Create a list of the DHCP packets in the order that they are utilized for a client obtaining an IP address.

# Question 18

You have installed another DHCP server on your Windows 2000 network to help with the allocation of IP addresses. The new DHCP server is installed on a Windows 2000 member server. The DHCP server has eliminated the need for the existing relay agent, so you have deleted the relay agent from the Routing and Remote Access Server configurations. When the first DHCP-enabled clients log on to the network, they cannot gain access to any of the network resources, yet they do not receive an error when obtaining the IP address. What is a possible reason for this behavior?

○ a. The DNS server scope option was not configured properly for the new DHCP server.

○ b. The relay agent needed the new DHCP IP address configured.

○ c. The relay agent is necessary for DHCP-enabled clients to communicate on the network.

○ d. The DHCP server needs to be authorized.

# Question 19

You are the network administrator for the acme.local domain. You are trying to reconfigure some of the servers in your environment to reduce the administrative overhead related to IP configurations. You have decided to use the different features of the Windows 2000 DHCP server to help with this configuration.

You decide to create a reservation for each of these Windows 2000 and Windows NT member servers. What information must you obtain in order to create the reservations? [Check all correct answers]

❑  a.  NetBIOS name for each server

❑  b.  MAC address for each server

❑  c.  IP address for each server

❑  d.  Domain name for each server

# Question 20

There are many different client operating systems on your network, including Windows 2000, Windows NT, Windows 98, and Windows 95. Most of these clients are configured to be DHCP enabled, and they receive all of their IP address information from the DHCP server. You want to force the DHCP server to update all of the clients with DNS. What configurations will you make to achieve this result? [Check all correct answers]

❑  a.  Always update DNS.

❑  b.  Update DNS only if DHCP client requests.

❑  c.  Automatically update DHCP client information in DNS.

❑  d.  Enable updates for DNS clients that do not support dynamic update.

# Question 21

You have just made some additional changes and configurations to the DHCP server options. All of the clients on the network need these new configurations to communicate with the LAN and WAN computers. To ensure the clients get these new changes, you need to run the correct series of commands to get the new changes. The clients should only run the command(s) that are required to obtain the new configurations. Arrange the following list in the correct order for the clients to obtain the new configurations:

**ipconfig**

**ipconfig /release**

**ipconfig /renew**

**ipconfig /all**

# Question 22

You are the network administrator responsible for the remote access users in the enterprise. The current network infrastructure consists of 10 Windows 2000 domain controllers, 2 Windows NT backup domain controllers, 4 Windows 2000 DNS servers, and 3 DHCP servers. You need to configure the new Routing and Remote Access Server on a Windows 2000 member server.

To configure the server, you perform the following configurations:

- Configure the RRAS server to accept incoming connections.
- Configure the RRAS server to only support the IP protocol.
- Configure the IP routing feature.
- Configure the BAP feature.
- Leave the existing RRAS policy with the default settings.

What additional configurations need to be made?

- ○ a. Install the DHCP relay agent on the Windows 2000 servers.
- ○ b. Authorize the RRAS server with the Active Directory.
- ○ c. Install NAT on the RRAS server.
- ○ d. Enable the DHCP server to Always Update DNS for the client.

# Question 23

You are the network administrator responsible for controlling the remote access into your Windows 2000 network. You are expanding your remote access capabilities by adding a VPN to the network. You would like to control the access through the VPN separately from the typical dial-up remote access users. The current remote access dial-up policy is just the default remote access policy.

You decide to use a remote access policy to control the access. The desired goals for the remote access users are:

- Existing dial-up clients are not affected.

- The VPN clients that are using L2TP can access the network.

- The VPN clients that are using PPTP cannot access the network.

- The VPN clients will use MS-CHAP v2 as the authentication type.

You perform the following configurations:

- Configure the routing and remote access server to use MS-CHAP v2.

- Create a new remote access policy called "L2TP clients."

- Create a new remote access policy called "PPTP clients."

- Configure the L2TP clients policy to allow remote access if the NAS-Port-Type is set to VPN and the Tunnel-Type is set to L2TP.

- Configure the PPTP clients policy to deny remote access if the NAS-Port-Type is set to VPN and the Tunnel-Type is set to PPTP.

- Configure the L2TP clients policy profile to use MS-CHAP v2 authentication.

- Configure the policy order to be PPTP clients, L2TP clients, and default remote access policy.

Which of the required conditions were met? [Check all correct answers]

- ❑ a. Existing dial-up clients are not affected.

- ❑ b. The VPN clients that are using L2TP can access the network.

- ❑ c. The VPN clients that are using PPTP cannot access the network.

- ❑ d. The VPN clients will use MS-CHAP v2 as the authentication type.

## Question 24

You are the network administrator responsible for controlling the remote access into your Windows 2000 network. You are expanding your remote access capabilities by adding a VPN to the network. You would like to control the access through the VPN separately from the typical dial-up remote access users. The current remote access dial-up policy is just the default remote access policy.

You decide to use a remote access policy to control the access. The desired goals for the remote access users are:

- Existing dial-up clients are not affected.

- The VPN clients that are using L2TP can access the network.

- The VPN clients that are using PPTP cannot access the network.

- The VPN clients will use MS-CHAP v2 as the authentication type.

You perform the following configurations:

- Configure the routing and remote access server to use MS-CHAP and MS-CHAP v2.

- Create a new remote access policy called "VPN clients."

- Configure the VPN clients policy to allow remote access if the NAS-Port-Type is set to VPN.

- Configure the VPN clients policy profile to use MS-CHAP v2 authentication.

- Configure the policy order to be VPN clients, then the default remote access policy.

Which of the required conditions were met? [Check all correct answers]

❏ a. Existing dial-up clients are not affected.

❏ b. The VPN clients that are using L2TP can access the network.

❏ c. The VPN clients that are using PPTP cannot access the network.

❏ d. The VPN clients will use MS-CHAP v2 as the authentication type.

# Question 25

You are configuring the remote access policies for your routing and remote access server. You are faced with the dilemma of determining whether you want the remote access policy to decide the access or the user configuration for the dial-up properties. During the evaluation of which decision to make, you must create a flow of how the RRAS server completes the process. Create a list of the appropriate steps from the following list, and order the steps in the correct sequence:

Check policy profile settings.

Check user dial-up property configuration.

Check computer dial-up property configuration.

Check remote access policy conditions.

# Question 26

You are planning your remote access topology for the network. The current network consists of a Windows 2000 native-mode domain. There are five domain controllers and two DNS servers. All of the DNS servers are located on Windows 2000 member servers. A single routing and remote access server will be the server you configure for the remote access users. You have the following requirements for the remote access users:

- Users have dynamic allocation of the connection bandwidth.

- The RRAS server needs to support Caller ID.

- The RRAS server needs to support Smart Card authentication.

- The RRAS server supports only IPSec communication for VPN connections.

You make the following configurations:

- Configure Multilink for the PPP options.

- Configure LCP for the PPP options.

- Configure the EAP authentication to support MD5-Challenge.

- Configure the 128 PPTP and 128 L2TP ports.

Which of the requirements are met with the configurations that were made? [Check all correct answers]

- ❑ a. Users have dynamic allocation of the connection bandwidth.

- ❑ b. The RRAS server needs to support Caller ID.

- ❑ c. The RRAS server needs to support Smart Card authentication.

- ❑ d. The RRAS server supports only IPSec communication for VPN connections.

## Question 27

You are planning your remote access topology for the network. The current network consists of a Windows 2000 native-mode domain. There are five domain controllers and two DNS servers. All of the DNS servers are located on Windows 2000 member servers. A single routing and remote access server will be the server you configure for the remote access users. You have the following requirements for the remote access users:

- Users have dynamic allocation of the connection bandwidth.

- The RRAS server needs to support Caller ID.

- The RRAS server needs to support Smart Card authentication.

- The RRAS server supports only IPSec communication for VPN connections.

You make the following configurations:

- Configure Multilink for the PPP options.

- Configure BAP for the PPP options.

- Configure MS-CHAP v2 and PAP authentication.

- Configure the 128 L2TP ports.

Which of the requirements are met with the configurations that were made? [Check all correct answers]

❑ a. Users have dynamic allocation of the connection bandwidth.

❑ b. The RRAS server needs to support Caller ID.

❑ c. The RRAS server needs to support Smart Card authentication.

❑ d. The RRAS server supports only IPSec communication for VPN connections.

# Question 28

As the network administrator of the acme.local domain, you have implemented serious security for the remote access users who enter the network. You have a new challenge, which is to give a group of users access to the network with less security than the other users. The desire is to keep the current users with the high security requirements and only allow the new group on the network with less security. How will you accomplish this configuration?

○ a.  Use an IAS server for authentication instead of the RRAS server.

○ b.  Configure a Windows Group condition in a new remote access policy that is applied before the other remote access policies.

○ c.  Reconfigure the default remote access policy, and make sure it is first in the list of remote access policies.

○ d.  Reconfigure the default remote access policy profile to reduce the security requirements, and make sure it is first in the list of remote access policies.

# Question 29

Your network consists of three locations: North America, South America, and Asia. Each of these three locations will use a standalone DNS to provide name-resolution services to the entire network. Each location must have fault tolerance for DNS in the event of a WAN link failure. Server maintenance and hostname registration will occur in North America. Place the appropriate server type for installation in the appropriate location.

Locations:

North America

South America

Asia

Server Types:

Standalone primary

Standalone secondary

Standalone caching-only

# Question 30

---

Your network consists of seven DNS servers in various geographic locations. Currently, all DNS servers are hosted on a domain controller as either
a standalone primary (1) or a standalone secondary (6). To provide for the
greatest fault tolerance and flexibility of configuration, what should you do?

○ a.  Convert the primary zone server to Active Directory integrated.

○ b.  Convert the secondary zone servers to Active Directory integrated.

○ c.  Convert all zone servers to Active Directory integrated.

○ d.  Convert nothing, leaving the zone servers as configured.

# Question 31

---

You have configured all Windows 2000 Professional machines as members
of your domain corp.com. However, you also want to have select Windows
2000 Professional computers contribute to the corporate intranet as members of the intranet.cc DNS domain. What configuration change is necessary to accomplish this?

○ a.  Configure the select intranet computers with an alternate domain
       suffix.

○ b.  Configure all computers not contributing to the intranet with an
       alternate domain suffix.

○ c.  Configure an additional A record entry for the select computers
       in DNS.

○ d.  Configure an additional CNAME record entry for the select
       computers in DNS.

○ e.  Configure a separate scope for the select computers in DHCP.

# Question 32

---

Which of the following are required for configuring secure dynamic update
in Windows 2000? [Check all correct answers]

❑ a.  Enable DHCP.

❑ b.  Enable secure dynamic updates on all clients.

❑ c.  Enable secure dynamic updates on the DNS server.

❑ d.  Create standalone primary and secondary zones.

❑ e.  Create Active Directory integrated zones.

# Question 33

To maintain compatibility and connectivity for all client computers not yet migrated to Windows 2000, you decide to continue using WINS until all migration is complete. What configuration is required to maintain connectivity between all computers on the network? [Check all correct answers]

- ❑ a.  Configure all WINS servers with static entries for all Windows 2000 domain controllers.

- ❑ b.  Configure all Windows 2000 client computers as WINS clients.

- ❑ c.  Configure all DNS servers with a WINS lookup record.

- ❑ d.  Configure all DNS servers for secure dynamic update.

- ❑ e.  Configure all DNS servers to host an Active Directory integrated zone.

- ❑ f.  Configure at least one secondary zone DNS on the network.

# Question 34

Your company has recently acquired a former competitor whose DNS must now be combined with your own. Both domains are Windows 2000. You will not have redundant entries in the respective DNS server zones for computers in other zones, nor will you transfer zone information from one DNS to another. How will you configure the DNS servers in each domain to provide name-resolution services for computers in the other domains?

- ○ a.  Configure each domain to have Active Directory integrated zones.

- ○ b.  Configure each primary DNS to boot from Registry.

- ○ c.  Configure each primary DNS to boot from file.

- ○ d.  Configure each primary DNS to boot from Active Directory and Registry.

## Question 35

You are the administrator of your network. Your responsibility is to oversee the migration of your existing NT 4 domain to Windows 2000. Some clients and application servers, including DHCP, WINS, and Exchange, remain on NT 4. All domain controllers have been migrated to Windows 2000. Users on Windows NT 4 client machines report that they are able to access some shared files, but not others. You can successfully ping all computers on the network via their FQDN. What should you do to solve the problem? [Check all correct answers]

❑ a. Configure all computers to register their PTR records with DNS.

❑ b. Configure all computers with the appropriate domain name suffix.

❑ c. Configure the Windows 2000 DHCP servers to Enable Support For Clients That Do Not Support Dynamic Update.

❑ d. Upgrade the legacy DHCP servers to Windows 2000.

❑ e. Add Windows 2000-compliant network cards to all legacy client computers.

❑ f. Upgrade the legacy WINS servers to Windows 2000.

## Question 36

Which of the following are appropriate NetBIOS names? [Check all correct answers]

❑ a. www.coriolis.com

❑ b. FREDDY

❑ c. BLDG_5_POLE_3

❑ d. SERVER\3

## Question 37

If you have a system configured as H-node, in which order will it try to resolve a NetBIOS name?

○ a. cache, local broadcast, WINS, LMHOSTS, HOSTS, DNS

○ b. local broadcast, cache, WINS, DNS, LMHOSTS, HOSTS

○ c. cache, WINS, local broadcast, LMHOSTS, HOSTS, DNS

○ d. local broadcast, WINS, LMHOSTS, HOSTS, cache, DNS

# Question 38

Where is the LMHOSTS file found by default?

○ a.  In the %systemroot%\system32\repl\import\scripts directory

○ b.  In the %systemroot%\help\common directory

○ c.  In the %systemroot% directory

○ d.  In the %systemroot%\system32\drivers\etc directory

# Question 39

Which of the following tags designates where there is a centrally located LMHOSTS file that all the systems in the local network use?

○ a.  **#PRE**

○ b.  **#INCLUDE**

○ c.  **#DOM**

○ d.  **#MH**

# Question 40

In Windows 2000 WINS, what gets registered with the database? [Check all correct answers]

❑ a.  Computer name

❑ b.  Workstation service

❑ c.  Server service

❑ d.  Messenger service

❑ e.  Name of user logged onto machine that is registering

❑ f.  Workgroup or domain of machine

## Question 41

Which of the following are valid IP addresses? [Check all correct answers]

❑ a.  131.107.2.200

❑ b.  10.0.0.256

❑ c.  0.5.6.9

❑ d.  1.2.3.4

❑ e.  200.200.254.254

## Question 42

NetBEUI can be routed in an IBM Token-Ring network.

○ a.  True

○ b.  False

## Question 43

Several contract employees have finished their project and no longer require access to network resources. For security purposes, their accounts have been disabled. How should you configure Certificate Services in the Active Directory to ensure that their existing digital certificates can no longer be used on the network?

○ a.  Add the usernames of the contractors to the Certificate Revocation List in Group Policy.

○ b.  Delete their certificates through Group Policy.

○ c.  Add the usernames of the contractors to the deny list on the enterprise CA.

○ d.  Delete their certificates from the enterprise CA.

# Question 44

You want to deny the global ability to encrypt files in the domain. What should you do in Group Policy to prohibit encryption?

- ○ a.  Remove the recovery agent from the default domain policy.
- ○ b.  Restrict the usage properties for the recovery agent.
- ○ c.  Remove the issuance of certificates for all users.
- ○ d.  Restrict the usage properties for all users.

# Question 45

You want to provide the highest levels of security possible for communication on your network. This security must include remote users. Which of the following must be done to ensure a high-security result? [Check all correct answers]

- ❏ a.  Enable EAP-TLS.
- ❏ b.  Enable AH.
- ❏ c.  Install Certificate Services.
- ❏ d.  Create a standalone CA.
- ❏ e.  Create an enterprise CA.
- ❏ f.  Create a subordinate standalone CA.
- ❏ g.  Create a subordinate enterprise CA.

# Question 46

As part of your Windows 2000 deployment, you are implementing Microsoft Certificate Services to increase security by validating user logon with Smart Cards. You want to make the creation of these certificates as efficient as possible. What should you do?

- ○ a.  Configure an auto-enrollment policy for all users and computers.
- ○ b.  Configure the Enforce Smart Card Logon for all users.
- ○ c.  Configure a domain controller as the enterprise root CA.
- ○ d.  Configure a domain controller policy to enforce Smart Card logon.

## Question 47

You have four different certificate authorities in your multiple-domain enterprise, each issuing certificates to both users and computers. You want to allow any user or computer to gain appropriate certificates from any authority, as needed. Which of the following is the key consideration in achieving this goal?

- ○ a. Add at least one certificate policy per domain.
- ○ b. Do not institute the use of Smart Cards.
- ○ c. Configure all certificate authorities to be mutually trusted.
- ○ d. Copy all issued certificates to the enterprise root certificate authority computer.

## Question 48

Your company's network must now connect to another due to a recent acquisition. Both networks utilize similar certificate service strategies but use different certificate authorities. What must be done to allow client access from one network to the other while maintaining the use of certificates?

- ○ a. Add each CA to the trust list for the other cooperating domain's CA.
- ○ b. Back up the certificates in each domain. Restore the certificates to the cooperating domain.
- ○ c. Delete the CA in one of the domains. Re-create the CA using the same naming structure as the cooperating domain.
- ○ d. Create an explicit trust between the two cooperating domains.

## Question 49

You want to rename your domain and reconfigure the DNS namespace. What configuration, if any, is necessary for Certificate Services?

- ○ a. No reconfiguration is necessary.
- ○ b. All certificate authorities must be configured to the new name.
- ○ c. The enterprise root certificate authority must be reinstalled.
- ○ d. All certificates must be reissued by a new certificate authority.

# Question 50

You have been asked to prepare a report of what functions IPSec implementation will provide. Which of the following are component features of IPSec? [Check all correct answers]

- ❑ a. Authentication of network packets
- ❑ b. Routing of network packets
- ❑ c. Encryption of network packets
- ❑ d. Assurance that no network packets have been intercepted
- ❑ e. Assurance that all network packets will only be accepted if valid
- ❑ f. Assurance that all network packets received are from a trusted source

# Question 51

You want to ensure that the appropriate network packets sent from computers on your network are properly processed through IPSec for encryption and signing. What should you configure on these computers?

- ○ a. An IPSec Group Policy
- ○ b. An IPSec filter
- ○ c. An IPSec profile
- ○ d. An IPSec protocol

# Question 52

Your Internet server has been experiencing attacks from various sources on the Web using an ICMP-based attack. Which of the following will maintain the availability of your Web site yet prohibit these attacks from significantly affecting your Internet server?

- ○ a. Configure a Group Policy to filter ICMP packets.
- ○ b. Configure an IPSec policy for a secure server.
- ○ c. Configure an IPSec filter for ICMP packets.
- ○ d. Configure SSL for your Web pages.

# Question 53

After reconfiguring your IPSec filters and policies, some packets that are configured to be filtered out are reaching computers in the network, causing service interruption. What should you do to identify and correct the problem?

○ a.  Use the Security Policy Management snap-in to verify policy link integrity.

○ b.  Reset all IPSec configurations to the default.

○ c.  Use the IPSec Monitor to modify IPSec session activity.

○ d.  Verify appropriate filter configuration with the ping utility.

# Answer Key

| | | |
|---|---|---|
| 1. c | 19. b, c | 37. c |
| 2. a, d | 20. a, c, d | 38. d |
| 3. d | 21. * | 39. b |
| 4. b | 22. a | 40. a, b, c, d, e, f |
| 5. a | 23. a, b, c, d | 41. a, d, e |
| 6. b | 24. a, b, d | 42. a |
| 7. a | 25. * | 43. a |
| 8. c | 26. b | 44. a |
| 9. a, b, c, d | 27. a, d | 45. a, b, c, e |
| 10. b, c | 28. b | 46. a |
| 11. d | 29. * | 47. c |
| 12. c | 30. c | 48. a |
| 13. b | 31. d | 49. d |
| 14. * | 32. c, e | 50. a, c, e |
| 15. a, b, c, d | 33. a, c | 51. b |
| 16. d | 34. c | 52. c |
| 17. * | 35. c, d | 53. a |
| 18. d | 36. b, c | |

## Question 1

The correct answer is c. The Network Interface layer is responsible for putting raw data onto network media. The Internet layer is responsible for determining the route a packet takes to get to its destination. Therefore, answer a is incorrect. The Transport layer is responsible for ensuring that data is delivered error free. Therefore, answer b is incorrect. The Session layer is not a part of the TCP/IP model, but of the OSI reference model. Therefore, answer d is incorrect.

## Question 2

The correct answers are a and d. The Network Interface layer puts raw data onto network media. The Transport layer ensures that data is delivered error free. The Session layer and the Presentation layer are both layers in the OSI reference model; therefore, answers b and c are incorrect.

## Question 3

The correct answer is d. If there is no response from the WINS server after the first attempt to renew its name (which happens at one-eighth the TTL expiration value), the client attempts to renew its name every two minutes until half of the TTL has expired. The time intervals for answers a and b are simply incorrect. The time period for answer c is the time interval that occurs when the client makes its first attempt. Therefore, answer c is incorrect.

## Question 4

The correct answer is b. NWLink is the Microsoft 32-bit NDIS 4.0 compliant version of Novell's IPX/SPX protocol. TCP/IP is a flexible suite of protocols designed for wide area networks. Therefore, answer a is incorrect. NetBEUI is a non-routable, broadcast-based protocol designed for small departmental LANs. Therefore, answer c is incorrect. DLC is used as an interface with SNA mainframes and printers that are connected directly to the network. It cannot be used to establish file and print connections to another computer. Therefore, answer d is incorrect.

## Question 5

The correct answer is a. To enable a computer to act as a WINS proxy, you must edit the Registry by setting the **EnableProxy** entry to 1. There is no such setting as **EnableWINS**, so answer b is incorrect. Installing a network interface card for each network ID will make the computer multihomed but will not make it a WINS proxy. Therefore, answer c is incorrect. Removing all protocols except NetBEUI will do nothing except make the computer unable to route. Therefore, answer d is incorrect.

## Question 6

The correct answer is b. The number in the first octet is 191, which falls into the range of Class B (128 to 191). The range of the first octet for Class A addresses is from 1 to 126, so answer a is incorrect. The range for the first octet of a Class C address is from 192 to 223, so answer c is incorrect. The range for the first octet of a Class D address is from 224 to 239, so answer d is incorrect.

## Question 7

The correct answer is a. AppleTalk can be used as a transport protocol in Windows 2000.

## Question 8

The correct answer is c. When the answering computer views the possible DD interfaces, it looks for a DD interface with the same name as the user account that attempted the connection. This is why the DD interface and the user account need to be the same. The interfaces do not need to be the same for a two-way DD connection. Therefore, answer a is incorrect. The user account does not need to be the same for a two-way DD connection. Therefore, answer b is incorrect. The issue of native mode does not play a role in the determination of the DD interfaces. Therefore, answer d is incorrect.

## Question 9

The correct answers are a, b, c, and d. All of the requirements are met with the use of NAT and the configurations as specified. Because the DHCP server is configured with new information, it is obvious that the existing scope currently serving the clients is not affected. With the RRAS server configured to use DHCP, the clients receive their addresses as before.

## Question 10

The correct answers are b and c. The clients will still obtain the IP address from the DHCP server from the existing scope. The Windows 2000 RRAS server was configured with ICS, which will not function if DHCP is on the network. There-fore, the clients will not be able to gain access to the Internet. So answer a is incorrect. There was no mention of a DNS server on any computer. Therefore, if the private interface of the RRAS server is set as the DNS server, there might not be any DNS resolution, outside of the fact that the RRAS server will resolve for the client. Therefore, answer d is incorrect.

## Question 11

The correct answer is d. The scope-based boundary for multicasting can specify a range of IP addresses that the multicast traffic should be forwarded to. Any DNS entry for TTL would not enable a multicast route. Therefore, answer a is incor-rect. Auto-static routing is for static routes that are updated using RIP. There-fore, answer b is incorrect. RIP v2 is an actual routing table that is dynamically updated and that uses password authentication for the replication of the route tables. Therefore, answer c is incorrect.

## Question 12

The correct answer is c. IP-in-IP tunneling is a logical interface that will trans-mit traffic that normally does not traverse an intranet or the Internet. RIP v1 and v2 are dynamic configurations of IP routing tables. RIP does not support IP multicasting. Therefore, answers a and b are incorrect. OSPF is a dynamic con-figuration of IP routing tables, which does not support IP multicasting. There-fore, answer d is incorrect.

## Question 13

The correct answer is b. Because the two-way demand-dial configuration is made between all routes, the WAN link costs will be reduced. RIP v1 does not allow any type of security for the replication of the RIP route table and it has issues with routing loops, which can cause loss of connectivity on the network. There-fore, answers a and c are incorrect. RIP does not group the routers or subnets; it simply broadcasts the route table on the network and receives other RIP route table broadcasts. Therefore, answer d is incorrect.

# Question 14

The correct answer is:

Server Options

    DNS

        10.1.2.5 or 10.1.2.3

        10.1.3.7

    WINS

        10.1.2.5

        10.1.3.7

Scope 1 Options

    Router

        10.1.2.1

Scope 2 Options

    Router

        10.1.3.1

Scope 3 Options

    Router

        10.2.0.1

        10.2.0.2

Either of the 10.1.2.x DNS servers can be used with the other DNS server, providing fault tolerance across the segments. Both WINS servers are required. This makes it easy for the administrator to configure the DHCP option. Each scope needs independent router configurations because the router is unique to each segment.

# Question 15

The correct answers are a, b, c, and d. The combination of RIP v2 and the demand-dial interface configuration will meet all of the criteria posed in the scenario.

## Question 16

The correct answer is d. A domain member server will support dynamic updates for DHCP clients. The member server will also eliminate any security issues with the ownership of DNS entries. Because the computer that updates DNS is the owner of the entry, it is best to configure this on a Windows 2000 domain member server. Therefore, answer a is incorrect. A Windows NT DHCP server cannot dynamically update DNS, independent of the membership in the domain. If the DHCP server is located on a domain controller, all of the entries will be insecure because of the enrollment in the DNSUpdateProxy group. This should be avoided. Therefore, answer b is incorrect. A Windows 2000 standalone server cannot be authorized and therefore cannot function properly on the Windows 2000 network. Therefore, answer c is incorrect.

## Question 17

The correct answers are:

DHCPDISCOVER

DHCPOFFER

DHCPREQUEST

DHCPACK

The client computer must first discover a DHCP server, which then offers a configuration. Once the client request to accept the offer is presented, the configuration is acknowledged. There is no DHCPINFORM packet type, so that choice is incorrect.

## Question 18

The correct answer is d. The DHCP server must be authorized to start allocating addresses to clients on the network. The clients will get an IP address from the APIPA range without any indication of a communication problem with the DHCP server. The clients would still be able to access most of the network resources without DNS. Therefore, answer a is incorrect. The relay agent is not needed if the DHCP server is on the same segment as the clients. Therefore, answer b is incorrect. The relay agent is not needed if the DHCP server is on the same segment as the clients. Therefore, answer c is incorrect.

## Question 19

The correct answers are b and c. The MAC address for the server network card and the IP address that will be reserved for the server are the only two required configurations for a DHCP reservation. The NetBIOS name is not a requirement, although a name can be associated with the reservation. Therefore, answer a is incorrect. The domain name is independent of the reservation. The domain name could be a reservation option that is allocated to the server when it comes on the network and obtains the pertinent information from the DHCP server. Therefore, answer d is incorrect.

## Question 20

The correct answers are a, c, and d. To update the Windows 2000 clients properly in DNS, you must choose to always update DNS and automatically update DHCP client information in DNS. To update the remaining Windows clients with DNS, you must enable updates for DNS clients that do not support dynamic update. The DHCP server will update both the A and PTR records for all of the DHCP clients with this configuration. Updating DNS only if the DHCP client requests it will only update the forward lookup zone resource record for the Windows 2000 clients, not the reverse lookup zone resource record. Therefore, answer b is incorrect.

## Question 21

The correct answer is:

**ipconfig /renew**

To obtain the new configurations from the DHCP server, the client only needs to run the command with the **/renew** switch. The command run without any switches simply displays the IP configuration to the command prompt window. Therefore, the answer **ipconfig** is incorrect. The **/release** switch actually releases the IP configuration. Therefore, the answer **ipconfig /release** is incorrect. Running this command will achieve the goal of obtaining the new configurations, but it is an extra step and causes overhead on the network and DHCP servers. The **/all** switch is used to list the IP configuration to the command prompt window, in complete detail. Therefore, the answer **ipconfig /all** is incorrect.

## Question 22

The correct answer is a. The DHCP relay agent is a critical configuration for the remote access servers that use the DHCP server to allocate IP addresses to the clients. The relay agent will allow the remote access client to communicate directly with the DHCP server to obtain the additional scope and server options required to communicate on the network. RRAS servers are not authorized; only RIS and DHCP servers are authorized. Therefore, answer b is incorrect. NAT is used to route internal clients to another network, which is not useful for this scenario. Therefore, answer c is incorrect. The DHCP server does not have to be configured to Always Update DNS for the clients. Therefore, answer d is incorrect.

## Question 23

The correct answers are a, b, c, and d. With the policies configured as shown, the entire plan of action will be configured properly. The existing dial-up remote clients will be able to gain access as before, using the default policy. Only the L2TP VPN clients will be able to gain access using the MS-CHAP v2 authentication method, and the PPTP VPN clients will not be able to access the network.

## Question 24

The correct answers are a, b, and d. With the policies configured as shown, all of the conditions are met, except that the PPTP clients can also access the network. The existing dial-up remote clients will be able to gain access as before, using the default policy. The L2TP VPN clients will be able to gain access using the MS-CHAP v2 authentication method. Another policy must be configured to deny the PPTP client's access to the network. Therefore, answer c is incorrect.

## Question 25

The correct answer is:

    Check remote access policy conditions.

    Check user dial-up property configuration.

    Check policy profile settings.

First, the conditions of the remote access policy must be met. If the conditions are not met, the user must meet the next policy conditions. If no policy condition is met, the user is denied access. The user dial-up property is then checked. If the user is allowed access, the profile is then created for the policy. If the user configurations do not match the profile, the user is denied access. The computer does not have any configurations for dial-up access, so the answer "Check computer dial-up property configuration" is incorrect.

## Question 26

The correct answer is b. The only requirement that is supported is the Caller ID for the server. BAP is required for the support of dynamic multilink. Therefore, answer a is incorrect. Even though EAP is configured for authentication, the Smart Card option must be selected, not the MD5-Challenge option. Therefore, answer c is incorrect. If only IPSec VPN connections are going to be supported, there should be no PPTP ports or a policy should be configured to deny the PPTP connections. Therefore, answer d is incorrect.

## Question 27

The correct answers are a and d. Users who can support multilink can also take advantage of the BAP protocol, which dynamically configures the multiple lines used to make a remote access connection using multilink. IPSec is supported by the L2TP protocol, not PPTP. Because PPTP is not an option, the IPSec requirement is met. The LCP option of the PPP configuration is required for the Caller ID support of the server. Therefore, answer b is incorrect. EAP with Smart Card authentication selected is required for Smart Card support. Because it is not selected, Smart Card authentication is not an option. Therefore, answer c is incorrect.

## Question 28

The correct answer is b. The solution can be made with little change to the other policies. The condition for Windows Group can filter out the new group of users and allow them access to the network with less security. This policy needs to be first in the list of remote access policies. IAS would not add any benefit to this solution. Therefore, answer a is incorrect. If the default remote access policy was first in the list, it would match the user configuration and take precedence. This would not meet the requirements of the scenario. Therefore, answers c and d are incorrect.

# Question 29

The correct answers are:

North America

   Standalone primary

South America

   Standalone secondary

Asia

   Standalone secondary

Only one standalone primary server may exist for the domain. Secondary servers are required for both name resolution and fault tolerance. A caching-only server will not provide fault tolerance, so that answer is incorrect.

# Question 30

The correct answer is c. Active Directory integration of DNS utilizes the multimaster replication and fault tolerance of Active Directory. It also allows for later configuration of secure dynamic update. Converting only the primary server would alienate the secondary servers. Therefore, answer a is incorrect. Converting the secondary zone servers to Active Directory integrated would force primary status, causing DNS failures. Therefore, answer b is incorrect. Converting nothing provides for no flexibility in later configuration and less fault tolerance due to the lack of multimaster capabilities granted through Active Directory integration. Therefore, answer d is incorrect.

# Question 31

The correct answer is d. Configuring an additional CNAME record entry for the select computers in DNS will centralize the configuration, making administration more efficient. Configuring the select intranet computers with an alternate domain suffix will allow for additional searches in DNS from the servers, but the clients will not be able to reach them because they do not have the additional settings. Therefore, answer a is incorrect. Configuring all the computers not contributing to the intranet with an alternate domain suffix will allow for the clients to find the servers, but the servers will not have a PTR record to get back to the client. Therefore, answer b is incorrect. These additional A records will not have FQDNs for the needed domain in the DNS. Therefore, answer c is incorrect. DHCP scopes have no effect on this scenario. Therefore, answer e is incorrect.

# Question 32

The correct answers are c and e. Active Directory integrated zones are required for secure dynamic updates, which can then be configured on the DNS zone. This will propagate the changes to all domain controllers running DNS. Enabling DHCP will allow the client to receive correct configuration, but does nothing to influence secure dynamic update. Therefore, answer a is incorrect. Secure dynamic updates are not configured from the client side. Therefore, answer b is incorrect. Standalone zones cannot accept secure dynamic updates. Therefore, answer d is incorrect.

# Question 33

The correct answers are a and c. The WINS servers must be able to resolve domain controllers for the legacy clients. The WINS lookup will allow for computers not yet in DNS to be found through their legacy NetBIOS name-resolution scheme. The Windows 2000 clients will use DNS, not WINS. Therefore, answer b is incorrect. Secure dynamic update is irrelevant for legacy clients not updating DNS. Therefore, answer d is incorrect. An Active Directory integrated zone will not solve the legacy client name-resolution issue. Therefore, answer e is incorrect. Secondary zones will be irrelevant if the functional primary zone is integrated into Active Directory. Therefore, answer f is incorrect.

# Question 34

The correct answer is c. To find computers in other DNS zones through this DNS, the root hints must be added to DNS, and then DNS must be configured to boot from file. This will copy the needed information into the file, which will be read anew on every boot. The default is for DNS in Windows 2000 is to read the root hint information from either the Active Directory (if integrated) or the Registry. Therefore, answers a, b, and d are incorrect.

# Question 35

The correct answers are c and d. Upgrading the DHCP servers solves the problem of legacy clients getting information from a legacy DHCP server (and thus not being updated). Once upgraded, all DHCP servers can then be configured to completely update DNS with legacy client information. Two problems exist in this situation: The legacy DHCP servers do not support updating PTR or A records in DNS, and the legacy clients do not support updating DNS with their information, either, making answer a incorrect. The domain name suffix does not solve the problem of updating of records in DNS, making answer b incorrect. If the network cards were not compatible, no communication would be occurring at all, and updating is still an additional configuration step, making answer e incorrect. WINS name resolution does not influence the dynamic updating of DNS records. Therefore, answer f is incorrect.

## Question 36

The correct answers are b and c. A NetBIOS name is a name that identifies a single host on a network. NetBIOS names belong to one and only one host. A NetBIOS name can be up to 16 bytes in length (15 characters plus an additional character to identify the service or application that is registering the name). Answer a is more than 15 characters, so it is incorrect. Answer d contains an invalid character (the backslash). Therefore, answer d is incorrect.

## Question 37

The correct answer is c. Configured as H-node, a system will resolve a NetBIOS name in the order cache, WINS, local broadcast, LMHOSTS, HOSTS, DNS. Answer a represents a system configured as M-node, so it is incorrect. Answers b and d are incorrect, because a system cannot be configured to resolve NetBIOS names in those manners.

## Question 38

The correct answer is d. The LMHOSTS file is found in the %systemroot%\system32\drivers\etc directory. The %systemroot%\system32\repl\import\scripts directory is the path where Windows NT 4 system policies and logon scripts are kept. Therefore, answer a is incorrect. The help files do not house the LMHOSTS file, so answer b is incorrect. The %systemroot% directory does not hold the LMHOSTS file by default, so answer c is incorrect.

## Question 39

The correct answer is b. The **#INCLUDE** tag means that there is a centrally located LMHOSTS file that all the systems use. An entry followed by **#PRE** will be preloaded into the NetBIOS name cache and remain in cache. Therefore, answer a is incorrect. An entry followed by **#DOM** will be considered a domain controller, so answer c is incorrect. The **#MH** tag tells the system that multiple entries exist due to one or more multihomed computers. Therefore, answer d is incorrect.

# Question 40

The correct answers are a, b, c, d, e, and f. All of these parameters are registered with the Windows 2000 database.

# Question 41

The correct answers are a, d, and e. An IP octet can range from 0 to 255 unless it is in the first or last octet. Then, the number cannot be 0 or 255. The final octet in answer b is higher than 255, so answer b is incorrect. The first octet in answer c is 0, so answer c is incorrect.

# Question 42

The correct answer is a. NBF, Microsoft's implementation of the NetBEUI protocol, does support routing in an IBM Token-Ring network.

# Question 43

The correct answer is a. Certificates should not be deleted but must go through the revocation process, which is implemented from the appropriate group policy object governing certificates. Deleting the certificates through Group Policy will cause invalid validation attempts from computers expecting a certificate to process. Therefore, answer b is incorrect. Any denying of certificates simply prohibits their issue. It will not revoke certificates. Therefore, answer c is incorrect. Deleting the certificates using the enterprise CA will cause invalid validation attempts from computers expecting a certificate to process. Therefore, answer d is incorrect.

# Question 44

The correct answer is a. Before any files can be encrypted, a recovery agent certificate must be issued. If there is no recovery agent certificate issued, encryption will fail. A recovery agent certificate is issued, by default, at the domain level. The properties of the recovery agent will not prohibit encryption. Therefore, answer b is incorrect. Removing the issuance of certificates for all users would prohibit proper use of certificates in many ways, but without the removal of the recovery agent, the user certificates could be re-created. Therefore, answer c is incorrect. Usage-related group policies will not prohibit encryption. Therefore, answer d is incorrect.

# Question 45

The correct answers are a, b, c, and e. Using both AH and EAP, in this case, would configure high security. Certificate Services and an enterprise CA provide the infrastructure components for this configuration. A standalone CA would not graft into Active Directory for the security of local objects. Therefore, answer d is incorrect. Standalone CAs are useful in many configurations but do not provide additional security. Therefore, answer f is incorrect. Enterprise CAs do not provide additional security. Therefore, answer g is incorrect.

# Question 46

The correct answer is a. Auto-enrollment allows for computers and users in the domain to request certificates. Once all users and computers are successfully enrolled, certificates are issued through the CA. Smart Card logon can be made available, but this is separate from the issuance of a certificate. Therefore, answer b is incorrect. Simply having an enterprise CA does not provide on-demand, efficient certificate issuance. Therefore, answer c is incorrect. Smart Card logon can be enforced or optional, but this is separate from the issuance of a certificate. Therefore, answer d is incorrect.

# Question 47

The correct answer is c. When multiple CAs are involved in the issuance of certificates, and they are not contained in a single PKI hierarchy, trusts between them must be established. Certificate policy is per domain and provides no interoperability. Therefore, answer a is incorrect. Although Smart Cards use certificates, they are still at the mercy of a CA. Therefore, answer b is incorrect. Copying all issued certificates to the enterprise root certificate authority computer is a bad idea. Certificates are domain name dependent, so you invite a lot of errors with this move. Therefore, answer d is incorrect.

# Question 48

The correct answer is a. The only possible solution is to establish a certificate trust between the issuing entities. Any other method will fail. Backing up the certificates is a wise practice, but will not integrate the certificates from another entity. Therefore, answer b is incorrect. CAs from separate entities must trust each other, similar structure or naming not withstanding (in fact, this would likely be harmful). Therefore, answer c is incorrect. Domain trusts are not the same as trusts between certificate authorities, and perform different functions. Therefore, answer d is incorrect.

## Question 49

The correct answer is d. Because certificates are name and domain specific, any renaming of a domain requires a tear-down and rebuild of both the domain (Windows 2000) and Certificate Services. As certificate services are established by name, any time that a domain name is changed certificate services must be re-configured. Therefore, answer a is incorrect. You cannot change the name identification of certificate services after it is configured. Therefore, answer b is incorrect. The naming context of the certificates is the issue, not the existence of the service itself, so reinstallation of the service is not necessary. Therefore, answer c is incorrect.

## Question 50

The correct answers are a, c, and e. IPSec provides authentication, encryption, and filtering of packets. IPSec is not responsible for routing packets. Therefore, answer b is incorrect. Network packets interception cannot be prevented. Therefore, answer d is incorrect. Trusted source determination is made based on the contents of the packets, not prior to their transmission. Therefore, answer f is incorrect.

## Question 51

The correct answer is b. Filtering defines which types of packets will be processed through IPSec and which will not. The Group Policy sets global IPSec behaviors, of which filters are only a part. Many additional settings come into use with a policy, so answer a is incorrect. Profiles are for users; filters are for machines. Therefore, answer c is incorrect. The IPSec protocol pieces perform the functions that the filters define, so answer d is incorrect.

## Question 52

The correct answer is c. An IPSec filter will prohibit ICMP packets, in this case, from being processed. Implementing the filter on these packets requires some resources, but the server will not be severely impacted. You can configure a protocol filter, but it will block all traffic of a type or to a port. Therefore, answer a is incorrect. Configuring an IPSec policy for a secure server will do more blocking than intended by this scenario. Therefore, answer b is incorrect. SSL is unrelated to packet filtering. Therefore, answer d is incorrect.

## Question 53

The correct answer is a. Filter integrity can be viewed and checked with the Security Policy Management tool. The problem is, it is likely that different people edited filters at approximately the same time, and dependencies (links) between filters are out of alignment. Resetting all the IPSec configurations to the default is a bad idea. There went all of the work you just did. Therefore, answer b is incorrect. The IPSec Monitor tool monitors sessions but cannot modify them. It might give you a clue about where the problem is, if you had documented your filter changes correctly, but you cannot fix the problem here. Therefore, answer c is incorrect. Ping will do you little good because the filter might be blocking this kind of traffic. Even if it were not blocking it, replies would only verify that a low level of direct connectivity is possible. Therefore, answer d is incorrect.

# Glossary

## Application layer
The seventh (top) layer of the OSI reference model and the fourth (top) layer in the DoD (TCP/IP) model. This layer is responsible for providing network services to application processes.

## Authorize
To register the Remote Installation Server (RIS) or the DHCP server with the Active Directory.

## Automatic Private IP Addressing (APIPA)
A client-side feature for Windows 98 and Windows 2000 DHCP clients. If the client's attempt to negotiate with a DHCP server fails, the client automatically receives an IP address from the 169.254.0.0 Class B range.

## Bandwidth Allocation Protocol (BAP)
A PPP control protocol that allows the dynamic addition and removal of multiprocessing connected links through multilink. The dynamic links can be controlled by remote access policies, which are based on the percent of line utilization and the length of time the bandwidth is reduced.

## Basic strength encryption
An encryption method that allows for MPPE 40-bit key encryption over PPTP VPN connections and dial-up connections. If L2TP over IPSec is the protocol for the VPN connection, 56-bit DES encryption is used.

## Binding
A logical connection between a network interface card and a protocol.

## BOOTP
A protocol originally designed for client computers that did not have disks. The configuration of BOOTP support consists of allowing a client machine to discover its own IP address, the address of a server host, and the name of a file to be loaded into memory and executed.

## Broadcast
A transmission sent simultaneously to more than one recipient. In communication and on networks, a broadcast

message is one distributed to all stations or computers on the network.

## Broadcast node (B-node)

One of four node types that can be set for NetBIOS name resolution.

## Cache

A part of RAM in which frequently accessed data is stored for quick access.

## Challenge Handshake Authentication Protocol (CHAP)

A one-way challenge-response authentication protocol for PPP connections. A connection using CHAP can also use additional types of encryption, such as MD5 and DES. Windows operating systems such as Windows NT, Windows 9x, and Windows for Workgroups always use CHAP when communicating with each other.

## Ciphertext

Clear-text passed through an algorithm to be encrypted.

## Clear-text

Unencrypted text.

## Data Encryption Standard (DES)

A popular symmetric-key encryption method developed in 1975 that uses a 56-bit key.

## Data Link layer

The second layer of the OSI reference model. This layer is responsible for taking raw bits from the Physical layer and packaging them into data frames.

## DHCP scope

A range of IP addresses within a specified subnet that are allocated to DHCP-enabled clients.

## DHCP server

A service that assigns TCP/IP configuration when requested.

## DHCPACK

Final message sent from the server to the client in the initial lease process, where the server acknowledges that the IP address is assigned to the client.

## DHCPDISCOVER

Initial broadcast message sent from the client to obtain an IP address.

## DHCPINFORM

A new message type for Windows 2000. This message is used for clients to obtain IP information (typically options) for their local configuration. The client might have an IP address for the network, which was not received by DHCP, but needs the options from the DHCP server to function on the network.

## DHCPNAK

A negative acknowledgement message sent from the DHCP server to the client indicating that the IP address requested is no longer valid.

## DHCPOFFER

A message from the DHCP server that contains a possible IP address for the client.

## DHCPRELEASE

A message from the client to the server requesting that the current IP address be canceled and the lease expired.

### DHCPREQUEST

A message from the client to the DHCP server indicating that the client wants to receive the offered IP address.

### Dial-up access

The kind of access employed when a remote client uses a public telephone line or ISDN line to create a connection to a Windows 2000 remote access server.

### Digital signatures

Data packets that provide, through shared keys and hashing algorithms, the means to assure that a related data packet originated from a specific source.

### Domain Name System (DNS)

A service used primarily for resolving fully qualified domain names (FQDNs) to IP addresses.

### Dynamic Host Configuration Protocol (DHCP)

A protocol that allows clients to receive TCP/IP configuration information from a centralized server. In Windows 2000, DHCP can also update DNS with a configuration that has been provided to a client computer.

### Encapsulated Security Payload (ESP)

An IPSec mechanism that provides L2TP encryption.

### Enterprise certificate authority

A digital certificate provider and authenticator that serves accounts within a domain.

### Extensible Authentication Protocol (EAP)

A mutual authentication protocol that is an extension to the PPP protocol. The extension allows for arbitrary authentication mechanisms such as Smart Cards and MD5 Challenge encryption.

### Forward lookup zone

A DNS zone that provides hostname-to-TCP/IP address resolution.

### Fully qualified domain name (FQDN)

A domain name that is part of a specified domain namespace tree. FQDNs have periods (.) in their names to designate their place in the namespace tree.

### Hash Message Authentication Code (HMAC) Message Digest 5 (MD5)

A hash algorithm producing a 128-bit hash of the authenticated payload.

### HMAC Secure Hash Algorithm (SHA)

A hash algorithm using a 160-bit hash of the authenticated payload.

### Hybrid node (H-node)

One of four node types that can be set for NetBIOS name resolution.

### Internet Authentication Service (IAS)

A server that provides the central management capabilities to control the access remote users have to the remote access server itself as well as to network resources.

### Internet Protocol (IP)

One of the protocols of the TCP/IP suite. IP is responsible for determining whether a packet is for the local network or a remote network. If the packet is for a remote network, IP finds a route for it.

### Internet Protocol Security (IPSec)
TCP/IP security mechanisms.

### IP address
A 32-bit binary address used to identify a host's network and host ID. The network portion can contain either a network ID or a network ID and a subnet ID.

### ipconfig
A command used to view, renegotiate, and configure IP address information for a Windows NT or Windows 2000 computer.

### Layer 2 Tunneling Protocol (L2TP)
A communication protocol that tunnels through another network such as IP, X.25, Frame Relay, and so on. L2TP is a combination of PPTP and Layer 2 Forwarding technology, which encapsulates PPP packets and provides additional security functionality.

### Link Control Protocol (LCP)
A PPP control protocol that dynamically configures after negotiating link and PPP parameters. The protocol controls the Data Link layer of the connection.

### Microsoft Challenge Handshake Authentication Protocol (MS-CHAP) v1
A special version of CHAP used by Microsoft. The encryption is still two-way and consists of a challenge from the server to the client that contains a session ID. The client uses a Message Digest 4 (MD4) hash to return the user name to the server.

### Microsoft Challenge Handshake Authentication Protocol (MS-CHAP) v2
A protocol that offers more secure encryption than CHAP or MS-CHAP v1, through mutual authentication and asymmetric encryption keys.

### Microsoft Point-to-Point Encryption (MPPE)
The link encryption used with MS-CHAP v2 or EAP-TLS authentication. This encryption takes advantage of 40-bit, 56-bit, and 128-bit encryption keys.

### Multicasting
A directed transmission from a single point to many points. The multicast address range is Class D, which uses the addresses from 224.0.0.0 to 239.255.255.255.

### Multilink
A technology that aggregates multiple physical links into a single logical link for data communication. Multilink is commonly used with dial-up and ISDN connections.

### Name resolution
The process of translating a name into an IP address. The name could be either a fully qualified domain name (FQDN) or a NetBIOS name.

### Network Basic Input/Output System (NetBIOS)
An application programming interface (API) used by programs on a local area network (LAN).

### Network layer
The third layer of the OSI reference model. This layer is responsible for addressing messages and translating

logical addresses and names into physical addresses. This layer also determines the route from the source computer to the destination computer.

### Open Systems Interconnection (OSI) reference model

A model comprising seven layers that standardize the type of communication between computers on a network.

### Password Authentication Protocol (PAP)

The protocol that allows clear-text authentication.

### Physical layer

The first layer of the OSI reference model. This layer is responsible for putting information as raw bits on network media and taking raw bits off the network media and passing them up to the Data Link layer.

### Point-to-Point Protocol (PPP)

An industry-standard protocol suite that is used to transport multiprotocol packets over point-to-point links.

### Point-to-Point Tunneling Protocol (PPTP)

A communication protocol that tunnels through another connection, encapsulating PPP packets. The encapsulated packets are IP datagrams capable of being transmitted over IP-based networks, such as the Internet.

### Presentation layer

The sixth layer of the OSI reference model. This layer is responsible for the method and form used to exchange data between two hosts. This layer also manages data encryption and compression.

### Public-Key Infrastructure (PKI)

Managed environments within which digital certificates, public keys, and private keys are used to provide the secure transmission of data.

### Relay agent

An agent that passes the DHCPDISCOVER packet to a DHCP server on a segment other than the DHCP client.

### Remote Authentication Dial-In User Service (RADIUS)

A protocol used by IAS to enable the communication of authentication, authorization, and accounting to the homogeneous and heterogeneous dial-up or VPN equipment in the enterprise.

### Reverse lookup zone

A DNS zone that provides TCP/IP address-to-hostname resolution.

### Serial Line Internet Protocol (SLIP)

An older remote access communication protocol used in Windows 2000 for outbound communication only.

### Session layer

The fifth layer of the OSI reference model. This layer is responsible for establishing a connection between two hosts.

### Shiva Password Authentication Protocol (SPAP)

A protocol typically used by third-party clients and servers. The encryption for the protocol is two-way, but it is not as good as CHAP.

## Smart Card

A hardware device used to provide additional verification of a user's identity. The Smart Card usually contains the user's digital certificate.

## Standalone certificate authority

A digital certificate provider and authenticator that serves accounts outside a domain.

## Static pool

A range of IP addresses configured on the remote access server allowing the server to allocate IP addresses to the remote access clients.

## Strong encryption

An encryption method that allows for MPPE 128-bit key encryption over PPTP VPN connections and dial-up connections. If L2TP over IPSec is the protocol for the VPN connection, 56-bit 3DES encryption is used.

## Superscope

A grouping of individual DHCP scopes. The individual member scopes are responsible for allocating IP addresses to different IP logical subnets functioning on the same network.

## Transport layer

The fourth layer of the OSI reference model. This layer is responsible for ensuring that messages are delivered error-free.

## Virtual private network (VPN) access

A remote client connection over an IP internetwork to create a virtual connection to a Windows 2000 remote access server.

## Windows Internet Naming Service (WINS)

A service that dynamically maps NetBIOS names to IP addresses.

## Zone transfer

To copy DNS database information from one DNS server to another.

# Index

# The Coriolis Exam Cram Personal Trainer

## An exciting new category in certification training products

The Exam Cram Personal Trainer is the first certification-specific testing product that completely links learning with testing to:

- **Increase your comprehension**
- **Decrease the time it takes you to learn**

No system blends learning content with test questions as effectively as the Exam Cram Personal Trainer.

Only the Exam Cram Personal Trainer offers this much power at this price.

Its unique Personalized Practice Test Engine provides a real-time test environment and an authentic representation of what you will encounter during your actual certification exams.

### Much More than Just Another CBT!

Most current CBT learning systems offer simple review questions at the end of a chapter with an overall test at the end of the course, with no links back to the lessons. But Exam Cram Personal Trainer takes learning to a higher level.

### Its four main components are:

- The complete text of an Exam Cram study guide in HTML format
- A Personalized Practice Test Engine with multiple test methods
- A database of 150 questions linked directly to an Exam Cram chapter

### Plus, additional features include:

- **Hint:** Not sure of your answer? Click Hint and the software goes to the text that covers that topic.
- **Lesson:** Still not enough detail? Click Lesson and the software goes to the beginning of the chapter.
- **Update feature:** Need even more questions? Click Update to download more questions from the Coriolis Web site.
- **Notes:** Create your own memory joggers.

- **Graphic analysis:** How did you do? View your score, the required score to pass, and other information.
- **Personalized Cram Sheet:** Print unique study information just for you.

---

**Windows 2000 Server**
**Exam Cram Personal Trainer**
ISBN: 1-57610-735-3

**Windows 2000 Professional**
**Exam Cram Personal Trainer**
ISBN: 1-57610-734-5

**Windows 2000 Directory Services**
**Exam Cram Personal Trainer**
ISBN: 1-57610-732-9

**Windows 2000 Security Design**
**Exam Cram Personal Trainer**
ISBN: 1-57610-772-8

**Windows 2000 Network**
**Exam Cram Personal Trainer**
ISBN: 1-57610-733-7

**Windows 2000 Migrating from NT4**
**Exam Cram Personal Trainer**
ISBN: 1-57610-773-6

**A+ Exam Cram Personal Trainer**
ISBN: 1-57610-658-6

**CCNA Routing and Switching**
**Exam Cram Personal Trainer**
ISBN: 1-57610-781-7

$99.99 U.S. • $149.99 Canada

Available: November 2000

**CORIOLIS**™
*Certification Insider Press*

**The Smartest Way to Get Certified**
**Just Got Smarter**™

# Look for All of the Exam Cram Brand Certification Study Systems

## ALL NEW! Exam Cram Personal Trainer Systems

The Exam Cram Personal Trainer systems are an exciting new category in certification training products. These CD-ROM based systems offer extensive capabilities at a moderate price and are the first certification-specific testing product to completely link learning with testing.

This Exam Cram study guide turned interactive course lets you customize the way you learn.

**Each system includes:**

- A Personalized Practice Test engine with multiple test methods
- A database of nearly 300 questions linked directly to the subject matter within the Exam Cram

## Exam Cram Audio Review Systems

Written and read by certification instructors, each set contains four cassettes jam-packed with the certification exam information you must have. Designed to be used on their own or as a complement to our Exam Cram study guides, Flash Cards, and Practice Tests.

**Each system includes:**

- Study preparation tips with an essential last-minute review for the exam
- Hours of lessons highlighting key terms and techniques
- A comprehensive overview of all exam objectives
- 45 minutes of review questions, complete with answers and explanations

## Exam Cram Flash Cards

These pocket-sized study tools are 100% focused on exams. Key questions appear on side one of each card and in-depth answers on side two. Each card features either a cross-reference to the appropriate Exam Cram study guide chapter or to another valuable resource. Comes with a CD-ROM featuring electronic versions of the flash cards and a complete practice exam.

## Exam Cram Practice Tests

Our readers told us that extra practice exams were vital to certification success, so we created the perfect companion book for certification study material.

**Each book contains:**

- Several practice exams
- Electronic versions of practice exams on the accompanying CD-ROM presented in an interactive format, enabling practice in an environment similar to that of the actual exam
- Each practice question is followed by the corresponding answer (why the right answers are right and the wrong answers are wrong)
- References to the Exam Cram study guide chapter or other resource for that topic

**CORIOLIS™**

*Certification Insider Press*

**The Smartest Way to Get Certified™**